ON TRACK/ OFF TRACK

ON TRACK/ OFF TRACK

PLAYING THE HORSES IN TROUBLED TIMES

JAMES QUINN

WILLIAM MORROW AND COMPANY, INC.

NEW YORK

Library of Congress Cataloging-in-Publication Data

Quinn, James, 1943–
    On track/off track : playing the horses in troubled times / James Quinn.—1st ed.
        p. cm.
    ISBN 0-688-07512-6 (alk. paper)
    1. Horse racing—Betting.   2. Horse racing—Betting—United States. I. Title.
SF331.Q554   1996
798.401—dc20   96-33872
                                                              CIP

Printed in the United States of America

First Edition

1 2 3 4 5 6 7 8 9 10

BOOK DESIGN BY MICHAEL MENDELSOHN OF MM DESIGN 2000, INC.

CONTENTS

PREFACE

"Why don't you write more often about racing's personalities, special topics, and the issues? The handicapping material has been great, but a handicapper's point of view regarding the game's most interesting people and events would be fascinating."

Authors continually engage suggestions about the next delivery, and no request to me has been pressed by colleagues at racetracks as frequently or as enthusiastically as the notion that I might write more broadly about the sport, the game, and the industry. The hints have been dropped ever more fervently in recent years, ostensibly because the troubled times confronting the sport and industry are having serious consequences for handicappers.

In this double-barreled anthology I have intended therefore to deal comprehensively and constructively with the interests and concerns of modern racegoers both on track and off. The first part of the book ("On Track") treats numerous highly specific, relatively narrow topics in handicapping that have gathered an especially contemporary force. Many of the ideas have achieved prominence among practitioners within the past half-dozen seasons.

The longer second part ("Off Track") is concerned with people, events, and the issues, all of it given a handicapper's shine, and was a delight to compose. I trust handicappers will enjoy taking this tour de force. Where necessary, in my judgment, criticism of the status quo has been sprinkled throughout these pages, but I have attempted to be constructive with it. I especially enjoyed taking the occasion to write generously and appreciatively about Charlie, Laz, and Laffit, three of the most remarkable and outstanding personalities to grace this sport of clay-footed kings.

In a third small concluding section I take a wry, ironic peek at the high-tech high jinks currently proliferating among handicappers and their PCs. So much of it amounts to handicappers in toyland. It's a convenient chance to sound off with my disappointment at the high-tech state of the art. I grab the opportunity as well to present my hopes for the next generation.

I did enjoy it all.

ON TRACK/ OFF TRACK

Del Mar

8

ONE MILE. WINDY SANDS STAKES. $
Year Olds and Upward which are non-wi
subscription of $50 each, which must ac
entry box, with $60,000 Added, of which
fourth and $1,500 to fifth. Weights Mond.
entry box, by the closing time of entries. *
closed Saturday, August 10 by 12:00 Noon

(1 mile)

start & finish

LETTHEBIGHOSS

3yo (May) gelding, gray
Trainer: Bob
Owner: Micha

Flying Paster ($35,000)
by Gummo
Moonlight Jig
by Jig Time

Wet:
Turf:
Dist:

111 Co

8Jun91	6Del	ft												ncussy 119	5.4
															Sc
27May91	8Bel	ft												107 b	13.3
			Gr.I Metropolitan Handicap												G
24Apr91	8Hol	ft	3	Stk71050	7f	21.50	44.10	1:08.70	1:21.30	88	3½ 3 3½ 3¾		4no 123	E Delahoussy 123 8b	1.1
			Harry Henson Stakes												
11Apr91	8CG	ft	3	Stk53700	6f	21.90	45.30	57.50	1:10.30	87	2f 5 4½ 3½	1½ 14	C Nakatan	122 8b	0.4
			Piedmont Stakes												
29Mar91	8SA	ft	2	Stk58000	6½f	21.30	44.10	1:09.70	1:16.10	88	57 7 3¾ 3¼	2no	1½ 1no	E Delahoussy 117 8b	1.4

ENTER THE MIGHTY PICK 3

As the 1990s unwind, the technological advances that promised to alter the racetrack experience evermore—personal computers, software, satellites, communications devices (modems), databases, on-line information services—have shaped up as comparatively inconsequential in relation to developments that have altered my racetrack experience.

My edge had begun to recede.

For fifteen years I have argued that successful handicappers must not abandon their edge. That edge is hinged to handicapping proficiency, and it occurs, predictably, year after year after year after year in the win pools. The exacta, the trifecta, the Pick 6, and other exotica aside, winners get that way first of all by demonstrating firm footing in the win pool.

As mundane as betting to win in exotic circumstances may sound, that advantage consists of picking 35 percent winners (roughly) at 5–2 average odds (approximately), and thereby collecting annual profits equal to 22.5 percent of the total amount wagered to win. The profits vary from $20,000 to $50,000, depending upon bet-size, number of plays, and actual proficiency.

Handicappers who imagine they can plunder the exotic pools while floundering in the straight pools will take a counterpunch soon enough from the law of large numbers. Exotic wagers are low-probability bets. Success depends more upon value than proficiency. Not fair value, mind you, but excellent value. Losses in exotic wagering can string together for weeks or months, and they do.

A pair of 2–1 shots has a 10 percent chance of running one-two in either direction in the exacta. That means even a competent handicapper combining 2–1 shots can be wrong in eighty of one hundred attempts. The winners are not destined to occur in the first fifty races either, only at a 20 percent rate over time. Barry Meadow has suggested Pick 6 players can anticipate six consecutive months of losing.

The relative predictability of successful win-wagering serves as an antidote to the caprice of exotic wagering. Handicappers dependent upon exotic wagering may be impressively successful this year, but sorrowfully unsuccessful next year, and the next, and the next. Bettors who live and die in the exotic pools know the pattern all too well.

The predictable profits of effective win-wagering, in contrast, accumulate with modest variations from year to year. If bet-size increases and the number of plays increases, profits increase correspondingly, assuming proficiency endures. The escalating pattern can be considered characteristic of most successful handicappers.

The 1990s have not been accommodating. First, small fields in numerous nonclaiming races have presented handicappers with an unprecedented number of underlays, notably in the stakes and allowance territories I prefer. If an odds-on stickout wins a stakes by half a furlong, so what? The most likely winner of the season is not a good bet if it's not a fair price.

Second, the year-long calendar of southern California, an isolated circuit bereft of shippers, has resulted in an unprecedented regimen of bad races and slow horses. This subverts handicapping effectiveness. It's fool's play to attempt to isolate the least slow among a herd of goats.

Third, the decline in racetrack attendance has reduced the playing field virtually to a contest among peers. Regular handicappers of today compete primarily against other regular handicappers, most of them well informed and heavily equipped with knowledge and skill. A complicated game has become intensely competitive, further blunting everybody's edge.

In recent seasons handicappers have found themselves confronting more underlays, passing more races, and getting fewer winners. My game has suffered more than I'd like to admit. A win-wagering ROI (return on investment) from 20 to 40 percent has been sliced almost by half.

Enter the Mighty Pick 3.

It's remarkable how an innovative wager that makes sense can resuscitate the days at the racetrack. With so many bottom-of-the-barrel claiming races, 3YO claiming races, and maiden-claiming races cluttering the programs in southern California, turning the weekday cards to dreary doldrums, it's refreshing to imagine that several of the awful races might contribute to Pick 3 payoffs upward of a thousand dollars. Not a few of them pay several thousand dollars.

In southern California the Pick 3 became an instant success. Not only did the payoffs routinely exceed those of trifectas and the corresponding parlays, but also the exotic wager was eminently hittable.

Within a year of its birth I had concluded the Pick 3 represented the ideal exotic wager. Exciting payoffs, combined with reasonably strong probabilities of winning. If riches were to come to me from racetrack speculation, this bet probably would be the source. In an unlikely circumstance heavy with irony, the Pick 3 was invented by Santa Anita Park, a track that took a rather retrograde view of exotic wagering during its formative days. Santa Anita once opposed multiple exactas on the same card.

As the weeks, months, and seasons passed, the Pick 3 continued to generate windfalls and boxcars. Whatever learning curve applies, the bettors have not yet rendered the wager ineffective, as they have so routinely the Pick 6. It's instructive to ruminate on the explanation. I would cite several advantages:

1. It's a $3 bet, in southern California at least.
    The pools are therefore half again as large as they would be with no disincentive to play. The $2 bettors do not buy $5 exactas, but they will buy $3 Pick 3s. Typical Pick 3 pools in southern California approximate $100,000. The take is 20 percent. Roughly $80,000 is returned to winning bettors.
    Outside southern California, Pick 3 pools have not grown nearly as large. No regrets. Smaller pools may be overly sensitive to combinations of favorites, but combinations of non-favorites pay extraordinarily well.
2. No probable payoffs are projected.
3. Big-ticket syndicates do not play.
    Pick 3 payoffs may be generous, but they are not swell enough to arouse the purchase of full fields. Excellent handicappers retain the edge.
4. Odds-on horses aside, combinations of favorites and non-favorites can pay surprisingly well.
5. Combinations of medium-priced winners pay extravagant amounts, at least much of the time.
6. Only winners must be tabbed, not the second and third finishers.

7. The probability of hitting any leg regularly exceeds 50 percent simply by covering the main contenders.
8. The probability of hitting the three legs in combination can be high, and significantly higher than is typically true of other exotic bets.

That's quite a laundry list. The last two advantages can be considered decisive. Exotic wagers are characterized as high-value low-probability propositions. The Pick 3 connects high value with a decent probability of success. Indeed the Pick 3 stands apart primarily because the probabilities of winning frequently favor the bettor. This is true of no other exotic wager. Regardless of odds, the chance of completing the Pick 6 has been estimated below 2 percent.

In playing Pick 3s, strategy is critical. In one approach a key horse in each of three consecutive races is identified. If each key horse is linked to the contenders in the other two legs, in effect three Pick 3s have been constructed.

To win, one of the key horses must prevail. In the other legs the contenders must survive. If two key horses win, and the contenders in the third leg have been covered successfully, the bettor has covered the winning combination twice. I like that. The strategy works amazingly well, and at moderate cost. If all three key horses win, the bettor collects the payoff multiplied by three. It happens.

Moreover, if one of the key horses represents a prime bet to win as well, and is a nonfavorite, the bettor is well advised to double down. Prime bets get that way because they win enough at good prices to throw substantial profits. The Pick 3 allows handicappers to compound those profits. Do it.

I first applied this strategy in the sixth, seventh, and eighth races at Del Mar during summer in the late 1980s. In one sequence the winner of the sixth, a key horse, paid 5–2. The seventh winner, a contender, paid 5–1. The eighth winner, another key, paid 9–2. The eighth winner, a nonfavorite, also qualified as a prime bet to win.

The exact cost eludes me, but it amounted to roughly $90. The Pick 3 returned $1100. Two winning keys meant I held two winning tickets. By doubling down, the prime bet in the eighth was converted to a pair of winning tickets in the Pick 3. The gross profit exceeded $3300. The three winners paid 5–1 and lower.

In 1993 the tracks of southern California began presenting bettors with the roll-over Pick 3. Beginning at the first race, bettors now can play a series of Pick 3s throughout the program. It's a fabulous advance.

In pursuing the roll-over Pick 3s, strategy will be even more critical. What to do with unpredictable races, where even the contenders will be unclear? Should top selections be singled, or used in combination with other contenders, and when? Which favorites should be included, and which should be excluded? Which races should be passed? How to deal with small fields? Obviously, alternative strategies must be invoked.

Only two seasons have passed since the roll-over Pick 3s have been offered. My experience with the roll overs has lasted approximately eighteen months. The first season was wonderful, but I'm trapped now (1995) in the midst of a lengthy losing run. The empirical evidence remains incomplete and inconclusive.

I intend to persevere. The ability to withstand losing runs is part and parcel of the racetrack experience. When challenging the exotics, it's a fundamental talent. As the loss-patterns continue and the losses inflict greater financial pain, I console myself by reviewing a few important Pick 3 statistics for the entirety of 1994.

Take a look at the table below.

Track	No. of Pick 3s	Pick 3 Average	Parlay Average	Pick 3 Median
Santa Anita	540	$1537	$1126	$440
Hollywood Park	487	1098	723	371
Del Mar	301	917	753	370
Oak Tree	158	1215	802	510
Hollywood Fall	252	698	521	304
1994 Totals	1738	$1156	$ 831	$395

NOTE: Southern California Handicapper and CPA Kermit Hollingsworth contributed the statistics.

The data indicate the Pick 3s on average paid 1.39 as great as the corresponding parlays. When the comparative takeouts have been considered, the Pick 3 afforded bettors a 33 percent edge. But averages can be deceiving, a cliché that applies forcefully here.

Because average Pick 3 payoffs exceed median payoffs (half above, half below) by a wide margin, the wager can be considered sensitive to extremes. Huge, unrepresentative payoffs that might have skewed the data have been eliminated. Still, the Pick 3 average payoffs proved dramatic across all tracks throughout the year. The average payoff when 1738 bets had been placed was an amazing $1156, approximately three times the median payoff.

Certain implications are plain. Whenever nonfavorites can be combined intelligently in Pick 3 wagering, handicappers should proceed. A compounding effect occurs, and payoffs regularly soar. Favorites can be used, but odds-on horses are taboo. In addition, in reducing the cost of tickets, handicappers should eliminate lower-priced horses first, favorites especially. Odds-on favorites revealing any flaw should be challenged automatically. Do not eliminate the higher-priced contenders.

Last weekend at Golden Gate Fields I liked a horse in the fifth race that won and paid $32.20.

I had covered the fourth race successfully by using a first starter ridden by leading jockey Russell Baze. The horse paid 2–1. Now I was alive in the Pick 3 concluding in the sixth to three contenders. One of them won, paying $12. The Pick 3 ($2) paid $794! The bet cost $6.

What happened a half hour later would make the day memorable. The seventh race at Golden Gate Fields was upset by a bettable 12–1 shot. The horse was among five contenders I had marked. I had keyed the $32 overlay I did prefer in the fifth to my three contenders in the sixth race, and in turn hooked those horses to the five contenders I had preferred in the seventh race. The fifteen combinations cost $30.

The Pick 3 paid $5700!

Now *that* was a day at the races!

BEYER SPEED FIGURES

How might handicappers best benefit from the Beyer Speed Figures? The numbers have appeared now in the *Daily Racing Form* for several seasons, but too many handicappers continue to testify they do not receive sufficient nourishment from them. The accelerated trend toward full-card simulcasting means the figures have obtained greater utility value than ever. It's convenient for handicappers in Chicago to know which horses entered today at Churchill Downs have run the fastest. Yet a dependence upon high-figure horses last out gets the figure handicapper nowhere.

In relying upon speed figures, handicappers make two serious mistakes repeatedly. One, they compare horses' speed figures with one another, before comparing each horse's figures with an absolute standard, such as a par figure. This guarantees an oversupply of figure bets, as one horse will often look superior to the others. If the contenders' speed figures all remain below par, however, the figures will be less decisive, and the race may not be susceptible to speed handicapping.

Second, and more importantly, speed figures should not be interpreted in a vacuum or out of context. The figures are best related to other salient factors of handicapping, especially class, pace, and form, critical fundamentals. Before examining the horses' speed figures, handicappers prepare themselves for a more reliable interpretation by asking what the several circumstances of this specific race imply for interpreting the numbers.

If the race will be seven furlongs, maybe figures recorded by certain horses at six furlongs should be discounted. If the race goes on grass, should handicappers rely upon dirt figures, and what other factors might be more prominent than speed figures? If three-year-olds are moving ahead in class dramatically, how might handicappers determine whether recent speed figures should be repeated? And on and on, the myriad of race conditions that influence how handicappers interpret and use the Beyer Speed Figures (see page 10).

Table 1 Beyer Speed-Figure Pars at Hollywood Park for Horses 3up at Six Regularly Run Distances

Class	Sprints			Routes		
	6f	6.5f	7f	7.5f	8.5f	9f
(claiming prices in thousands)						
Clm 10	80	80	80	80	80	80
Clm 12.5	83	82	82	82	82	82
Clm 16	86	85	85	84	84	84
Clm 20	88	87	87	89	88	87
Clm 25	91	90	90	91	89	89
Clm 32	94	92	92	93	91	91
Clm 40	97	95	94	95	93	93
Clm 50	100	97	97	98	95	94
Mdg Clm 50	80	80	80	80	80	80
Mdn Clm 32	74	75	75	76	76	76
Maiden	88	87	87	89	88	87
Alw, NW1X	94	92	92	93	91	91
Alw, NW2X	100	97	97	98	95	94
Alw, NW3X	102	100	99	102	99	98
Clf Alw	105	102	102	104	103	100
Stakes	111	107	106	109	105	103
Gr. 1/Gr. 2	116	112	111	113	109	107

Standard Adjustments

F & M	−6	−5	−5	−5	−6	−6
3YO Races*	−8	−7	−7	−7	−9	−9

*Adjustments to par figures in races limited to 3YOs include claiming races, stakes races, and classified allowance races, but not maiden, maiden-claiming, or nonwinners allowance races.

Legend	6f	six furlongs	Alw, NW1X	allowance race, for non-winners of one allowance race, etc.
	Clm	claiming		
	Mdn Clm	maiden-claiming	Clf Alw	Classified allowance race
	F & M	fillies and mares	Gr. 1/Gr. 2	Grade 1 and Grade 2 stakes

The solution to the first mistake is relatively elementary. It consists of developing a chart of Beyer Speed Pars. Examine Table 1 above, which contains Beyer Speed Pars for Hollywood Park 1994–1995. Table 1 assigns a Beyer 80 to $10,000 claiming horses, and I recommend that class level as a point of origin for major, medium-sized, and many smaller tracks.

Table 2 Beyer Turf Pars at Hollywood Park
for Horses 3up at Five Regularly Run Distances

Class	5.5f	1M	8.5f	9f	10f
Maiden	92	88	88	87	x
Al2, NW1X Alw, NW2X Clm 50 & Lower	99	93	91	91	90
Alw, NW3X Clf Alw Above Clm 50	105	97	95	94	93
Stakes	111	101	99	98	96
Gr.1/Gr. 2	120	107	105	103	101

Standard Adjustments

	5.5f	1M	8.5f	9f	10f
F & M	−6	−6	−6	−5	−5
3YO Races	−9	−10	−9	−9	−8

Table 3

		Mdn	Stk/Alw
Beyer Pars	5f	76	x
	5.5f	77	84
Races for 2YOs	6f	80	86
	Fillies & mares (6f)	−6	

Notice the large differences among class levels (columns) and the slighter differences among distances (rows). Beyer speed charts are characterized by wide variations in the numbers, a strength of the method. Standard adjustments for fillies and mares and for races limited to three-year-olds (claiming, stakes, and classified allowance only) are provided at the bottom. Tables 2 and 3 above present the Beyer Pars for Hollywood's grass races and races for juveniles. Pars should be considered vital for interpreting the Beyer Speed Figures of the *Daily Racing Form*. Without pars, too many of the figures defy interpretation.

Handicappers have no way of knowing whether a performance (a 74, an 80, an 85, a 92, a 99, a 103, a 110) has been strong, average, or weak. Mistakes of interpretation and use will be inevitable, and may run rampant. Many high-figure horses are bogus, and handicappers need to recognize that.

Constructing the par charts is not overly complicated. Obtain a set of par times for the local tracks and for simulcast tracks. Following Beyer, calculate the value of one fifth of a second at each of the regularly run distances for a common class level. Assign a value of 80 to each par time at that class level. Using the value of one fifth at each distance, and the various par times, fill in the par figures for each class level.

If handicappers do not want to calculate the value of one fifth at each distance, using the par times for $10,000 claiming horses and a speed figure of 80 as a point of origin, add 2.5 points for each faster length in sprints, and 2 points for each faster length in routes. The approximations will sacrifice some useful precision, but will work satisfactorily, at least much of the time.

The solution to the second mistake depends upon the player's knowledge and skill in handicapping. The more and varied the experience with speed figures in combination with other facets of handicapping, the better, especially in evaluating the unfamiliar races and unfamiliar horses introduced by full-card simulcasting.

On a marathon weekend in June 1995, Hollywood Park carded fourteen races on Saturday and another fourteen races on Sunday. Utilizing the par charts provided, handicappers can deal effectively with the Beyer Speed Figures for the two days. The discussion will be limited by the races under review and by my experience in using Beyer Speed Figures. I'm uncertain as to which limitation is greater, but let's assume it's the first.

The first on Saturday was one of the most intriguing. It was a $50,000 claiming sprint at six furlongs limited to 3YO fillies. The Beyer Par was 86.

Which of these two do handicappers prefer?

Rona Prospect
Own: Burke Gary W & Timothy R
VALENZUELA F H (152 15 18 8 .10) $50,000
Ro. f. 3 (Mar)
Sire: Allen's Prospect (Mr. Prospector)
Dam: Glen Orchy (Believe It)
Br: Truman C. Welling (Md)
Tr: Machowsky Michael (16 5 2 3 .31)
L 118

Lifetime Record :	6 2 2 0	$55,000		
1995	5 2 2 0	$54,200	Turf	0 0 0 0
1994	1 M 0 0	$800	Wet	0 0 0 0
Hol	2 1 0 0	$22,250	Dist	3 1 1 0

7May95-1Hol fst 6f :213 :442 :563 1:10 (F)Clm 50000 86 7 2 12½ 11 11½ 1½ Valenzuela F H LB 118 4.50 90-11 Rona Prospect118½ Lisa Mac115no Miss Kyama1162½ Stead
22Apr95-7SA fst 6f :21 :44 :56 1:091 (F)Alw 42000N1X 71 1 3 21 23 26 710½ Valenzuela P A LB 120 5.20 81-11 Desert Princess1204 Marfa Smeralda117¾ Sunsamia120hd G
22Mar95-1SA fst 6½f :22 :45 1:094 1:163 (F)Md Sp Wt 78 4 1 11 12½ 16 15½ Desormeaux K J LB 117 *.90 89-09 Rona Prospect1175½ Five O'clock1175 Danceroundthemine117nk
9Feb95-6SA fst 6½f :214 :45 1:102 1:17 (F)Md 50000 76 7 1 1½ 2hd 2½ 2½ Desormeaux K J LB 118 *1.30 86-17 Counterpane117½ Rona Prospect118¾ Redeployed1173½ Cau
15Jan95-4SA gd 6f :213 :451 :572 1:10 (F)Md Sp Wt 62 1 3 11 1hd 21½ 211 Desormeaux K J B 117 5.00 76-11 Texinadress11711 Rona Prospect1176½ Sunsamia117½ Rail,
25Jun94-3Hol fst 5f :22 :45 :572 (F)Md Sp Wt 25 4 4 2½ 22½ 39½ 520 Flores D R B 118 10.90 77-10 Serena's Song11810 Valid Attraction118hd Guise1183½ In
WORKOUTS: Jun 2 Hol 5f fst :593 H 4/32 May 26 Hol 5f fst 1:004 H 4/30 May 20 Hol 4f fst :50 H 29/44 May 4 Hol 3f fst :352 H 2/21 ●Apr 14 Hol 5f fst :582 H 1/14 Apr 8 Hol 6f fst 1:152 H 6/10

Bueno
Own: Zillmann Judith
PEDROZA M A (192 15 16 32 .08) $50,000
Dk. b or br f. 3 (Apr)
Sire: Society Max (Mr. Prospector)
Dam: Neat Choice (First Draft Choice)
Br: Triple AAA Ranch (Ariz)
Tr: Eikleberry Kevin (1 0 0 0 .00)
L 118

Lifetime Record :	8 4 1 1	$43,119		
1995	3 1 0 1	$7,770	Turf	0 0 0 0
1994	5 3 1 0	$35,349	Wet	1 0 0 0
Hol	1 0 0 0	$1,100	Dist	4 3 1 0

28May95-7Hol fst 6½f :212 :44 1:091 1:154 (F)Clm 62500 64 7 3 55 67 59 513 Pedroza M A LB 118 7.60 77-15 Shreveport1211¼ Valid Symmetry1162¾ Lisa Mac1154½ Wide
15May95-11TuP fst 6½f :22 :442 1:084 1:15 (F)Alw 9500N2X 70 3 4 31 31½ 3½ 12½ Martinez F III L 115 2.10 94-11 Bueno1152½ Shu Biz Annie115no Selbyville1201¼
20Jan95-12TuP fst 1 :222 :452 1:10 1:354 (F)Alw 9700N1m 72 7 3 34½ 21½ 2hd 3½ Lidberg D W L 120 6.40 86-19 Whataninspiration117nk Dancin At The Wire120nk Bueno12010
31Dec94-6TuP sl 6½f :223 :463 1:123 1:193 (F)To The Post12k 52 5 5 52¾ 41½ 56¾ 58¼ Lidberg D W L 121 *.50 64-27 Refasten1173 June Jones1162 Luree's Baby1173 Wide into l
27Nov94-12TuP fst 6f :213 :441 :564 1:094 [S]ArizBrdrsFty53k 67 6 5 42½ 31 1hd 13½ Lidberg D W L 117 2.40 85-16 Bueno1173½ Speed Predicted120no I Rate120¾
Bit fract. in gate, drvg.
15Nov94-11TuP fst 6f :214 :45 :571 1:094 [S]FutTrl 66 8 3 2½ 2hd 2hd 2nk Lidberg D W L 117 *.30 85-19 Bangthedrumboldly120nk Bueno1176 Speed Predicted1202
28Oct94-3TuP fst 6f :214 :434 :563 1:093 (F)Alw 6000N2L 64 4 6 1hd 21½ 21½ 13 Lidberg D W 117 *.70 86-10 Bueno1173 Refasten1207 Heber1171
3Oct94-3TuP fst 6f :213 :442 :56 1:093 (F)[S]Md c-12500 64 6 2 2½ 1½ 12 111 Lidberg D W 118 *.50 86-15 Bueno11811 Real Meri118½ Misselegantrhythum1189 Bit gree
Claimed from Triple A A A Ranch, Johnson Joseph E Trainer
WORKOUTS: May 2 TuP 4f fst :471 H 4/31 Apr 23 TuP 4f fst :482 H 16/25 Apr 14 TuP 4f fst :492 H 22/32 Apr 3 TuP 3f fst :38 B 14/14 Mar 21 TuP 4f fst :481 H 24/40

Figure handicappers prefer Rona Prospect. The winner, however, was Bueno, the longest price on the board. Rona Prospect finished a game second, beaten by a head.

A shipper from Turf Paradise creamed at Hollywood Park on May 28, Bueno had never approached par for this race, but was not as wild an upset as her 14–1 odds intimate. First examine Bueno's record at Turf Paradise, where she was an odds-on favorite in four of her first five, and in the other captured the Arizona Breeders Futurity, purse of $53,000, by three and one-half lengths. Consistent, impressive, and extremely well backed.

When consistent, versatile, impressive, well-backed shippers from minor tracks lose their first start at a major track, handicappers should forgive the pratfall. One of the shrewdest handicappers I have met supports this kind on their second and third attempts at the major track, confident the odds will be unrealistically high.

Besides, Rona Prospect was stuck on the Hollywood rail, which had proved dead at six furlongs for most of the 1995 spring meeting. Crucial to know! The Beyer 86 satisfies par, but the figure had been recorded wire-to-wire from an outside post. Outside-to-inside was not the preferred running style at Hollywood Park 1995.

Third, shippers from minor tracks have frequently recorded higher Beyer Speed Figures in southern California than they managed at the shipping tracks. That's an anomaly local handicappers simply must be aware of. Regarding local knowledge, many simulcast handicappers will be kept in the dark, at least for a time.

So Bueno upset Rona Prospect, a favorite which was not a reasonable bet from the detestable rail post.

Saturday's second was a maiden-claiming affair for bottom-of-the-barrel types. The Beyer par was 74. The fastest experienced horses showed Beyer Speed Figures of 71 and 64. Are handicappers surprised that a first-starter won and paid $9.60? I implore figure analysts to discount speed figures whenever the contenders display figures more than two lengths below par. Speed figures will be unreliable frequently in maiden-claiming events. Speed figures many lengths below par will be meaningless.

The third was a classified allowance route on the dirt, for nonwinners of $22,500 since Christmas. The Beyer par was 100. Review the three below. Any preference?

As impressively as Straight to Bed has performed in 1995, the six-year-old is a claiming horse tried-and-true that should be outgunned in classified circumstances, unless form is peaking and the distance and probable pace will be comfortable.

Extended beyond a mile, Straight to Bed had been all out to survive in his last. He has flirted with today's par regularly and equaled the par recently. But his Beyer Speed Figure declined three to four lengths last out, not a ringing endorsement for a significant class rise. At 2–1, no thanks.

Luthier Fever and Polar Route both qualify. Polar Route's pattern looks to be improving. One sprint and one route following a three-month absence, the second start improved, indicates a strong effort today. The 5YO has surpassed par three times against today's class or better.

Luthier Fever has surpassed par once, but that race, four back, occurred on dirt, and the change from turf to dirt today hides the performance well. Something else. Look at the pattern of speed figures. In every other race Luthier Fever's figures rise and fall. A rise from 72 to par or better would continue the pattern.

Patterns of speed figures mean more than any figure standing independently. At four, after being so consistent at three, Luthier Fever has become an in-and-outer. Until that pattern disappears, handicappers best honor it.

If both horses deliver their best, Polar Route should prevail. It's close, however, and Polar Route was offered at 9–5, while Luthier Fever was 7–2. In close situations take the higher odds. I also prefer supporting the younger horse on the upturn of a nicely hidden up-down figure pattern.

Luthier Fever took the early lead easily from Straight to Bed and won going away.

The next was another maiden sprint with the experienced starters below the Beyer par of 87. Surprise, surprise, another first-starter won. The favorite at 7–10 looked best in the past performances, including a seemingly high Beyer of 82. The 82 falls two lengths short of the maiden par at Hollywood Park. It's not an intelligent bet.

I blew the fifth, an allowance race for nonwinners other than maiden or claiming. The Beyer par was 91. The easy winner looked like this, a type I rarely support.

Geri
Own: Paulson Allen E
PINCAY L JR (178 19 29 26 .11)

Ch. c. 3 (Feb)
Sire: Theatrical (Ire) (Nureyev)
Dam: Garimpeiro (Mr. Prospector)
Br: Paulson Allen E (Ky)
Tr: Shoemaker Bill (17 2 1 4 .12)

113

Lifetime Record:	3	1	1	1	$34,400					
1995	3	1	1	1	$34,400	Turf	0	0	0	0
1994	0	M	0	0		Wet	0	0	0	0
Hol	0	0	0	0		Dist	0	0	0	0

21Apr95-6SA	fst	1	:22	:451	1:103	1:353	3↑ Md Sp Wt	98	6	5	46	32½	11½	13½	Pincay L Jr	B 117	*.80	91-12	Geri1173½ Double Up1166½ Mindlikaseive1233	Cl(
26Mar95-6SA	fst	6½f	:22	:451	1:092	1:153	Md Sp Wt	86	2	10	84½	62½	42½	21¾	Delahoussaye E	B 118	2.50	92-09	Tru's Heritage1181¾ Geri1183½ Silent Majority1185	(
11Feb95-6SA	fst	6f	:212	:443	:564	1:094	Md Sp Wt	76	8	10	1016	1016	913	35¾	Delahoussaye E	B 118	4.70	82-11	Go Gary Go1181¼ Conquest1184½ Geri118no	Broke slow

WORKOUTS: Jun 12 Hol 7f fst 1:291 H *3/3* ●Jun 7 Hol 6f fst 1:13 H *1/19* Jun 2 Hol 5f fst 1:031 H *28/32* May 28 Hol 4f fst :50 H *47/66* May 21 Hol 3f fst :371 H *17/28* Apr 20 SA 3f fst :39 H *36/38*

Geri had won smartly on April 21. Today is June 17. The gap extends for fifty-seven days. I will allow a six weeks' respite following a big win, but not much longer. Why the layup?

Geri had exceeded today's allowance par by three lengths in its maiden romp. Handicappers should like that. Maidens who impress with allowance figures, especially following a par-or-faster pace, can be trusted in allowance company, and often will be underbet. Two other horses in the field flashed par figures, but both looked ordinary otherwise.

Despite the suspicious layoff, Geri impressed again. The maiden grad paid even-money. No play.

Odds-on high-figure horses won the seventh and eighth, fooling nobody and enriching nobody.

In the seventh the high-figure favorite was actually tied by another contender. Of the two, only the winner figured to improve. It's an important, if evident, point. If two, three, or four contenders look similar on speed figures, prefer any that should improve. Improving form translates to improving speed figures.

The ninth was fascinating. It was an allowance sprint at seven furlongs, for fillies and mares, 3up, that had not won other than maiden or claiming. The Beyer par was 87. Two contenders had equaled par, but neither could be trusted. Examine the 2–1 favorite.

Smooth Wine
Own: Marshall Robert
PINCAY L JR (178 19 29 26 .11)

Ch. f. 4
Sire: Prospect North (Mr. Prospector)
Dam: Smooth N Lovely (Pappagallo)
Br: Lea Dennis & Jim (Wash)
Tr: Marshall Robert W (21 3 6 5 .14)

L 118

Lifetime Record:	26	9	5	3	$54,151					
1995	8	4	1	0	$35,451	Turf	0	0	0	0
1994	18	5	4	3	$18,700	Wet	3	1	2	0
Hol	3	2	0	0	$25,225	Dist	1	0	0	0

3Jun95-1Hol	fst	6½f	:22	:444	1:093	1:154	ⒻClm c-20000	87	7	3	31½	31	13	15½	Desormeaux K J	LB 118 b	*1.40	90-08	Smooth Wine1185½ Musical Pal116hd Toast The Table1161½	Clear
Claimed from Team Green, Stein Roger M Trainer																				
17May95-8Hol	fst	1 1/16 ⊗	:232	:47	1:112	1:432	ⒻAlw 43000N1X	67	6	3	42½	21½	22	49	Desormeaux K J	LB 117 b	2.50	75-17	Cathy's Dynasty1176 Whatawoman1171 Wadjit1172	4 wide :
1May95-1Hol	fst	6½f	:223	:452	1:101	1:164	ⒻClm 20000	86	5	3	22½	23	11½	16½	Desormeaux K J	LB 117 b	3.00	85-15	Smooth Wine1176½ Kata Did1172 Musical Pal1161	
12Apr95-6SA	fst	6f	:221	:45	:57	1:093	ⒻClm c-16000	46	6	6	54¼	55½	510	817¾	Desormeaux K J	L 117 b	2.70	71-13	Stach Sr.11711 ⒹSophi's Favorite1161½ Point Position116½	W
Claimed from Harrington Mike, Harrington Mike Trainer																				
15Mar95-5SA	fst	6f	:22	:451	:573	1:103	ⒻClm c-10000	79	1	6	45	34½	23½	12½	Desormeaux K J	LB 116 b	3.90	84-12	Smooth Wine1162½ Magic Moon116½ Investinu1173	Cle:
Claimed from Team Green, Stein Roger M Trainer																				
28Jan95-5SA	fst	7f	:23	:463	1:11	1:231	ⒻClm 12500	51	6	3	21	32	57½	613	Desormeaux K J	LB 117 b	5.60	73-11	Sarita Sarita116½ Canfield's Girl1154½ Toast The Table1174	W
21Jan95-6YM	sl	6f	:234	:49	1:014	1:153	ⒻClm c-10000	65	3	4	45	31	21	2hd	Ward V M	B 120 b	2.10	66-30	Granger Gal117hd Smooth Wine120nk Fast And Sassy1155	Finis
Claimed from Doc's Racing Stable 19, Burlingame Tom Trainer																				
7Jan95-7YM	gd	6f	:223	:461	:591	1:123	ⒻClm 10000	61	2	7	78¼	56¼	42½	11	Ward V M	B 116 b	*2.30	81-16	Smooth Wine1161 Classy Rolls1161½ Barbafire112¾	
23Dec94-8YM	sl	6f	:231	:464	:593	1:13	3↑ ⒻClm 8000	71	2	6	66	55¼	25	25½	Ward V M	B 115 b	3.00	73-28	Swan River Daisy1175½ Smooth Wine1155½ Stelliena110¾	Cl(
25Nov94-8YM	sl	5½f	:232	:474	1:011	1:082	ⒻClm 8000	61	3	5	58	56½	35½	1hd	Ward V M	B 116 b	6.40	73-29	Smooth Wine116hd Kristybooshay1196 Hot Hanna1182½	Up fin:

WORKOUTS: May 10 Hol 4f fst :474 H *5/63* Apr 9 Hol 3f fst :351 H *5/26* Apr 3 Hol 4f fst :521 H *11/11*

It's crucial to know the claiming pars that are comparable to the nonwinners' allowance pars at the local track. At Hollywood Park, nonwinners once allowance pars are comparable to $32,000 claiming pars, not $20,000 claiming pars. Smooth Wine will be rising high following the big win on June 3. She had attempted to rise just as high following the big win on May 1. What happened on May 17 should happen again. The extended record reflects a low-priced claiming competitor that tops out at the $20,000 claiming level. That is not an allowance contender.

The 4–1 second choice looked like this:

Continental Mood	Gr. f. 4		Lifetime Record: 2 1 0 0 $19,575
Own: Budget Stable	Sire: Darn That Alarm (Jig Time) Dam: Present Ace (For The Moment)		1995 1 1 0 0 $18,700 Turf 0 0 0 0
SORENSON D (55 5 8 4 .09)	Br: Dizney Donald R (Fla) Tr: Lloyd Kim (17 3 1 3 .18)	L 120	1994 1 M 0 0 $875 Wet 0 0 0 0 Hol 1 1 0 0 $18,700 Dist 0 0 0 0

3Jun95–6Hol fst 6½f :21⁴ :44² 1:09² 1:15⁴ 3↑ ⑦Md Sp Wt 87 4 4 3½ 2²½ 2ʰᵈ 1⁴ Sorenson D LB 122 f 54.00 90 – 08 Continental Mood122⁴ Sensuality116½ Stylish Society116ⁿᵏ Clear
12Jun94–1AP fst 6½f :22 :45² 1:11⁴ 1:18⁴ 3↑ ⑦Md Sp Wt 47 4 6 6²½ 54½ 3⁵ 4⁷½ Gryder A T L 114 f 19.00 71 – 16 Legafino114½ Darn Gorgeous114½ Burned Dividend114½ Brief w
WORKOUTS: May 27 Hol 4f fst :48⁴ H 17/52 May 20 Hol 5f fst 1:00¹ H 15/42 May 13 Hol 5f fst 1:00³ H 19/54 May 6 Hol 5f fst :59³ H 5/42 Apr 30 Hol 5f fst 1:00⁴ H 18/42 Apr 23 Hol 4f fst :47² H 3/26

Away a year, Continental Mood had won going away on her comeback, earning a Beyer par for today's allowance race. Nothing doing. Figure handicappers recognize a probable bounce at first glance. The filly wears fronts. Figure analysts rarely fail to anticipate this kind of obvious bounce due to overexertion following a layoff. For every horse that does not disappoint, a half dozen do. The odds are usually low. Why fight it?

The 16–1 winner looked like this:

Soy De Verdad	Ch. f. 4		Lifetime Record: 2 1 0 0 $1,266
Own: Camargo Julio G A	Sire: Ferdinand (Nijinsky II) Dam: Riasly (Raise A Native)		1994 1 0 0 0 Turf 1 0 0 0
ALMEIDA G F (136 13 17 19 .10)	Br: Thompson Roland E (Ky) Tr: McAnally Ronald (49 10 8 8 .20)	120	1993 1 1 0 0 $1,266 Wet 0 0 0 0 Hol 0 0 0 0 Dist 0 0 0 0

31Jly94–5Dmr fm 1⅛ ① :23¹ :47³ 1:13² 1:44⁴ ⑦Alw 44534N2L 61 4 4 5¹½ 4½ 54½ 61¹½ Almeida G F B 117 b 16.30 68 – 22 La Frontera120½ Wood Of Binn117⁴½ Sydney Explorer117⁴½ W
1Dec93↑Cdad Jardim(Brz) fst *6f 1:14² ⑦Premio Balerine d'Oro–Mdn 1 119 – Further Information unavailable
WORKOUTS: Jun 9 SA 7f fst 1:29⁴ H 6/6 Jun 4 SA 7f fst 1:29³ H 3/3 May 29 SA 7f fst 1:32³ H 3/3 May 23 SA 6f fst 1:14² H 3/13 May 18 SA 6f fst 1:17³ H 13/17 May 12 SA 5f fst :59³ H 2/36

I took no interest in Soy De Verdad, but she was a lightly raced 4YO from a hall-of-fame barn showing sharp, regular workouts. The Beyer Speed Figure of 61 means nothing, the point to be stressed. One low figure cannot be interpreted reliably. Second-starters might improve dramatically. If Smooth Wine and Continental Mood form the main contention in this allowance, Soy De Verdad can be used instead, as an angle bet, in exotics, or as a longshot to win.

The tenth was the Valkyr Handicap, a $100,000 stakes sprint at five and one-half furlongs on the turf, for fillies and mares, 3UP, limited to Cal-breds. The Beyer par was 99. The race featured the comeback of the sensational Soviet Problem. Review her record.

Itching to bet against this brilliant sprinter (second in the Breeders' Cup Sprint), I sat chilly when I could not find a figure horse capable of the upset. Soviet Problem's speed figures consistently exceed the stakes par, but that was hardly the point. The leaders of the division are not intended to do their best after a lengthy layoff. Bigger objectives await their peaking form. Soviet Problem went 2–5 in this heat.

Unfortunately none of the opposing Cal-breds showed a speed figure above par, let alone a figure comparable to any of Soviet Problem's numbers. If another filly or mare had been almost as fast, and keenly sharp, I would gladly have accepted the odds. And I would have won my bet. Soviet Problem tired visibly late, but survived against the lackluster competition.

When champions, near champions, and division leaders return from a long rest, they will be vulnerable, and may be unintended. Prefer horses having slightly lower speed figures, but sharp form, and a style well suited to today's distance, surface, and probable pace.

The thirteenth was an allowance sprint, for nonwinners three times other than maiden or claiming, 4UP, and I liked Fu Man Slew to upset Abaginone. It was strictly a figure play. How many handicappers agree?

Fu Man Slew
Own: Fisher & Isom & Moore
SORENSON D (55 5 8 4 .09)

Dk. b or br g. 4
Sire: Slew's Royalty (Seattle Slew)
Dam: Miss Shuga (To the Quick)
Br: Schwartz Stable (Cal)
Tr: Lloyd Kim (17 3 1 3 .18)

L 116

Lifetime Record:	10	3	1	2	$120,086					
1995	1	0	0	0		Turf	0	0	0	0
1994	9	3	1	2	$120,086	Wet	1	0	0	0
Hol	3	1	1	0	$37,550	Dist	2	0	0	1

27May95-9Hol	fst	6f	:21^3	:44^4	:56^4	1:09^1	3↑ Alw 51000N3X	70	8	2	2^{½}	1^{hd}	2^{hd}	9^{13¼}	Sorenson D	B 116	7.60	81–11	In Case116½ Beautiful Crown1161¼ Argolid116nk	Dueled, ga
29Oct94-5SA	fst	6f	:21^1	:43^4	:56	1:09^1	3↑ [S]CalCupSprntH100k	58	7	6	3^{½}	4^{2¾}	11^{7½}	12^{15¼}	Sorenson D	B 115	9.70	76–09	Uncaged Fury116hd Ke Express115½ Wild Gold1161¾	Brief
24Sep94-10TP	my	6f	:22	:45^3	:57^3	1:09^4	KyCup Sprint144k	84	3	3	1^{½}	1^{hd}	4^{2½}	5^{7¼}	Sorenson D	118	8.20	86–13	End Sweep120hd ExclusivePraline1221½ ChimesBand1221	Pace, wea
31Aug94-8Dmr	fst	6½f	:22	:44^2	1:08^1	1:14^2	[R]InvernessDrv60k	97	6	1	1^{hd}	2^1	2^1	3^{2¾}	Desormeaux K J	B 121	*1.40	96–08	Uncaged Fury119¾ Flying Sensation1152 Fu Man Slew1212¾	Wea
16Jly94-9Lrl	fst	6f	:21^4	:44^4	:56^3	1:08^4	3↑ DeFrancsMem-G2	107	6	2	1^1	1^{hd}	2^1	3^{2¾}	Bravo J	107	9.10	93–12	Cherokee Run1142¼ Boom Towner119½ Fu Man Slew107½	Wea
17Jun94-7Hol	fst	7½f	:22	:44^2	1:09	1:28^3	Harry Henson82k	106	5	1	1^1	1^{1½}	1^1	2^{hd}	Sorenson D	B 118	5.60	91–15	IndividulStyle121hd FuMnSlew118½ BeutifulCrown1171¼	Held stub
21May94-7Hol	fst	6f	:21^4	:44^2	:56^1	1:08^3	3↑ Alw 41000N2X	107	1	2	1^{½}	1^{hd}	1^{hd}	1^{¾}	Sorenson D	B 115	3.10	97–10	Fu Man Slew115¾ Westcot116¾ Winning Pact1136	(
24Apr94-4SA	fst	6f	:21^1	:44^3	:57	1:09^3	[S]Alw 37000N1X	94	1	4	1^1	1^1	1^2	1^{3½}	Sorenson D	B 120	15.00	89–13	Fu Man Slew1203½ I'ma Game Master1173 Royal Issue120¾	Clear
10Apr94-6SA	fst	6f	:21^3	:44^3	:57	1:09^3	Md Sp Wt	86	2	5	1^1	1^{hd}	1^{hd}	1^1	Sorenson D	B 118	38.20	89–11	Fu Man Slew1181 Devon Dancer1181¼ Nucay118¾	Game
13Mar94-2SA	fst	6½f	:21^4	:44^4	1:09^4	1:16^2	[S]Md Sp Wt	64	4	11	5^{3½}	6^{3¾}	4^{4½}	4^7	Black C A	118	20.00	83–12	Pie AlaRoad1181¼ Commander'sCode1185½ HillsboroRoad118hd	No l

WORKOUTS: Jun 11 Hol 5f fst 1:00^1 H *5/56* ●May 22 Hol 5f fst :59^4 H *1/29* ●May 15 Hol 6f fst 1:12 H *1/8* May 10 Hol 6f fst 1:15 H *5/22* May 4 Hol 6f fst 1:15^3 H *15/19* Apr 28 Hol 5f fst 1:02 H *22/43*

The Beyer par was 102.

Abaginone must be expected to bounce, and Fu Man Slew shows a trio of speed figures impressively superior to today's allowance par. He has the talent. The gelding also gets his second start following a seven-month rest. He had pressed a rapid pace first back, before tiring, and should improve, maybe tremendously.

Abaginone was 3–10, and Fu Man Slew 8–1. I bet with gusto. Abaginone did not bounce. He slaughtered Fu Man Slew on the front, my hope finishing last. So what? At 8–1 versus 3–10, if I take those odds repeatedly, I'm a winner.

In Sunday's first, a $40,000 claiming sprint having a Beyer par of 97, this horse upset a figure standout and hard-knocker favored at 3–5.

Rubin's Champion
Own: Smith Joanna T
VALENZUELA P A (84 11 14 16 .13) $40,000

B. g. 5
Sire: The Carpenter (Gummo)
Dam: Our Sweet Sham (Nostrum)
Br: Brown Ruben (Cal)
Tr: Bernstein David (23 2 3 4 .09)

L 116

Lifetime Record:	19	4	7	3	$132,944					
1995	5	1	0	2	$36,900	Turf	1	0	0	0
1993	12	2	6	1	$82,944	Wet	3	1	0	1
Hol	7	0	4	1	$31,550	Dist	10	4	3	2

4Jun95-7Hol	fst	7½f	:22^1	:44^3	1:09^2	1:28^2	3↑ [S]Alw 45000N2X	70	1	6	1^{½}	1^{hd}	8^{8¼}	9^{13}	Flores D R	LB 116 b	41.80	79–10	Pumpkin House1142 Saros' Triumph1162 Desert Pirate1143	Ins
29Apr95-3Hol	fst	7½f	:22^4	:45^3	1:09^4	1:28^3	3↑ [S]Alw 45000N2X	85	4	2	1^{½}	1^{½}	3^{2½}	[illegible]	Valenzuela P A	LB 117 b	4.60	84–13	Lucky Lit116½ Dancing Torch1196½ Rubin's Champion1173½	
Steadied, pinched back near 1/8																				
5Mar95-3SA	sly	6f	:22	:45^4	:58^1	1:11^1	Alw 47000N2X	88	3	6	6^{3¾}	4^{4½}	4^4	3^4	Steiner J J	LB 116 b	14.50	77–22	Kern Ridge1162½ Desert Act1171½ Rubin's Champion1162	Alon
11Feb95-7SA	fst	6½f	:21^1	:44	1:08^4	1:15^1	Alw 47000N2X	50	2	6	6^{5½}	8^{5¾}	8^{11}	7^{22¼}	Pedroza M A	LB 116 fb	26.10	74–11	Blumin Affair1172 Desert Act1178½ Tajo115no	Checked mi
6Jan95-7SA	sl	6f	:21^4	:45^2	:58	1:12	[S]Alw 42000N1X	82	3	5	3^3	2^{2½}	2^2	1^{1¾}	Pedroza M A	LB 118 fb	6.10	77–25	Rubin'sChampion1181¾ Airlaunch118½ Superfluously1201	Stumb
11Dec93-9Hol	sly	6f	:22^3	:45^4	:58^3	1:11^3	3↑ [S]Alw 30000N1X	52	5	3	6^{4½}	6^{6½}	5^{8½}	6^{13}	Pedroza M A	LB 116 fb	*1.60	69–19	Bold And Lacey119¾ Ke Express1175 Kolbe's Gold1181¼	Climb
21Nov93-9Hol	fm	1 (T)	:23^2	:46^3	1:10^4	1:35^3	3↑ Alw 33000N1X	69	5	5	3^4	3^3	4^{1½}	5^{6½}	Pedroza M A	LB 115 fb	9.80	80–11	Justtofit115nk Tutts118nk [DH]Gambler's Way118	W
2Oct93-8Fpx	fst	6½f	:21^4	:45^2	1:09^4	1:16^1	3↑ Alw 36000N1X	78	4	3	2^2	2^1	2^{2½}	2^6	Pedroza M A	LB 114 b	*1.80	89–09	Quotion1146 Rubin's Champion1143 Video Alert1131	Intimidat
16Sep93-10Fpx	fst	6½f	:21^1	:44^2	1:10^3	1:17	Foothill50k	81	1	7	8^{7½}	7^{5½}	5^{4½}	2^2	Lopez A D	LB 114 fb	12.20	89–11	Town Caper1142 Rubin's Champion114½ Dale's Best117½	
2Sep93-6Dmr	fst	6f	:21^3	:44^2	:56^4	1:09^3	Clm 50000	87	6	1	3^1	3^{½}	1^{½}	1^3	Pedroza M A	LB 115 b	3.20	91–09	Rbn'sChmpon1153 WstrnSct110nk TwntyIsPlnty1162½	Wide earl

WORKOUTS: Jun 12 Hol 3f fst :37^4 H *19/26* May 26 Hol 5f fst 1:03^4 H *28/30* May 19 Hol 4f fst :46^3 H *2/41* Apr 24 SA 4f fst :48^2 H *15/36* Apr 18 SA 5f gd 1:01^3 H *9/43* Apr 10 SA 5f fst 1:00^4 H *18/50*

The 5YO had not finished within four lengths of today's par in its last ten attempts. He started from the dead Hollywood rail. His pace figures were also lower than the favorite's by as many as four lengths. Rubin's Champion nonetheless grabbed the early lead and withstood the hard knocker's pressure by half a length.

No explanation satisfies. It just happens. At two, Rubin's Champion had impressed sufficiently to imagine the horse might amount to something. He did not develop. He entered today's fray a dispiriting zero-for-seven at Hollywood Park. He stole the race. Chalk it up to the mystique of early speed.

It's convenient to remember as well that when his Beyer Speed Figure has been published, and it's a 97 or higher, Rubin's Champion becomes a prime candidate to regress next time. The 97 will stick out like a detour sign in Rubin's Champion's past performances, an exceptional figure an ordinary horse does not replicate.

The hard knocker who finished second was Appendix Joe, whose record reflects a couple of interesting figure patterns.

Keep in mind that a Beyer Speed Figure in sprints can be worth as much as two and one-half points.

When a high-priced claimer dispenses comparably strong speed figures repetitively, especially while running on the front, where variations in the early pace can play havoc with the final numbers, handicappers have found one of the most reliable figure plays in the game. Appendix Joe may have lost by three-quarters to Rubin's Champion, but he will probably repeat his customary speed figures next out. The high-priced hard knockers run within two lengths of their top reliably.

If Appendix Joe and his kind suddenly dispense a performance more than three lengths below their top, beware. Unless a special excuse accompanies the performance (suicidal pace, badly outclassed), the hard knockers at last need a rest. Get off.

Appendix Joe had also shipped to southern California from Yakima Meadows, in Washington, a minor track that prospered following the wholesale migration there of Longacres horses. The gelding's Beyers had been persistently lower at Yakima Meadows than they have been at Hollywood Park and Santa Anita. It's a shipping phenomenon peculiar to several Beyer Speed Figures in southern California, and presumptively a phenomenon at other shipping and receiving ovals.

If handicappers discover as a rule the Beyer Speed Figures have been higher or lower at the local tracks than they were at the shipping tracks, accept the deviations and record them mentally. The mental adaptations protect a downside, and occasionally can trigger a fantastic overlay, as when Appendix Joe shipped to Santa Anita on January 29, moved up in class, and promptly surprised at 38–1. His pace fraction that day was a blistering 43 ⅘, his turn time just as eye-catching at 22⅖. I had not recognized Appendix Joe as a good thing on January 29, but might have if the Yakima successes had not occurred on wet tracks.

Remember this: If claiming shippers from lower-class ovals have been consistent, versatile, and impressive, especially after moving ahead in class, they have every right to impress at the higher-class oval as well. If they lose at first crack, play them back the next time, and the next. The odds will be juicy. Lower speed figures at the shipping track will not prevent the eventual upset.

The next was a Cal-bred maiden sprint, having a Beyer par of 82. The winner was Contentment. Take a quick look.

Whenever a maiden has exceeded par, that maiden will be difficult to defeat. Contentment's 87 Beyer reflects a performance two lengths better-than-par. First-starters will be severely stretched to overcome that. Handicappers should identify the Beyer pars for maidens at their tracks, and adhere to this guideline closely.

Fast-forward to the seventh race, a dash on the grass at five-and-a-half furlongs for $62,500 claiming horses, which means good horses. The Beyer par was 99.

The predictable winner looked like this:

Stately Warrior
Own: Cavanagh Marguerite F & Thomas M
ANTLEY C W (146 20 23 13 .14) $62,500

B. g. 5
Sire: Stately Don (Nureyev)
Dam: Really Fancy (In Reality)
Br: Cavanagh Mr–Mrs Thomas M (Ky)
Tr: Peterson Douglas R (10 1 1 1 .10)

L 117

Lifetime Record:	35	5	3	6	$164,878					
1995	8	1	1	2	$58,225	Turf	14	1	2	3
1994	11	2	0	1	$39,078	Wet	2	0	0	0
Hol Ⓣ	5	0	1	1	$22,525	Dist Ⓣ	1	0	0	0

1Jun95-8Hol	fm	5½f	Ⓣ	:213	:441	:552	1:014		Alw 55000N$Y	99	2	4	2½	1hd	1hd	52½	Antley C W	LB 118 b	23.80	96-02	Cyrano Storme116no Pembroke1161¾ Tychonic116½	Dueled, ou
10May95-8Hol	fm	1	Ⓣ	:231	:46	1:094	1:334		Alw 54000N3X	90	1	1	15	12	2hd	64½	Black C A	LB 116 b	13.20	89-06	Sharman1152 Geenger Man115½ Saltgrass1151	Speed, w
24Apr95-4SA	fm	*6½f	Ⓣ	:214	:44	1:072	1:133		Alw 47000N2X	101	4	1	2hd	1hd	1½	11¼	Antley C W	LB 115 b	4.70	90-13	Stately Warrior1151¼ Saturnino1152 Le Dome1163½	V
9Apr95-2SA	fm	*6½f	Ⓣ	:214	:434	1:064	1:13		Clm 62500	94	1	2	42½	43½	33½	34¾	Antley C W	LB 116 b	2.70	88-07	Three Peat1164 Saturnino116¾ Stately Warrior1162¼	
5Mar95-3SA	sly	6f		:22	:454	:581	1:111		Alw 47000N2X	83	6	1	21	31½	33½	46	Valenzuela P A	LB 117 b	3.20	75-22	Kern Ridge1162½ Desert Act1171½ Rubin's Champion1162	W
19Feb95-7SA	fm	*6½f	Ⓣ	:212	:44	1:074	1:141		Alw 47000N2X	98	5	1	1hd	12	15	2hd	Black C A	LB 116 b	8.10	87-13	Lynton116hd Stately Warrior1162 I'm Checkin' Out117½	Los
1Feb95-5SA	gd	*6½f	Ⓣ	:214	:44	1:082	1:15		Alw 47000N2X	94	8	1	3nk	31½	1hd	3½	Black C A	LB 116 b	23.30	83-17	Geenger Man117hd Golden Post117nk Stately Warrior116no	Gav
18Jan95-3SA	fst	6½f		:212	:441	1:09	1:154		Alw 53000N3X	77	6	2	41	43	66	47½	Antley C W	LB 116 b	12.70	86-14	Lit De Justice1182½ Virtuous Regent1172¾ Marmoe1162	
29Dec94-8SA	fst	6f		:213	:441	:562	1:084	3↑	Alw 47000N2X	65	8	1	43½	43	88¾	814¼	Antley C W	LB 119 b	12.40	79-14	Isitingood1161¾ Desert Act1173 Heavenly Crusade1151¾	Took u
Placed 7th through disqualification.																						
14Dec94-7Hol	gd	6f		:221	:46	:583	1:114	3↑	Alw 40000N2X	85	3	6	64½	63¼	31½	33	Antley C W	LB 119 b	8.80	78-21	VirtuousRegent1171¼ SkimTheGravy1171¾ StatelyWarrior119hd	4

WORKOUTS: Apr 7 SA 3f fst :374 H *30/39*

Handicappers should appreciate the differences between Stately Warrior's dirt figures and his grass figures. The gelding prefers turf, notwithstanding his modest achievements on that surface.

Beyer Speed Figures do an exceptionally good job of distinguishing horses at the various distances and on different surfaces. If today's race will be seven furlongs, a mile, or a mile and one-quarter, handicappers should pay attention to any speed figures recorded at those exact distances.

The same guideline bolsters the handicapping on wet tracks, in the mud, and on the grass. Rely upon speed figures that have impressed under those conditions, notably if the performances were underscored by lofty odds. The good races were not expected, not routine. They therefore constitute excellent figure plays.

Next comes a fine point of class handicapping not well comprehended by handicappers, and informed absolutely by speed figures. The Sunday feature was a Grade 2 event for 3YO fillies, offering a $100,000 pot at a mile and one-sixteenth. The Beyer par was 94.

The 8–5 favorite looked like this and was highly likely to disappoint.

Sleep Easy
Own: Juddmonte Farms
NAKATANI C S (190 47 34 23 .25)

B. f. 3 (May)
Sire: Seattle Slew (Bold Reasoning)
Dam: Dokki (Northern Dancer)
Br: Juddmonte Farms Inc (Ky)
Tr: Frankel Robert (64 17 3 13 .27)

L 117

Lifetime Record:	3	2	0	0	$87,950					
1995	3	2	0	0	$87,950	Turf	0	0	0	0
1994	0	M	0	0		Wet	0	0	0	0
Hol	2	1	0	0	$67,600	Dist	0	0	0	0

27May95-4Hol	fst	7f	:22	:443	1:092	1:222		ⒻRailbird-G2	94	8	2	53	54	41½	1¾	Nakatani C S	LB 113	*1.70	90-11	Sleep Easy113¾ Texinadress1182½ Laguna Seca115½	4 wide,determ
6May95-6Hol	fst	7f	:221	:45	1:094	1:224	3↑	ⒻAlw 40000N1X	80	4	3	3½	31½	63¾	43¼	Solis A	B 114	*.70	85-12	Cee's Maryanne120¾ Pharos Discovery115¾ Bello Cielo1161¾	
Fell back turn, in tight 1/16, came back																					
1Apr95-6SA	fst	6½f	:22	:442	1:091	1:153		ⒻMd Sp Wt	95	1	2	1hd	1½	12½	16½	Flores D R	B 117	6.30	94-10	Sleep Easy1176½ Danathunder1172¼ Toga Toga Toga117no	Rid

WORKOUTS: Jun 13 Hol 5f fst 1:004 H *5/37* Jun 7 Hol 5f fst 1:003 H *6/43* May 22 Hol 5f fst 1:01 H *12/29* May 16 Hol 4f fst :484 H *6/11* May 2 Hol 5f fst 1:013 H *12/32* Apr 26 Hol 6f fst 1:13 H *3/17*

Lightly raced, improving, beautifully bred, and trained by the remarkable Bobby Frankel, Sleep Easy has just recorded today's Grade 2 par in a Grade 2 sprint. Isn't the translation to the route matter of fact? It is not.

I just cautioned that Beyer Speed Figures can be excellent indicators of ability at exact distances. A horizontal, high-class move from sprint to route, as from a Grade 2 sprint to a Grade 2 route, is not acceptable unless the sprint figure clearly exceeds par, preferably by three lengths.

The route will demand greater displays of endurance and determination. Obvious reserves of speed will be needed. The reserves suggest the horse can stretch out effectively, as par figures do not. Sleep Easy had captured the Grade 2 Railbird in a determined effort, which resulted in a par figure. For unseasoned 3YOs, par going short does not often translate into an above-par performance at the same high class at a longer distance. Trainer specialists might also concede that Frankel has never fared as well with 3YOs as he has with mature older horses.

I could not isolate the winner of this Grade 2 route, but I was not lured into an 8–5 wager on Sleep Easy. Sleep Easy finished third, a decent effort, but not a winning effort, as the Beyer Speed Figures might have warned.

The ninth was another maiden sprint, the Beyer par 88. None of the experienced runners had yet exceeded a Beyer 82. Guess what? Again a first-starter won. I trust this lesson will not be lost.

The next was a seven-furlong sprint for $8,000 platers, 4up, the bottom class at Hollywood Park. The Beyer par was 78. Six of ten entrants had exceeded par recently, but none stood apart on the figures. One stood apart, however, on a pace analysis. Check out the last running line.

Distinguished Bid — B. g. 6
Own: Hansen Yuliya
PEDROZA M A (195 15 16 32 .08) — $8,000
Sire: Baederwood (Tentam)
Dam: Truly Brilliant (Brilliant Protege)
Br: Parson Edmund L (Md)
Tr: Sahadi Jenine (23 5 2 2 .22)
L 116

Lifetime Record:	34	13	1	3	$75,785					
1995	3	0	0	1	$1,470	Turf	1	0	0	1
1994	13	9	1	1	$55,385	Wet	3	2	0	0
Hol	1	0	0	0		Dist	1	0	0	0

10May95-5Hol	fst	7f		:22	:443	1:09	1:22	Clm 10000	54	6	1	2hd	2hd	24	718	Pedroza M A	LB 116 f	4.90	74-11	Dragster1167 Luckscaliber1161¾ Harrisburg1161¼	Dueled, g
22Apr95-13RD	fst	6f	⊗	:23	:463	1:00	1:132 3↑	Alw 8040N1Y	52	4	4	3nk	1½	1½	36½	Marte I	LB 118 f	*.90	75-15	TisAndy'sTurn1181½ ThdddyofthmAll1185 DistingushdBd118½	W
6Apr95-7TP	fst	6f		:221	:452	:573	1:103	Alw 10000s	80	4	4	43	33½	32½	44¾	Marte I	L 114 f	10.00	87-19	More Traffic1132½ Long Suit113¾ Joe's Dollar1191½	
14Aug94-4EIP	fst	6½f		:223	:46	1:103	1:171 3↑	Alw 5000s	77	3	4	41¾	21½	31½	45¼	Marte I	L 116 f	*1.70	86-14	Jcqulyn'sGroom114hd ThrsholdTrffic119no Boozing1165	Bid, flatt
24Jly94-6FP	fst	1		:242	:48	1:131	1:40 3↑	Alw 4000s	66	1	5	61	46½	32	24	Marte I	L 119 f	*.40	83-19	BldeOfThBll1164 DistinguishdBid1194½ Jolly'sDncrs1191½	Lugge
13Jly94-14RD	sly	170		:232	:472	1:123	1:442 3↑	Alw 5000s	76	6	3	33	21½	13	1¾	Marte I	LB 116 f	*.70	84-22	Distinguished Bid116¾ Mr. Nice Sky116¾ Cathaoir Mor116hd	
3Jly94-6EIP	fm	1$\frac{1}{16}$	Ⓣ	:233	:47	1:103	1:403 3↑	Alw 5000s	80	5	1	1hd	1hd	11	3½	Marte I	L 112 f	*.70	98-01	Jeffrey'sProspect112no MrryLink112½ DistinguishdBid1123	Hel
27May94-10RD	fst	170		:24	:481	1:14	1:45 3↑	Alw 4000s	84	4	3	2½	1½	15	14	Marte I	LB 119 f	*.40	81-19	Distinguished Bid1194 Turning Hawk1226 Fight AtNoon1164	Ri
23Apr94-8Pim	fst	1⅛		:461	1:101	1:36	1:492 3↑	[S]Jennings H100k	84	7	2	32½	45	68	815½	Marte I	L 114 f	9.20	82-16	Taking Risks1143 Frottage117nk Tidal Surge1125	(
5Apr94-9TP	fst	1		:23	:461	1:10	1:351	Alw 19400N$Y	93	3	1	1hd	1hd	12½	15	Marte I	L 115 f	*1.40	96-12	DstngushdBd1155 SchoolboyRow1212½ StylshSnor11813	Sharp, ri

WORKOUTS: Jun 13 Hol 3f fst :38 H *25/29* Jun 1 Hol 5f fst :593 H *2/41* May 25 Hol 3f fst :36 H *5/21* May 2 RD 5f my 1:06 B *1/2*

None of the other contenders had equaled 45 flat to the pace call. Several ran slower to the pace call by a couple of lengths. Distinguished Bid was dropping a peg out of a hot pace at today's distance against a better field. Moreover, the 6YO's route figures at various midclass tracks last season had easily exceeded Hollywood's $8000 par. The gelding had won three times going longer, while showing speed to the pace call.

When the Beyer Speed Figures look contentious, especially at lower class levels, handicappers should immediately conduct a pace analysis. If pace figures must improve, final figures should decline, and vice versa. If one horse stands out on pace, à la Distinguished Bid, the handicapping is practically done.

Distinguished Bid secured the front handily and cruised home by five. The only disappointment was the $6.40 mutuel. Apparently more handicappers than ever are becoming astute pace analysts.

Some figure plays just cannot be denied. This is an allowance sprint for Cal-bred fillies, nonwinners other than maiden or claiming. Par is 87. Which horse do handicappers prefer?

Bonjour Madame	Ch. f. 3 (Feb)		Lifetime Record :	3 1 0 0	$16,113
Own: Magnin & Relatively Stable	Sire: Beau's Eagle (Golden Eagle II) Dam: Madam Ask Us (Damascus)		1994 3 1 0 0 $16,113	Turf 0 0 0 0	
	Br: Harold Applebaum (Cal)		1993 0 M 0 0	Wet 0 0 0 0	
STEVENS G L (126 22 21 18 .17)	Tr: Drysdale Neil (29 9 4 3 .31)	114	Hol 0 0 0 0	Dist 0 0 0 0	

29Oct94-9SA fst 1¼ :22 :454 1:112 1:441 ⑧CalCupJuvFil100k 43 2 1 1¹ 4² 6⁶ 72¾ Delahoussaye E B 116 7.60 52-19 Fbulouspersusion115½Roujoleur1154¼Embroidrd1154½ Dueled, ga
25Sy94-2BM fst 6f :222 :45 :572 1:103 ⑥Md Sp Wt 77 7 1 43½ 43½ 3¹ 1² Baze R A B 117 3.20 88-12 Bonjour Madame117²Mari's Sheba117no Fare Value1174¼ Ralli
31Jly94-6Dmr fst 5f :221 :451 :572 ⑦⑥Md Sp Wt 76 3 3 41½ 41½ 44½ 44½ Delahoussaye E B 117 14.10 98-07 Vida Slew1171¾Regal Ruthie1171¼Candi's Star117hd Mild l
WORKOUTS: Jun 11 Hol 6f fst 1:153 H 19/21 Jun 5 Hol 6f fst 1:154 H 13/14 May 30 Hol 3f fst :372 H 13/24 May 25 Hol 5f fst 1:012 H 26/43 May 19 Hol 5f fst 1:032 H 44/44 May 13 Hol 5f fst 1:033 H 52/54

Juliandra	Dk. b or br f. 3 (Apr)		Lifetime Record :	1 1 0 0	$20,350
Own: Big Train Farm & Recachina	Sire: Bolger (Damascus) Dam: Beseya (Cajun Prince)		1995 1 1 0 0 $20,350	Turf 0 0 0 0	
	Br: Dion Recachina & John Forsythe (Cal)		1994 0 M 0 0	Wet 0 0 0 0	
NAKATANI C S (190 47 34 23 .25)	Tr: Peterson Douglas R (10 1 1 1 .10)	L 114	Hol 1 1 0 0 $20,350	Dist 1 1 0 0	

2Jun95-2Hol fst 6½f :214 :444 1:092 1:154 3↑ ⑧⑧Md Sp Wt 92 5 2 2½ 1½ 1¹ 12½ Nakatani C S LB 116 6.70 90-12 Juliandra116²½Contentment11710Shoshana11612
WORKOUTS: May 29 Hol 5f fst 1:05 H 38/38 May 24 Hol 5f fst 1:03 H 34/52 May 18 Hol 5f fst 1:02 Hg30/41 May 12 Hol 4f fst :493 Hg23/30 May 6 Hol 4f fst :471 H 3/49 Apr 30 Hol 3f fst :364 H 12/26

The faster horse won.

Notice the spread in the Beyer Speed Figures between Juliandra and Bonjour Madame, from 92 to 77, or 15 points, which means six lengths. When young 3YOs improve in a sudden spurt, the norm will be three to five lengths. That degree of improvement would not be enough to allow Bonjour Madame to overtake Juliandra. Juliandra, I trust handicappers have noticed, has already exceeded by two lengths today's allowance par. She is hardly outclassed in an NW1 allowance contest.

Keep those numerical differences in mind. Beyer Speed Figures are characterized by wide swings in the numbers, a strength of the method often perceived otherwise. If Horse A has improved by three lengths while Horse B has declined by three lengths, perfectly normal patterns, the numerical spread will be 15 points in sprints, and 12 points in routes.

In other words it's not unusual for an improving horse to reduce a 15-point difference on the Beyer scale to no difference at all. Full-dress handicapping should supersede any blind ambition tied to the figures.

Bonjour Madame did improve by five lengths. She lost to Juliandra by only a neck.

Handicappers should not underestimate the importance of placing the Beyer Speed Figures in a broader context. The importance of having Beyer pars cannot be overstated. They anchor many decisions hinged to the numbers and guide the analyses in ways that merely comparing horses' speed figures with one another cannot possibly achieve.

As the *Daily Racing Form* has not yet provided Beyer Speed Pars, handicappers must develop their own.

It's no longer painstakingly difficult, and does not resemble the time-and-energy drudgery traditionally required during a long afternoon of making the actual par times. Now figure handicappers can purchase par times, and convert them quickly to Beyer Speed Pars. The paybacks will commence immediately.

To conclude on a high note, one common situation which does not require illustration, but which handicappers should internalize and recall to mind in an instant, occurs at every track in several races every day. Two Beyer Speed Figures as strong or stronger than the figures of other horses will be more reliable than any figure standing alone. Beyer himself refers to the phenomenon as a "double-fig." The two high figures need not be consecutive, just related.

A single high Beyer may reflect a tactical advantage that will not be present today, but two top Beyers reflect authentic speed.

Countless other situations might be illustrated to provide a deeper perspective and broader context for interpreting the Beyer Speed Figures effectively. But it's unnecessary. If handicappers remember to use speed figures in their full-blown handicapping context, they have remembered the most important principle of figure handicapping.

PACE FIGURES

Of the several factors that influence final times, and therefore the associated speed figures, three are vital: (1) track surface; (2) relative class; and (3) pace. Many would include trips, a circumstantial factor that can obviously prevent horses from recording final times they otherwise might.

Regardless, the influence on time wielding the heaviest practical consequences for handicappers is pace. That's because the various leading figure methods dealing exclusively with adjusted final times ignore pace. Thousands of handicappers apply those methods. When pace figures should supersede speed figures, which happens frequently, final-figure analysts proceed at a disadvantage. Handicappers in possession of pace figures enjoy an enviable edge, perhaps the most underestimated edge in figure handicapping.

In addition, the utility value of pace figures is high. Horses carrying fancy pace figures win at every track virtually every racing day. It happened yesterday at each of two tracks I played, once on the grass at Santa Anita, and again in a classified allowance sprint at Golden Gate Fields.

It's instructive to revisit both races. The Golden Gate sprint (February 26) invited classified types that had not won $24,000 first money since November 2. The main contenders illustrate a common and clever aspect of pace analysis utilizing pace figures.

Review the past performances briefly and examine the speed and pace figures provided on page 27.

	Race	Pace	Speed	Class
Hornitos	Feb. 5	103	107	Hcp
Troyalty	Nov. 20	110	105	Gr. 3 (T)
Lil Sneeker	Feb. 9	108	106	Alw, NW4X

Relying upon my figures, Hornitos and Lil Sneeker both showed speed figures superior to Troyalty's. The Beyer Speed Figures assigned even greater advantages, especially to Hornitos, who went favored at 2–1.

But Troyalty figured to prevail in this spot and indeed he romped wire-to-wire by two lengths, paying $7.20. Lil Sneeker finished second. Hornitos did not fire, but would not have won regardless.

When horses show comparable speed figures, pace figures earned against clearly superior competition frequently deserve the nod. Troyalty, a colt that prefers dirt, had recorded a superb pace figure on grass at Hollywood Park against Grade 3 sprinters. If Hornitos had pressed Troyalty early, its speed figures would almost certainly have declined, a dynamic too few speed handicappers are willing to concede.

Lil Sneeker qualifies as a top-class claiming and allowance sprinter at Golden Gate Fields. Those kind will be smothered by stakes sprinters showing higher pace figures versus better at major tracks. Under a smart ride by Russell Baze, Lil Sneeker avoided a pace contest with Troyalty, staying several lengths back early, and came late for second.

Figure handicappers can tally repeatedly with this play. Whenever a few solid sprinters look competitive, favor the horse demonstrating a pace edge in clearly superior company. If the pace slackens, the speed figure of the classier horse usually improves. If the pace quickens, the speed figures of the lower-class horses typically decline.

In a fascinating variation of the Golden Gate race, switch now to Santa Anita, change from dirt to grass, and go from sprint to route. It's the same day. The Santa Anita turf event is an allowance affair, 4up, for nonwinners twice other than maiden or claiming. Majestic Style will be adding blinkers. Golden Post is the favorite.

Again, review the records and examine some interesting speed and pace figures.

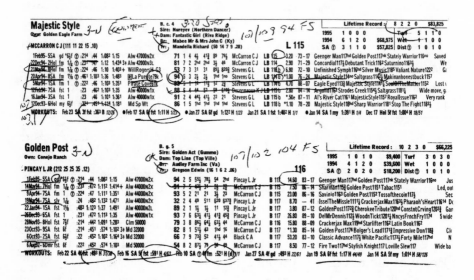

	Race	Pace	Speed	Class
Golden Post	Feb. 1	102	104	Alw, NW2X
	May 14	100	106	Alw, NW2X
Majestic Style	Feb. 1	109	94	Alw, NW2X
	Dec. 22	107	100	Alw, NW3X
	Apr. 20	116	106	Stk, Restricted

In the colt's third start following a long layoff, Majestic Style will be fitted with the blinkers he wore while winning a stakes last season, not to mention finishing within three-quarters of a length of Eagle Eyed, a Grade 2 winner. Trainer Richard Mandella is making a move.

But the telltale clue is Majestic Style's pace figure of 109 last out. When a horse has been away, is rounding into form, and delivers a high pace figure before tiring, the next start should be a major effort.

If that horse has beaten better, the high pace figure means still more. It means the horse is prepared to surpass today's lower-level conditions. Another horse may disrupt the plans, but the combination of fast pace, improved form, and back class will be difficult to deny.

Horses such as Golden Post will be outgunned early and late. After starting in maiden-claiming affairs and having lost four times under today's conditions, Golden Post's pace figures are particularly suspect. If Golden Post attempts to press Majestic Style approaching the pace call, its pace figure will be higher. Its final figure therefore will almost surely be lower, maybe many lengths lower.

Blinkers on, Majestic Style rushed to the front in the Santa Anita grass race and was never threatened. He paid a generous $8.40. Golden Post was no factor.

Pace figures can clarify numerous otherwise baffling situations, but none having a greater analytical force than in these examples. When high pace figures can be combined with back class and improving form, the synergism can be fantastic.

Both Troyalty and Majestic Style won by open lengths, never seriously threatened. In the same way, innumerable horses having high pace figures and competitive final figures win with surprising ease. Speed handicappers will often be caught looking another way. Pace handicappers have the edge, and they should be certain to exploit it.

Pace figures play various prominent roles in figure handicapping, virtually all of them underestimated by handicappers without pace figures. The odds crawl upward.

As a rule, pace figures will be more decisive than speed figures in cheaper races. Maiden-claiming races, bottom-of-the-barrel claiming races, and claiming races limited to 3YOs fill the bill. Speed figures of favorites and other contenders may be dismal to awful. All the horses have frequently run below par, maybe by several lengths. The races look unpredictable, unplayable.

But one of the horses may flash a superior pace figure. If those horses can wrestle the lead at the second call, they will be difficult to overtake. The others are plainly slow. The pace stickout lasts. It's a common scenario in bad races. Handicappers in possession of pace figures should never fail to identify the horse with the pace advantage in low-level company.

Pace figures are relevant, too, when nonclaiming horses move ahead in class. The swifter pace of the better races defeats dozens of overbet class-jumpers every season. The standard that counts is a pace figure within two lengths of today's par. If nonclaiming horses moving up reveal unacceptable pace figures, throw them out.

A group notoriously sensitive to low pace figures are the nonclaiming 3YOs. Every season the fancier threes make their way through the nonwinners' allowances to the stakes and the graded stakes, a few of them jumping into the classics. At each step the accompanying pace figure should be acceptable. If pace looms a problem, and the price is low, no play.

Alternately, if the pace figure has been solid, but the speed figure is slightly below par, beware. Handicappers are looking at evidence that a fast pace probably takes too high a toll. If pace analysis indicates today's pace should be faster than the colt or filly has engaged effectively, a 3YO is likely to disappoint.

The relationships will look like this: (Par 107)

| Pace 106 | Speed 111 | Alw, NW2X |
| Pace 112 | Speed 105 | Stakes, Gr. 2 |

The sizzling pace of the Grade 2 event extracts too much early and the horse finishes a couple of lengths below par. This 3YO can win multiple stakes, and will, but will probably be outrun in the important events and will be extended to succeed whenever the pace should be hard-pressed and faster-than-par. The majority of 3YO stakes candidates reveal speed and pace figures similar to these: (Par 105)

| Pace 101 | Speed 106 | Alw, NW1X |
| Pace 106 | Speed 102 | Alw, NW1X |

The horse is probably a claimer. Its ability to withstand allowance competition will depend upon the pace. If the early fractions are too slow, maybe. If the going's fast, very probably not. Numerous maiden graduates jam this category. To be sure, regardless of the speed figure, if the maiden win has featured a below-par pace figure, the graduate is not likely to advance in the allowances.

On the other hand, anytime a nonclaiming 3YO can improve its pace figure and speed figure simultaneously by two lengths or more while moving up in class, as from maiden to allowance conditions, that sophomore can probably move ahead again.

No one who has experimented with a quality brand of pace figures for six months will doubt their versatility and value again. Like converts of any kind, they will swear by pace figures. Methods aside, figure handicappers craving every edge have a definite financial incentive to develop pace figures, and to use them shrewdly.

TURN-TIME PLUS

E normous frustration at the racetrack is tied to realizing an overbet favorite should lose, without knowing which horse should win. The low-level claiming horse below was even-money in an $8500 claiming sprint at Golden Gate Fields. Look carefully at the last running line, the second line back, and the third line back.

Turn-time refers to the second fraction of the races, constitutes a crucial aspect of pace analysis in sprints, and can be calculated as the fractional-time difference between the first and second calls, modified by lengths gained or lost. Improving or declining turn-times often indicate to pace analysts whether form is positive or negative. Revisit Sucha Warrior's last three running lines. Calculate the turn-times.

Do handicappers agree the even-money shot has taken a negative turn? I hope so. Examine the turn-times of the races and of Sucha Warrior.

Race	Race	Horse	
Feb. 15	23 ⅖	23 ⅗	Lost by 6 ½
Feb. 4	22 ⅘	22 ⅘	Won by 2 ½
Jan. 22	22 ⅗	22 ⅗	Won by 3

When sharp, Sucha Warrior can negotiate the second fraction under twenty-three seconds, and win. Suddenly the horse is running fourth, beaten four lengths, at the first call. The turn-time of the February 15th race is an unexceptional 23 ⅖, and Sucha Warrior loses a length. That's potentially a horse in decline, the kind to attack at even-money.

For the record, Sucha Warrior finished out of the money in the $8500 race where I searched diligently, but unsuccessfully, for an alternative.

In *Modern Pace Handicapping* author Tom Brohamer introduced handicappers to the joys and advantages of turn-time. Brohamer flatly asserted the second is generally the most decisive fraction of sprints. By the second call the race is two-thirds complete.

During the second fraction the powerful front-runners and pressers exhaust the weaker kind. Pressers and stalkers gain ground on weaker front-runners. Off-pace types and closers maneuver into striking position, gaining on the early pace.

Turn-time can be connected to a couple of basic principles of pace analysis. If they hope to have a realistic chance of reaching the wire first, off-pace horses and closers should be gaining on the lead horse during the second fraction. Sucha Warrior's inability to gain on a sluggish second fraction provided a telltale clue of impending decline. An unaware betting public rendered the horse even-money.

In addition any horse that dispenses an impressive turn-time and subsequently wins or finishes close in par or faster has delivered an excellent performance. These horses will be a handful next time. They may look like this:

Jason H appeared on the same Golden Gate program as Sucha Warrior. Similar illustrations can be found at local tracks throughout the country.

Away since October 20, on February 4 Jason H returned and completed the turn of a maiden sprint in 22 ⅖ seconds, a splendid second fraction. Jason H then devoured the final fraction in 24 seconds flat. The 3YO gelding ran the final half mile in 46 ⅖.

This was not the late charge of a one-run closer. Such a charge normally finishes second or third. Jason H first gained on the pace, picking up three lengths on a 23-flat second fraction, which is one length faster-than-par for maidens at Golden Gate Fields.

This was a provocative maiden victory, so impressive to me, I backed Jason H at 7–1 in his next start, an allowance race for nonwinners of two lifetime. I expected to cash the bet, and would have except the allowance race occurred at a mile. Jason H grabbed the lead coming into the stretch, but flattened in the final sixteenth, and was passed by the favorite, who was exiting a minor stakes. Jason H held second.

No matter. If Jason H returns to six furlongs next, I'll be interested. The 22 ⅖ turn-time and fast finish of the maiden sprint will be partially hidden. I might get another chance at 7–1. If Jason H can run 22 ⅖ around the far turn and finish in 24 seconds, I'll take my chances.

Pace authority Brohamer has advised handicappers that horses that dominate on pace do so by controlling two pace segments, not just one. It's a significant detail. Early speed occurs from the start to the first call. Late speed occurs from the quarter pole to the wire. Both styles win races, but not as a function of pace analysis. That occurs only when the early speed has been linked to the second fraction, notably in sprints.

On pace analysis one-run closers will be particularly vulnerable in sprints if they fail to gain on the lead horse during the second fraction. The closers need striking position at the second call. Without striking position, without revealing a turn-time faster than the lead horse during the second fraction, deep closers retain only two possibilities. Either they enjoy an enormous class edge, or the early pace self-destructs. In the first instance, classy closers overtake lesser horses, usually in the stakes or on the grass. In the second, ordinary closers pick up the pieces.

Because horses must control two fractions to dominate on pace, a perfectably acceptable method of pace analysis links turn-time to another fraction. The technique is simple, and requires no information beyond the past performances of the *Daily Racing Form*. I have dubbed the method "turn-time plus."

The catch is subjective. Handicappers must make a judgment about today's probable pace. They must determine which should be more decisive, early pace or late pace. Once that judgment has been formed, calculate the turn-time and add it to either the first fraction or the third fraction. The fastest fractional time figures best, on pace at least.

The technique is appropriate for distinguishing frontrunners, pressers, and stalkers. As with Jason H, closers should always be rated by combining the second and third fractions, or turn-time plus the final fraction.

In general, cheaper races will be more susceptible to early-pace advantages, and better races will be more susceptible to late-pace advantages. Exceptions, as usual, will be numerous. By cheaper races is meant maiden-claiming, claiming races limited to 3YOs (especially January to June), and claiming races for older horses below the mid-level of the track's claiming division.

Brohamer himself uses turn-time impressively in mid-level to high-level claiming races. He does a similar analysis in stakes sprints, looking carefully for horses that can run the turn in 22 flat, 22 ⅕, and 22 ⅖ seconds. If those horses have finished close enough in competitive stakes, Brohamer waits eagerly for the next spot. He's consistently correct.

Brohamer also invokes turn-time quickly and effectively when playing at unfamiliar mid-level and minor tracks, especially in claiming races. Unless the track surface is favoring closers, claiming horses that can grab the advantage in cheap circumstances at the second call, or shortly after the second call, can be wickedly difficult to overtake. The chasers are simply slow.

In my play I apply the turn-time-plus technique when inspecting nonclaiming races. Assuming that quality animals are more likely to sort themselves out in the late stages, I add the turn-time and the final fraction. The method works especially well in nonclaiming routes. If a couple of good races for each contender have been examined using turn-time plus, and the same horse repeatedly rates the advantage, that's a double-advantage opportunity I favor.

As provocative as turn-time can be in numerous situations, Brohamer has been careful to post a couple of caution signs. Turn-time does not stand alone. It is not an independent factor of handicapping. A solid turn-time in combination with a noncompetitive speed figure, for example, is meaningless. If horses are unacceptably slow, a good turn-time does not redeem them. Turn-time is interpreted best in relation to other fundamentals, such as early speed, improving form, relative class, speed figures, and pace analysis.

Also, it's important to relate turn-times to turn-time pars, which vary slightly from cheaper races to better races. The turn-times of Sucha Warrior and Jason H at Golden Gate Fields become vividly more meaningful when juxtaposed with the relevant pars.

Class Levels	Pars	Sucha Warrior	Jason H
Clm $8500	23 ⅕	23 ⅖	
Maiden	23 ⅕		22 ⅖
Alw, NW1X	23		
Clm $40,000	23		
Stakes	22 ⅘		
Mdn Clm $12,500	23 ⅗		

Not a lot of variation. From top to bottom, stakes to maiden-claiming races, only a four-length difference. For this reason, turn-time pars are conveniently divided into two categories, better races and cheaper races, specifically an allowance race for nonwinners other than maiden or claiming and a low-level claiming race.

Handicappers can depend upon these turn-time pars for most races at Hollywood Park.

Alw, NW1X	22 ⅘
Clm $10,000	23 ⅖

If stakes times were listed for Hollywood Park, the par is 22 ⅗, just one length faster to the second call than minor allowance conditions.

Here are the turn-time pars at two levels of competition for 44 racetracks:

Track	A1w, NW1X	Low-Level Claiming
Ak-Sar-Ben	24	24
Arlington Park	23 ⅖	23 ⅗
Aqueduct	23 ⅕	23 ⅗
Atlantic City	23 ⅕	23 ⅗
Belmont Park	23 ⅕	23 ⅗
Bay Meadows	22 ⅘	23 ⅕
Churchill Downs	24 ⅕	24 ⅗
Calder Race Course	23 ⅕	23 ⅘
Detroit Race Course	23 ⅕	23 ⅕
Del Mar	23 ⅖	23 ⅗
Ellis Park	23 ⅘	23 ⅘
Fair Grounds	24	24 ⅕
Fairplex Park	23 ⅗	24
Golden Gate Fields	23	23 ¼
Gulfstream Park	23 ⅕	23 ⅗
Garden State	23 ⅘	24 ⅕
Hawthorne	23 ⅗	23 ⅘
Hialeah	23 ⅗	23 ⅘
Hollywood Park	23	23 ⅖
Keeneland	23 ⅖	23 ⅘
Louisiana Downs	23 ⅕	23 ⅗
Laurel	23 ⅖	23 ⅗
Meadowlands	23	23 ⅖
Monmouth Park	23 ⅕	23 ⅗
Oaklawn Park	23 ⅘	24 ⅕
Penn National	23 ⅗	24 ⅕
Philadelphia Park	23 ⅕	23 ⅗
Pimlico	23 ⅖	23 ⅗
Portland Meadows	23 ⅗	24 ⅕
River Downs	23 ⅘	24
Rockingham Park	23 ⅗	23 ⅘
Remington Park	23 ⅖	23 ⅘
Ruidoso	23	23
Santa Anita	23	23 ⅖
Saratoga	22 ⅘	23

(continued)

Track	A1w, NW1X	Low-Level Claiming
Sportsman's Park	23 ⅘	23 ⅘
Suffolk Downs	23 ⅘	24
Sunland Park	23	23 ⅖
Tampa Bay Downs	23 ⅖	23 ⅘
Thistledown	23 ⅘	23 ⅘
Turfway Park	23 ⅗	23 ⅘
Turf Paradise	22 ⅖	22 ⅘
Woodbine	23 ⅕	23 ⅖
Yakima Meadows	22 ⅗	23

Source: *Par Times,* by Gordon Pines, Cynthia Publishing Co., Los Angeles, Calif., 1994.

Finally, turn-time becomes a handy, useful tool for simulcast handicappers playing at unfamiliar tracks. If the Beyer Speed Figures look unimpressive, unreliable, or contradictory, and other evidence remains unclear, it's convenient to discover that one of the horses has a definite advantage during the second fraction.

That horse may figure to win, and frequently does.

THE HANDICAPPING FACTORS

W hy do talented handicappers lose? It's a fascinating riddle, and among highly experienced players, perplexing. This much is well documented, and fairly well known. The handicapper who can pick 35 percent winners at average odds of 5–2, attainable levels of proficiency by anyone who cares, has a 22.5 percent edge on the game.

That's a precious edge, the kind beyond the reach of most investors, savers, and businesses. If handicappers can occasionally pick 40 percent winners at average odds of 5–2, or 35 percent winners at slightly higher average odds, they have tapped a profit rate of 40 percent. If they sustain the investment for three to five years, it's meaningful money.

With so much profit at stake, why do talented handicappers manage to blow it, and lose money season after season? The explanation is multilayered and no doubt complicated, embedded in individual personality as well as the culture of the racetrack, but three reasons stand out.

The first and most debilitating by a wide margin is hinged to the dynamics of pari-mutuel wagering. Hell-bent to play winners, handicappers bet too much money on too many underlays. This guarantees a loss long-term.

The second has accompanied the advance of exotic wagering. Inexperienced and untutored regarding the machinations of the exacta, quinella, the trifecta, the Pick 3, the Pick 6, and even the daily double, handicappers rely upon betting strategies that are not only wrongheaded, but also punitive.

The third is connected to the art of handicapping. Aware that every race is a new puzzle, and that there can be several ways to skin the same race, handicappers conclude that anything goes, or that one method is just as good as another. They therefore put too much emphasis on the incidental or secondary factors of handicapping. In the jargon of athletics, they are not fundamentally sound.

Of the complicating matters of handicapping, none exceeds the bald reality that many factors do influence the outcomes of races. Inevitably the pedestrian wants to know, which is the most important factor in handicapping? The motive is understandable, to simplify the game. Or to overturn some partially hidden truth that might render matters less complicated; easy perhaps.

Of course, no factor is most important, and no factor is unimportant. The charm of handicapping is that all of the factors can be important some of the time, and none of the factors will be important all of the time. No wonder beginners become confused, veteran handicappers readily acknowledge, without wondering in the slightest whether, despite the years and lessons, they themselves might remain needlessly muddled as well.

For although no factor of handicapping can be dubbed most important, it's eminently fair to divide the several factors into two groups, the fundamentals and the secondary factors. The fundamentals deal with the abilities of horses. The secondary factors deal with the circumstances of races. The trap that catches most handicappers is that they routinely confuse the fundamental and the circumstantial.

Consider the scheme of the handicapping factors below:

The Fundamentals	Situational Factors
Speed	Distance
Class	Trips
Pace	Trainer
Form	Jockey
Special situations	Track surface
Track bias	Weight
Trainer patterns	Post position
	Pedigree
	Equipment/medication
	Age
	Sex
	Body language

Invite practitioners to analyze the seventh race today, and what can handicappers expect? References to the trainers, jockeys, track surface, and post positions and how these might affect the outcome are practically guaranteed to appear in the opening remarks. Before the horses can be examined on fundamental abilities, the human elements and circumstances have overwhelmed the analysis.

Already the game has been lost.

Having crammed their skulls with considerations that may or may not be pertinent, and certainly should be less important than other factors, few handicappers from that departure will be capable of straightening out their thinking well enough to beat this game.

The fundamental abilities of horses are always relevant, and usually important. The race analysis begins best if it begins with the fundamentals. The circumstances of races may be significant, even decisive, but they may not.

Emphases on trainers and jockeys can be particularly insidious to the handicapping process. Much of the trainer-jockey speculation is superfluous. In handicapping seminars and classes, participants can be heard routinely assessing trainers in ways that not only are vaguely understood but also contribute no meaningful insight to the race analysis. The trainer is good, or he's weak, or he's a good trainer on grass, or he's tough following layoffs, or he likes to use today's jockey, and so forth.

Handicappers who pollute their thinking early in the handicapping process with disjointed references to secondary factors have scarcely a hope of beating this game. Trainers, jockeys, and post positions play an obvious part in race outcomes, but to confuse that role with the basic abilities of the horses is to contort the handicapping process itself. Horses take precedence. Only then do jockeys and trainers count, either strengthening or weakening the fundamental case.

The upshot for handicappers is to become as expert as they possibly can on the fundamentals of handicapping. Not only is a working knowledge of the speed, class, pace, and form factors strongly recommended as the first line of defense, but also handicappers are strongly recommended to become truly expert with one of the fundamentals. It's no coincidence that the most impressive handicappers of all invariably stand apart in their ability to use one or two handicapping factors extraordinarily well. If those factors happen to be situational (trips, trainers, body language), the experts also reveal a keen and abiding respect for the fundamentals.

If a trip playback shows a below-par figure, or should be disadvantaged by the pace, or will be outgunned, it's no play. If the sharpest horse in the walking ring does not measure up on speed, class, and pace as well, the body language expert does not dive headlong into a serious win wager.

The handicapping process unravels best when it begins with concern for the fundamentals. In an eight-week handicapping program I've conducted with colleagues Tom Brohamer and Frank Romano at various tracks, the first four weeks are devoted to the fundamentals, such that the interrelationships among the factors can be clarified and better comprehended.

Once the abilities of horses have been carefully evaluated, the race circumstances and human elements deserve a fair hearing. The purpose is to confirm the basic analysis, or to dispute it. If the race occurs at seven furlongs, ability at the distance is obviously important, and may be decisive. If the race is limited to 3YOs, knowledge about a Thoroughbred's age will be important, and may be decisive.

Any of the secondary factors can play a meaningful role, or a decisive role, at any time. It's the misplaced emphasis too much of the time that subverts effective handicapping.

The scheme of handicapping factors recognizes that certain situations can be considered special. In those special circumstances a specific handicapping factor can take precedence over all else. Track bias leaps to mind. Whenever the track surface is severely biased, the bias alters the race outcomes radically. Track bias now takes precedence over speed, class, pace, and form.

Severe biases should not be confused with everyday references to the track surface. The track is favoring the inside, or it's favoring the outside. It's favoring the speed, or it's favoring the closers. Mild biases do not alter race outcomes. They are just another factor of handicapping. If handicappers confuse mild track biases with the horses that figure tops on speed, class, pace, and form, the game has been lost again.

It's possible as well to be fortified on the fundamentals of handicapping and miss too much of the rest. The speed handicapper who relies upon middle-distance speed figures to evaluate stakes contenders at a mile and one-quarter has not been adequately concerned about distance.

The class expert who expects an unproven front-running 3YO moving ahead in class to overcome an outside post in a large field at a flat mile has underestimated the influence of post position.

The form analyst who fails to discount a poor performance that resulted because a presser was forced wide on the clubhouse turn at a mile and one-sixteenth has been insensitive to trips.

The pace analyst who ignores the presence of a low-percentage rider at a route on the grass will probably be penalized for discounting the jockey factor at the wrong moment.

One of the challenges handicappers confront every day involves relating the multiple factors of handicapping to one another effectively. Handicappers who do it well persistently are probably the most talented handicappers of all.

Those handicappers are unlikely to confuse a horse's jockey and its speed, or its trainer and its class, or its post position and its pace advantages, or its weight and its form. They do not anticipate the probable influences of the trainer, jockey, and post positions before they have scrutinized the relative abilities of the horses.

In other words, the most talented handicappers recognize the difference between the fundamental and the incidental factors of handicapping, and how the two groups can be connected effectively.

BETTING STRATEGIES

The majority of practiced handicappers do not know how to bet. Another large percentage know how, but they forget. The awful habits persist primarily because the bettors do not appreciate how much money is at stake.

During a handicapping program conducted at Oak Tree 1994, a middle-aged lady liked a 40–1 shot in a race where the favorite was even-money. She bought a $20 quinella coupling the two.

The 40–1 shot won. The even-money favorite finished second. The quinella paid $65. The lady was ecstatic, and deservedly so. She collected $650.

The exacta paid $186. Keeping the investment constant, the seminar leaders suggested she might have split the bet, taking a $10 quinella and a $10 exacta with the longshot on top and the even-money shot underneath. Those combinations yielded $1255.

After the celebration had quieted, the prosperous lady's face changed to a grimace. By misplaying the wager, she had deprived her pocketbook of $600. The seminar leaders rubbed it in tenderly. They pointed out that within a year the miscue multiplied by ten would cost $6000.

The anecdote probably generalizes to casual bettors everywhere. They misplay races, penalizing their bankrolls even when winning. As exotic wagering expands and increasingly dominates a day at the races, it's convenient to review the betting strategies that have been recommended variously as effective. Also the habits that have been recognized as counterproductive.

THE EXACTA

Already a quarter of a century has lapsed since the exacta was introduced at Hollywood Park in 1969. The wager supports multiple purposes, primarily allowing handicappers to link combinations of contenders and marginal outsiders in contentious races. Astute handicappers can use exactas repeatedly to convert overbet favorites in the win pools (underlays) to overlays in the combination pools.

The exacta and other exotics also permit handicappers to interconnect the multiple information resources they bother to collect by covering an array of potentially positive outcomes.

Like all pari-mutuel wagers, the exacta is a good bet when it pays well in relation to the risk. It's a bad bet when it pays poorly, even when the combinations click, a stark reality racegoers do not easily grasp.

Unfortunately the most popular exacta strategies constitute poor bets. More often than not, the risk will be greater than the reward. How many handicappers recognize their personal plight in the three worst exacta bets?

1. The favorite on top of other contenders, second and third choices especially
2. Baseballs (three-horse boxes)
3. Pairs of long shots

The favorite on top represents a bad risk because handicappers tend to use other low-priced contenders underneath. These combinations do not pay enough. Overbet favorites will be similarly overbet on the top sides of exactas. Why bother? Long term, no edge.

If favorites are played on top, they must be coupled with attractive overlays. These combinations pay fairly well. There's a better way, however, to be mentioned momentarily.

The positive exacta strategies are two:

1. Pairs of medium-priced horses
2. Favorites on the bottom

Whenever the favorite is not the handicapper's first or second choice, opportunity has knocked. Couple the two nonfavorites. In addition, if the favorite is a third choice, play each nonfavorite atop the favorite.

If racegoers would alter their exacta habits to conform to these few strategies, profits would improve.

THE QUINELLA

Because the quinellas cost one-half an equal number of exacta combinations, the expected payoff is one-half the exacta payoff. That principle provides the key to quinella wagering. Whenever the quinella should outperform the exacta, favor it.

The ripest quinella strategies:

1. An overbet favorite with underbet contenders or overlays
2. Pairs of low-priced contenders
3. Pairs of longshots

The mistake handicappers indulge routinely is the same transgression committed by the seminar lady. They hook overbet and underbet contenders instinctively and equally in exactas, when the clever alternative puts the underbet contender on top of the overbet horse in exactas and couples the two in quinellas. When the low-priced favorite wins, the quinellas routinely pay more than 50 percent of the exactas, regardless of the second horse.

I once collected a generous finder's fee that was inadvertent and unexpected. A wealthy gentleman sat at the lunch table on the fall day at Oak Tree in 1993 when Hollywood Wildcat faced three opponents in the stakes that was preliminary to the Breeders' Cup Distaff. Asked for an opinion, I was confident Hollywood Wildcat would win and equally confident that the mare Re Toss would finish second.

My guest announced his intention to buy a one-way $500 exacta. I suggested he could win three-quarters as much at half the risk by playing quinellas instead. He debated the proposition and bought a $400 quinella and a $100 one-way exacta.

Hollywood Wildcat won, and Re Toss finished second. The exacta paid $15. The quinella paid $12, or 80 percent of the exacta. The gentleman collected a profit of $2650. If Re Toss had finished first and Hollywood Wildcat second, the gentleman would have received the same $2000 of quinella profits.

Pairs of low-priced contenders typically pay more than half of the exacta payoffs. Boxes cost half as much. Handicappers have intuited these advantages reasonably well, and not a few hardened veterans have determined to crush a pair of heavily bet co-favorites in the quinella pool.

A combination bet handicappers have not intuited as well is a pair of longshots. Longshot combinations pay depressingly low in exactas, but surprisingly well in quinellas. Perhaps handicappers just do not imagine that the exacta combos will be overbet. They therefore overbet them. The same longshot combinations are notoriously underbet in quinellas. Recently I saw an exacta coupling a 30–1 shot and a 20–1 shot pay $1700-plus. The quinella paid $1400-plus.

A useful strategy when pondering pairs of longshots is to bet each to win and couple the two in quinellas.

THE TRIFECTA

Barry Meadow urges handicappers to avoid the trifectas unless the favorite or second choice can be eliminated.

Andrew Beyer advises handicappers that favorites should be used to win only, not to finish second or third. Because so many racegoers box three horses in trifectas, payoffs will prove comparable whether the favorite runs first, second, or third.

So if handicappers like a 4–1 horse, a 15–1 shot, and the 8–5 favorite in that order, a trifecta box makes no sense. Instead box the pair of nonfavorites in exactas and play each on top of the favorite.

If trifectas are bought, take the favorite to win, and cover the two nonfavorites in the second and third slots. The show hole might also include other marginal horses at attractive prices or eliminate the favorite. Box the 4–1 horse and 15–1 shot to win and place, coupling the two with other overlays and contenders to show. Ineffective but popular trifecta strategies include boxing three horses, notably if the favorite is included, and playing the favorite in the place and show holes.

THE PICK 3

In structuring serial bets, an effective strategy divides each race's contention into A and B contenders. In any three-race sequence, the A contenders should include only one favorite.

The betting strategy combines the A horses in each leg on the main ticket. Next combine the B horses in one leg with the A horses in the other two. Or the A horses in any leg with the B horses in the other two. And so on, until the A and B lists have been exhausted to the bettor's satisfaction. If cost must be reduced, eliminate low-priced horses, not overlays, marginal horses, or longshots. If the odds are attractive, the strategy also combines the B horses in each leg on a minimum-cost, back-up ticket.

In my play, A horses are main contenders at overlay prices, and can include favorites that should be underbet or fairly bet plus any contenders having a relatively strong chance that might be seriously underbet. The B horses include overbet favorites I like plus other contenders, as well as marginal horses at irresistible prices.

Combinations of favorites in the Pick 3 pay poorly. Odds-on favorites usually drag down the payoffs regardless of what happens in the other two legs.

Whenever an odds-on favorite is false, the Pick 3 becomes the best play in town. Handicappers must respond. Cover the other contenders in that leg, linked to the main contenders and marginal horses in the remaining legs. The reward justifies the risk. If nonfavorites figure tops in the other legs, double-down on those combinations linked to the several contenders in the race where the odds-on horse looks bogus.

A NEW BETTING LINE

The main problem with betting lines is that the probabilities that horses will win represent a precarious estimate in the best of situations. Morning lines, to be sure, become seriously imbalanced when constructed by track employees who are not handicappers. Authentic handicappers' betting lines are more finely tuned but still problematic.

For years I have followed a two-step procedure for making a line. I first identify the contenders utilizing the handicapping factors I judge fundamental to the race at hand. I assign the contenders a probability of winning, leaving a 20 percent chance to the other horses. I then jiggle the line, adding some value, subtracting some value, based upon several handicapping factors and how strongly I imagine they apply. Finally, I determine the favorite to be a fair bet at 2–1, or 8–5, or 5–2, or whatever, and the other contenders a fair bet at somewhat higher values.

Perhaps the real problem occurs in the fine-tuning, perhaps in choosing the relevant fundamentals and weightings. Who knows? After all, the probabilities that horses will win contain inherent degrees of error. The handicapper's 2–1 favorite might be closer to 3–1 or to even-money, depending upon factors not included in the estimation, perhaps the trip on the track, unanticipated jockey errors, or irregularities in the form cycles. There's simply an abundance of noise.

Instead of fine-tuning, perhaps the initial betting line should be broadened. Horses' chances would be identified by a cluster of odds. Overlays would occur anytime a horse's actual odds slipped into a higher odds cluster. Consider the model below:

Level	Probability	Odds	Overlay
A	50%–42%	1–1 to 7–5	3–2
B	40%–33%	3–2 to 2–1	5–2
C	28%–25%	5–2 to 3–1	7–2
D	22%–20%	7–2 to 4–1	5–1
E	18%–15%	9–2 to 6–1	8–1
F	12%–10%	7–1 to 9–1	12–1

If handicappers judge the favorite to have a 50 percent chance, it's no bet until the odds reach 3–2.

If a contender is assigned a 20 percent chance, the bettable odds begin at 5–1.

A marginal type might be assigned a 10 percent chance. A 9–1 shot can be bet at 12–1 and higher.

As the win probabilities decrease, naturally the bettable odds increase. Because the horses will win less frequently, generating longer losing runs, payoffs must be correspondingly higher. To minimize confusion, handicappers can assign horses a letter grade A–F and memorize the accompanying overlay odds.

The A,B,C levels will contain the large majority of top choices and many contenders. If first choices become overlays, bet to win. If second and third choices become overlays, win betting often makes sense, notably when first choices and public favorites have become underlays. Any contender that becomes an overlay represents a potential play.

If handicappers keep records, they can quickly identify areas of strength and weakness. Flat bets are fine.

Not a few handicappers learn that their first choices are not the most profitable, if profitable at all. But second and third choices may return generous rates of profit when supported as overlays. As always, I recommend the strategy of win-betting on prime selections enthusiastically. Win-wagering applies to predictable races only, of course, not the indecipherable unpredictable puzzles.

The unstoppable advances of exotic wagering have placed severe pressures on betting shrewdly and intelligently. Handicappers should resolve to do the right thing. Without abandoning the positive edge that accompanies solid handicapping and effective win-wagering, playing the exotics with strategies that succeed means a difference of thousands of dollars a season.

Too many regular handicappers have already fallen far behind in exotic pools. Fortunately they can catch up. As Lee Rousso likes to emphasize, for good handicappers the losses always come back. The starting line is tomorrow.

TRACK PROFILES

A diligent keeper of track profiles for several seasons, I was stunned during Oak Tree at Santa Anita 1994 by a comment escaping from my friend and professional handicapper Frank Romano. Romano observed that if handicappers did not like the speed horses to win, they should not expect them to finish second either.

"Forget the early speed in the two hole in exactas," urged Romano, glancing at his detailed track profiles. "They haven't been able to hold the place position at any distance this meeting."

Numerous handicappers stay up-to-date with track profiles, which reflect the running styles that have been winning lately, but Romano is the single player I know who keeps careful track profiles to place. Beyond the obvious edge in exacta wagering during Oak Tree 1994, Romano insists the extra record keeping pays off handsomely in trifectas, his specialty.

Track profiles describe the running positions and beaten lengths of winners at the first call and second call at the various regularly run distances. Handicappers want to know whether the track surface has been favoring certain running styles at specific distances.

At a flat mile during the first half of Santa Anita 1995, for example, front-runners and pressers held an overwhelming advantage. Most of the winners ran within a length of the lead at both the first and second calls. Off-pace horses rarely threatened. Deep closers did not win once. It's nice to know.

The mile profile changed abruptly approaching the midpoint of the season, roughly forty days along. The new profile favored closers capable of gaining a striking position after six furlongs. That's especially nice to know.

Consider the track profile (beaten lengths) for seven mile races run at Santa Anita during the weekend following this sudden shift.

Saturday	B.L. 1	B.L. 2
1st	2	0.1 (hd)
2nd	5.7	3.6
5th	1.5	0.1 (hd)
8th	0	0

Sunday	B.L. 1	B.L. 2
2nd	5	0
4th	4.8	0.1 (hd)
8th	12.5	8

Only one winner had led or had run within a length at the first call. Two winners had remained far back at the second call. Surveying the three previous race days, the mile profile for the week had looked radically dissimilar to the mile profile for the preceding season. If the new profile persisted, handicappers keeping profiles understood that milers that had been disadvantaged earlier due to running styles might be upgraded now. Similarly, front-runners and pressers that had won the earlier miles might be discounted now.

An aspect of track profiles that has been underestimated generally regards the compatibility between recent races and the seasonal profile. Be aware of sudden movements. Recent races take precedence. Until, that is, the customary profile just as quickly reappears.

Handicappers have tended as well to overestimate the significance of the second call. Regardless of distance, winners as a group should be expected to be "up close" at the second call. To note that 70 or 80 percent of the recent winners have been within three lengths of the leader at the second call may not be as meaningful as it sounds. In the era of the small field especially, a high percentage of the starters typically cluster within three lengths of the leaders at the second call. If several consecutive winners have raced within a length at the second call, however, that may be decisive.

The small data describing seven Santa Anita miles indicate that the track favored off-pace closers that weekend, yet five of the seven winners had either led or advanced to within a head at the second call. When inspecting track profiles, before declaring an advantage for front-runners and pressers, handicappers must examine the beaten lengths at the first call.

As standard operating procedure, it's crucial to develop track profiles for each separate distance. Do not cluster sprints and routes. Six furlongs and six-and-a-half furlongs may be a sixteenth of a mile apart, yet highly dissimilar, and so might a mile and a mile and one-sixteenth. If handicappers construct meticulous profiles, vive la différence.

Of special interest will be the irregular distances of seven furlongs, a mile, and a mile and one-quarter. I like to provoke participants at handicapping seminars: "What's the track profile at seven furlongs for the past half-dozen races?" It's rare that anyone knows.

Casual handicappers can stay abreast of track profiles by consulting result charts for five minutes each racing day. In a notebook, for each distance, record the beaten lengths of the winners at the first and second calls. Exacta bettors are advised to mimic Romano and construct handy track profiles for the place holes.

In addition, if the track profile for related distances suddenly favors early speed at both the first and second calls, the evidence supports a speed bias. If the bias persists the next day at the same distances, handicappers may have secured a serious edge for a time. Consider the track profile for the nine races at Santa Anita on February 15, 1995.

Race		B.L. 1	B.L. 2
1st	6.5 fur.	0.5	0.5
2nd	1 mi.	0	0
3rd	1 mi.	0	0
4th	6 fur.	0	0
5th	8.5 fur.	0	0
6th	6 fur.	0.5	0
7th	6 fur.	0	0
8th	6 fur.	0	0
9th	7 fur.	0	0

Does that profile suggest a speed bias? Ordinarily handicappers would be impatient for the next afternoon's races. No need for a course specialist. The obvious prescription says to double-down on the early speed.

I resisted that urge, and gratefully. Only because I appreciate the machinations of Santa Anita track super Steve Wood. The first on February 16 was a dirt mile. The track profile changed abruptly: first call the winner was beaten by 11 lengths; second call the winner was beaten by 11.6 lengths. Wood does not tolerate severe speed biases. He alters the track surface immediately.

Most track superintendents do not act as quickly. Handicappers observing a severely biased track can adjust immediate plans to play the races. A severe bias amounts to a profit stream for as long as the bias endures. If handicappers need an incentive to stay current on their track profiles, let the occasional overbearing bias serve the purpose.

Regular handicappers should never be caught unawares. The time and energy requirements for recording track profiles is negligible, the advantages several and practical. Whenever the track surface assists front-runners, pressers, stalkers, or closers in abnormally skewed patterns, regular handicappers should know it. It's sufficiently important to qualify as standard operating procedure.

SECOND-STARTERS

Many practiced handicappers appreciate the extra-added attractions associated with second-starters in maiden races. A few seasons ago I began to focus on these horses deliberately. Now I emphasize second-starters in maiden races automatically. The reason is return on investment, which has proved substantial.

Two distinct patterns offer the sweetest opportunities. The first is conventional, though not as well comprehended as it should be. Two maidens have exited the same race. One has accumulated two, three, or four starts, maybe a few more. The other is a second-starter.

The more experienced maiden has recorded the better speed figure in the race each contested. The second-starter's figure is one, two, or three lengths slower than his experienced opponent's.

Favor the second-starter. The second-starter can be expected to improve by three to five lengths. The more experienced maiden should not be expected to improve. If second-starters improve as expected, they win. If figure handicappers have overbet the more experienced maiden having the higher figure, the odds on the second-starter may be tantalizing.

The second pattern gets comparable results, and juicier odds. In recent weeks at Santa Anita, I had noticed an atypical recurrence of the pattern, and virtually all of the second-starters have come shining through. Of the bunch, I liked the proposition below the most.

Examine the lines for the favorite (below) and the second-starter (page 56). The track surface had been labeled fast, but its base had been softened by prolonged intense rainstorms.

King's Marshall	Ch. c. 3 (Mar)		Lifetime Record:	3 M 1 1	$14,798

Own: N & M Boyce Racing Stable Inc — Sire: Flying Paster (Gun.mo) — Dam: Josette (Top Command)
Br: Neil Boyce & Michele Boyce (Cal) — Tr: Boyce Neil B (15 0 3 3 .00)

VALENZUELA F H (18 2 6 3 .11)

L 118

1995 1 M 1 0 $8,000 Turf 0 0 0 0
1994 2 M 0 1 $6,798 Wet   0 0 0 0
SA   1 0 1 0 $8,000 Dist 0 0 0 0

12Feb95–6SA fst 6f :21² :44³ :57 1:09³ ⑤Md Sp Wt 85 6 1 1hd 2hd 1hd 2² Hawley S LB 118 *2.50 87–10 Canyon Crest118² King's Marshall118² BelloBeau118¹½ Tired, dr
13Aug94–2Dmr fst 5½f :21⁴ :45¹ :57³ 1:04² ⑤Md Sp Wt 60 9 1 4½ 3½ 35½ 3⁴ Baze G LB 117 4.20 85–06 ProfitMargin117²½ Mr.Progressive117¹¾ King'sMarshll117⁴½ 4 wi
30Jly94–1Dmr fst 5f :22¹ :45⁴ :58¹ ⑤Md Sp Wt 52 5 2 2hd 2½ 31½ 57¼ Flores D R B 117 *1.60 91–05 Telefonazo117⁵ Strategist117¹ Chocolate Threads117½ Dueler

WORKOUTS: Mar 6 SA 5f my 1:01¹ H 2/8 Feb 28 SA 4f fst :46⁴ H 3/36 Feb 1 SA 5f fst 1:00² H 11/38 Feb 2 SA 6f fst 1:12³ Hg4/13 Jan 28 SA 5f gd 1:00³ H 8/78 ●Jan 23 SA tr.t 4f fst :47³ H 1/8

55

Polar Arrival

	Gr. g. 3 (May)			Lifetime Record :	1 M 0 0	$0
Own: Baker & Cravitz & Team Valor	Sire: Flying Paster (Gummo)					
	Dam: Kool Arrival (Relaunch)		1995	1 M 0 0	Turf	0 0 0 0
	Br: P. Valenti & J. Coelho (Cal)		1994	0 M 0 0	Wet	0 0 0 0
PEDROZA M A (195 20 25 20 .10)	Tr: Hennig Mark (13 1 2 4 .08)	118	SA	1 0 0 0	Dist	0 0 0 0

12Feb95–6SA fst 6f   :21² :44³ :57 1:09³   ⑤Md Sp Wt   65 8 11 11¹¹ 9¹³ 8⁹½ 6⁹¾ Pedroza M A   B 118   18.00   79–10 Canyon Crest118² King's Marshall118² Bello Beau118¹½   Late
WORKOUTS: Mar 7 Hol 4f fst :52¹ H 20/21   Feb 28 Hol 5f fst 1:00³ H 9/17   Feb 22 Hol 4f fst :48¹ H 3/16   Jan 27 Hol 5f gd 1:02 H 21/28   Jan 17 Hol 5f gd 1:02² H 11/18   Dec 31 Hol 5f fst 1:00⁴ H 16/57

Among the advantages presented by King's Marshall was a pace figure slightly above par and a speed figure one length below par. The two 3YOs are exiting the same race, but Polar Arrival was hardly competitive, and the gelding's odds had floated upward to 18–1.

The pattern I favor is an inexplicably dull try first out, coupled now with (a) a good barn and (b) a persuasive reason to imagine the horse might provide a dramatic reversal of form. The full context includes a vulnerable favorite and seductive odds.

Mark Hennig has been quite a solid horseman. No problem there. The persuasive factor is Polar Arrival's pedigree. The track surface at Santa Anita had been wet-fast, wet-slow, sloppy and muddy in recent days following a succession of winter rains. Not only is Flying Paster a top-rated wet-track sire, but also the broodmare sire Relaunch is more highly rated.

Using the 300-point scale from Tomlinson's *Mudders and Turfers*, Polar Arrival obtained a sensational wet-track rating. When the sire's rating was added to half the broodmare sire's rating, Polar Arrival gets a 365. King's Marshall was a son of Flying Paster as well, an intriguing coincidence. The 8–5 favorite King's Marshall obtained a Tomlinson rating of 320, which is excellent.

As often happens in second-starter situations, Polar Arrival should benefit as well from another source. Having broken eleventh on its maiden voyage, today Polar Arrival was adding blinkers. It was possible, too, that King's Marshall might "bounce" following a strong exertion after a six-month layoff, although the pattern is not classic.

I respected the favorite's dope enough to buy a quinella, but my betting choice was Polar Arrival, and when the bettors gave me 5–1, I grabbed it. The result chart is testimony to the charms of second-starters in maiden races. I endorse them enthusiastically.

SIXTH RACE

Santa Anita

MARCH 11, 1995

6½ FURLONGS. (1.14) MAIDEN SPECIAL WEIGHT. Purse $40,000 (includes $3,000 from California–bred race fund). 3–year–olds bred in California. Weight, 118 lbs. (Non–starters for a claiming price of $32,000 or less in their last three starts preferred.)

Value of Race: $40,000 Winner $22,000; second $8,000; third $6,000; fourth $3,000; fifth $1,000. Mutuel Pool $497,406.50 Exacta Pool $356,536.00 Trifecta Pool $319,631.00 Quinella Pool $64,656.00

Last Raced	Horse	M/Eqt. A.Wt	PP	St	¼	½	Str	Fin	Jockey	Odds $1
12Feb95 6SA6	Polar Arrival	Bb 3 118	8	6	66	4hd	22	12	Pedroza M A	5.40
26Nov94 6Hol4	To Be Khaled	LB 3 113	6	7	71½	78	32	22	Sanchez Obed5	12.80
26Feb95 5SA5	Windy's Halo	B 3 118	4	3	5hd	6hd	5hd	3½	Atkinson P	10.50
	Fancy Ticket	LB 3 118	5	1	11½	11	1½	42¾	Valenzuela P A	1.80
12Feb95 6SA2	King's Marshall	LB 3 118	3	4	3½	3hd	62	51½	Valenzuela F H	1.50
17Feb95 9SA2	Sharp Account	LB 3 118	7	2	21	21	4hd	63½	Sorenson D	17.10
26Feb95 5SA9	Librio	Bb 3 118	2	5	41½	52	712	711	Garcia M S	30.30
	Tagman	B 3 118	1	8	8	8	8	8	Pincay L Jr	25.00

OFF AT 2:54 Start Good. Won driving. Time, :214, :45, 1:102, 1:17 Track wet fast.

$2 Mutuel Prices:

8–POLAR ARRIVAL	12.80	6.20	4.40
6–TO BE KHALED		9.60	6.40
4–WINDY'S HALO			5.00

$2 EXACTA 8–6 PAID $144.60 $2 TRIFECTA 8–6–4 PAID $840.60 $2 QUINELLA 6–8 PAID $77.00

Gr. g, (May), by Flying Paster–Kool Arrival, by Relaunch. Trainer Hennig Mark. Bred by P. Valenti & J. Coelho (Cal).

POLAR ARRIVAL wide early, angled in to race outside WINDY'S HALO on the backstretch, advanced four wide early on the turn, entered the stretch outside SHARP ACCOUNT, gained the lead inside the furlong marker, got clear under urging and was hard ridden to win clear. TO BE KHALED well off the rail on the backstretch and turn, came four wide into the stretch and finished well for the place. WINDY'S HALO settled inside the winner but out from the rail on the backstretch, also came four wide into the stretch and just got the show. FANCY TICKET sped to the early lead while drifting out, set the pace off the rail to midstretch and weakened. KING'S MARSHALL bumped between foes early, continued outside LIBRIO leaving the backstretch, raced between rivals on the turn and weakened in the lane. SHARP ACCOUNT prompted the pace three deep on the backstretch, angled in on the turn and also weakened in the stretch. LIBRIO bumped after the start, had a rail trip and gave way. TAGMAN was off slowly, drifted wide down the backstretch and was outrun. No mud calks were reported.

Owners— 1, Baker & Cravitz & Team Valor; 2, Crownover L E; 3, Cumbari Stable & Mayer; 4, Halo Farms; 5, N & M Boyce Racing Stable Inc; 6, Cavanagh Marguerite F & Thomas M; 7, Valpredo John; 8, Elhami & Sweeney

Trainers—1, Hennig Mark; 2, Kiss Lou; 3, Mayer V James; 4, Sadler John W: 5, Boyce Neil B; 6, Peterson Douglas R; 7, Villagomez Jaime; 8, Sweeney Brian

Scratched— Fortunenick (12Feb95 6SA4)

The day after Polar Arrival upset King's Marshall and keyed a $124 Pick 3, the second at Santa Anita presented handicappers with another variation on the second-starter theme. Consider the past perform-ances:

Our Summer Bid		Lifetime Record: 4 M 3 0 $18,000

Own: Scolamieri & Woolery

SILVA J G (27 0 5 1 .00)   L 117

B. f. 3 (May)
Sire: Cause for Pause (Baldski)
Dam: Summer Sorrows Bid (Bold Bidder)
Br: Green Thumb Farm Stable (Cal)
Tr: Scolamieri Sam J (10 0 4 2 .00)

1995 2 M 1 0 $11,000 Turf 0 0 0 0
1994 2 M 2 0 $7,000 Wet 0 0 0 0
SA 2 0 1 0 $11,000 Dist 2 0 2 0

Bellicent		Lifetime Record: 1 M 1 0 $8,000

Own: Ridder Thoroughbred Stable

MCCARRON C J (135 17 26 17 .13)   L 117

Ro. f. 3 (Feb)
Sire: Moscow Ballet (Nijinsky II)
Dam: Astolat (Flying Paster)
Br: Ridder Thoroughbred Stable (Cal)
Tr: Hofmans David (33 4 7 2 .12)

1995 1 M 1 0 $8,000 Turf 0 0 0 0
1994 1 M 0 0 Wet 0 0 0 0
SA 1 0 1 0 $8,000 Dist 0 0 0 0

The handwritten markings indicate both fillies have recorded the same pace figures, which equaled par. Bellicent shows the stronger speed figure, although both numbers fall lengths below par, and she also represents leading connections. Neither Our Summer Bid's trainer nor her jockey have won a race at the meeting.

Bellicent becomes an obvious second-starter, and the bettors pushed her down to even-money. No play. In a more difficult battle than even-money warranted, Bellicent won.

But what if the human connections had been reversed? What if Our Summer Bid represented a leading trainer and jockey and Bellicent represented weak connections? Many bettors would probably have preferred Our Summer Bid. The second-starter still deserves the nod. The second-starter figures to improve, the five-start experienced filly does not.

Now eliminate the last running line of Our Summer Bid. Which filly should handicappers favor?

It's Bellicent regardless. Even though the experienced maiden shows a Beyer Speed Figure of 77, and the second-starter a 72 Beyer, that's exactly the conventional pattern acknowledged above. No real improvement should be expected of Our Summer Bid. Bellicent should be expected to improve by three to five lengths, maybe more. If so, Bellicent wins.

If the last running line were omitted and Our Summer Bid exited an attractive barn, to be ridden by a leading rider, the odds on that filly might be considerably lower. Bellicent could be an attractive alternate.

Before abandoning the topic, the recommended patterns feature second-starters in maiden races only, not in maiden-claiming affairs. Not much improvement can be anticipated among maiden-claiming horses, and although the patterns apply as rigorously to races for 2YOs, maiden races for 3YOs achieve much more prosperous results. Apparently the bettors are more firmly attached to second-starting juveniles than they are to second-starting older maidens.

RESTRICTED CLAIMERS

The full-card simulcasting from northern California to southern California has acquainted Santa Anita and Hollywood Park handicappers with claiming races they rarely engage, but should graciously welcome. The restricted claiming races.

The conditions below are the most commonly carded:

5 Bay Meadows

5½ Furlongs. (1:01³) CLAIMING. Purse $6,500. 4-year-olds and upward which have never won two races. Weight, 122 lbs. Non-winners of a race since January 15, allowed 3 lbs. A race since December 15, 5 lbs. Claiming price $6,250. (Maiden races, claiming, starter and classified handicap races for $5,000 or less not considered.)

The race invites older horses that have not yet won two races at the $6250 claiming level or higher. Multiple winners at the $5000 level or lower, however, are exempted. So are winners of maiden races.

The horse below resembles the most common kind of winner:

Will Meyers is dropping from an open claiming race at a higher class level to a restricted claiming race at a lower class level. Its performances at the higher levels have been competitive, and Will Meyers has even captured an allowance race.

Case closed. If handicappers observe decent efforts at open claiming levels and the horse is dropping to a lower level restricted to horses that have never won two races, that's a thunderous dropdown. The only remaining issue is price. Will Meyers won the Bay Meadows dash by half a furlong, and paid decently. Overnight one public selector had ignored Will Meyers and had listed his chances at 15–1.

On the day Will Meyers dominated his hapless foes, Bay Meadows carded four restricted claiming races. The handicapper's approach can be consistent and merciless. Scan down the past performances and circle the eligibility conditions of any horse that has lost more than one restricted claiming race. Eliminate all of them.

The worst kind of horse in a restricted claiming race looks like this:

Mydadscounteric was favored in the dash where Will Meyers romped. While dropping seriously in class, Mydadscounteric had lost three straight under restricted claiming conditions. A shipper from southern California, the gelding should have blasted the field on January 25 at the $12,500 level for nonwinners of two races lifetime (N2L).

Next Mydadscounteric drops again on February 4 to nonwinners twice at the $6500 claiming level, gets 30 percent jockey Russell Baze, and blows at 9–10. He's favored again on February 20, and blows again. The heavy betting on plugs is difficult to comprehend.

A situation that fools many handicappers finds horses dropping to today's restricted level from a restricted level a few steps higher, as with Mydadscounteric on February 4. Show no mercy. The putatively higher claiming level for nonwinners of two races is usually a mirage. Below $20,000 claiming, all the claiming prices can be considered lower-class levels, and absolutely so under restricted claiming conditions.

The horses cannot run well enough to defeat multiple winners. Handicappers who restrict their support to horses exiting open claiming races have arrived immediately at the nub of these races. Look first for good races at higher open claiming levels. If those types are absent, consider open claiming winners of multiple races at or slightly below the exemption price.

An exception handicappers might allow regards horses that reveal just one loss in a restricted claiming race. The finish should be close, preferably within two lengths if the horses have set or pressed the pace, within one length if horses have gained from behind the pace.

A circumstance that characterizes numerous restricted claiming races is a dearth of early speed. Speed horses win more than a fair share of the claiming races at every track, and these multiple winners have been barred. The leftovers do not reveal impressive speed. It's not unusual for the entire restricted-race lineup to be positioned behind the pace by a few to several lengths.

The lack of early speed can be exploited occasionally for substantial money. One of the best plays in a restricted claiming race in northern California during 1995 occurred at the commonly carded $6500 claiming level. The stunning surprise was the payoff. Take a look:

On February 4, Aquarian Star entered a restricted $6500 claiming race after exiting an open $8000 race where he had exhibited early speed. The other contenders in the restricted race revealed no early speed. Aquarian Star grabbed the front and led all the way. It was so easy and it typifies the quintessential dropdown handicappers should favor when analyzing restricted claiming races.

One reason Aquarian Star paid $35 was his status as a shipper from Hastings Park, formerly Exhibition Park. At Hastings, against 3YOs, Aquarian Star had beaten unrestricted $12,500 claimers. No doubt the northern California bettors discounted the $12,500 Hastings Park race as inferior.

It is not. At lower claiming levels, horses can ship from minor tracks and do rather well, not only at middle-class places such as Golden Gate Fields but also at major tracks. Moreover, in relation to races open to older horses, races restricted to 3YOs are less suspect at the lowest claiming levels. Whether claiming types are three, four, five, or six, they cannot run especially fast, long, or determined. Age will be less significant.

  Restricted claiming races should be recognized as good friends of simulcast handicappers. With the specific restrictions of the races now provided by *Daily Racing Form* symbols, handicappers who know what to scout for can plow through these fields with clarity and confidence. As easy as one, two, three, (a) eliminate the multiple losers under restricted claiming conditions; (b) compare and contrast the survivors; and (c) prefer the overlays, notably any displaying authentic early speed.

LAYOFFS

In a companion piece ("False Favorites") I observed that horses that have been absent for an unreasonable period following a win represent one of the worst bets at the track. That's because the pattern represents the worst kind of layoff. Look at the horse below. It's May 11.

Away almost five months following a towering score in which it completed the turn of a long sprint in 22 ⅕ and recorded its Beyer top, Bahatur has no reasonable excuse for his absence. The assumption must be an injury.

Regardless, Bahatur does not figure to win the $100,000 claiming race (entered for $75,000) in which he returned. If Bahatur had returned for a $50,000 tag instead, he would not figure to win that race either.

The extended layoff following a win presents an insidious situation to handicappers. Because the last race ended in victory, the horses look seductive. So they are sent to the post with paltry odds, and may be favored.

Yet they rarely repeat. Follow this guidepost: If horses have won last out, but stay inactive for more than six weeks, no play.

Bahatur ran second in his comeback, a strong effort in good time. No contradiction intended. When win types perform well following an unreasonable layoff, they invariably perform well enough to impress, but not well enough to win. Bahatur becomes an excellent illus-

63

tration of a negative layoff convertible to a positive pattern. His entry at the $100,000 claiming level sent a positive signal, and Bahatur ran a good race.

Nonetheless Bahatur lost. Next time the 6YO gelding might regain the form he displayed on December 18, and win unmistakably, especially if lowered to $80,000 claiming or returned to the $62,500 level. In a positive situation that's what handicappers should expect. First time back, however, forsake a bet to win.

In the negative form of the layoff pattern, the horses away too long after a win dispense an equally and unmistakably bad performance. Now the horses can be abandoned until they demonstrate renewed spirit.

On the same day (May 11) at Hollywood Park, this filly appeared in an allowance field for nonwinners other than maiden or claiming:

Big win. Top barn. Jockey Corey Black replaced Eddie Delahoussaye only because Neil Drysdale's stable rider happened to be out of town.

I tossed Bello Cielo in a blink. She should have raced weeks before May 11. No reason to speculate about possible explanations. Just assume these layoff types will not win on the comeback. Bello Cielo did not.

Horses that win impressively are extra sharp. The stables will be eager for the next spot. If an unlikely unreasonable layoff follows, something has gone wrong. The horses probably will be (a) overbet and (b) unable to repeat.

A variation of the pattern presents a tougher call. It's May 5:

This 4YO filly has been away for forty-seven days. She pops up in a stakes sprint on the lawn at Churchill Downs. No workouts show, but Kentucky can be notoriously negligent about publishing recent workouts.

I accepted Eichtercua on form.

An absence of more than six weeks following a big win should raise red flags. To be acceptable, horses should show a pattern of workouts similar to training patterns in the past, and today's start should help explain the delay.

If a young developing horse has been improving undeniably and the barn might be looking for the appropriate stakes conditions, be flexible. On March 19, Eichtercua had blasted a classified allowance field at Turfway Park, and twenty days before that she had won a non-winners' allowance race at the Fair Grounds. Obviously improving, Eichtercua's delaying tactics until today's opportunity going short on the grass make sense.

Eichtercua did not win at Churchill, but she should not have been eliminated on form.

Another kind of lengthy layoff fools handicappers repeatedly. It's May 17 and the filly below has been entered in a $10,000 claiming sprint. Is Paddy's Pick acceptable on form?

A lady handicapper told me she had liked Paddy's Pick, except for the extended layoffs. She was regretting having missed the 9–1 mutuel Paddy's Pick delivered on her comeback.

Unknown to the lady, Paddy's Pick was acceptable on form on May 17. Horses away for ninety days, six months, nine months, even a year can be accepted on form if they show a five-furlong workout within the past fourteen days. As with Paddy's Pick, the telltale workout is commonplace at major tracks, but it is uncommon at midsize and minor tracks. Data collected years ago by William L. Scott and lately by others indicate horses having the five-furlong workout win their fair share. When the five-furlong workout is part of a regular pattern, à la Paddy's Pick, form may be more than acceptable, it may be sharp.

The form-class nexus applies in this context. Paddy's Pick had won carrying a $32,000 maiden-claiming tag. Maiden-claiming graduates should be expected to win against winners at a claiming level approximately one-half the maiden-claiming price. Paddy's Pick might be expected therefore to handle $16,000 winners.

After Paddy's Pick had resurfaced from a February 17th layoff on September 4, she faced $32,000 winners. Not only had the filly been away for seven months, she had been entered ambitiously. The poor result can be attributed in part to the wrong class, not merely the layoff. At the $10,000 level, the class barrier has been removed. Form is acceptable, and may be sharp. The positive result should surprise no one.

Sticking with Paddy's Pick, suppose the September 4th comeback had not occurred. Now the May 17th date follows by fifteen months the filly's last start, a strong win against maiden-claiming foes. Is Paddy's Pick now acceptable on form?

She is. Until recently, at major tracks horses absent for longer than a year qualified as automatic throwouts. No longer. They may not win a rightful share, but they win enough. Handicappers need to hesitate. Invoke the form-class nexus. If the long-lost horse will be facing classier horses than the recent record supports, no play. But if the horse is trying cheaper, and the workouts impress, maybe.

As a rule, long standing now, handicappers should be liberal about layoffs and their form standards. Horses short of peaking form win races all the time. Horses returning from layoffs win their fair share, and many have an enviable edge.

Following are the records of five horses returning from layoffs. Which might handicappers judge acceptable? It's May 14.

If handicappers judged Alcovy acceptable, I disagree. Horses away for an unreasonable period following a win are never acceptable on form. Toss them out unmercifully.

Acceptable. It's been only five weeks since the March 31st win, an agreeable respite for sharp horses.

A closer call perhaps, but acceptable. The six-week deadline has been reached, but Gracious Granny not only shows a long workout, the filly's been on a roll and the barn is probably seeking the next convenient stakes opportunity.

Northwest Storm
Own: Scheumann Theiline P
VALENZUELA F H (11 2 1 2 .18) $62,500
Dk. b or br m. 5
Sire: Tsunami Slew (Seattle Slew)
Dam: Lady de Saron (Targowice-Fr)
Br: Arriola Joseph (Ky)
Tr: Glatt Ron (1 0 0 0 .00)
L 116

Lifetime Record:	18 6 5 1	$88,163		
1994	9 2 4 0	$70,377	Turf	8 1 4 0
1993	8 3 1 1	$15,146	Wet	0 0 0 0
Hol Ⓣ	5 1 3 0	$36,500	Dist Ⓣ	4 1 1 0

13Nov94-7Hol	fm	1	Ⓣ :24	:481	1:121	1:373	3↑ ⒻAlw 43000N3X	89	1	2	21½	22½	21	2hd	Delahoussaye E	LB 116 f	4.10	76-24	Desert Orchid116hd Northwest Storm1161¾ Tansaui116hd	
14Oct94-8SA	fm	1	Ⓣ :23	:462	1:111	1:351	3↑ ⒻAlw 47000N3X	87	2	2	31½	21½	21½	22½	Nakatani C S	L 116 f	8.30	86-11	Dance For Vanny1162½ Northwest Storm116½ Tansaui116nk	
3Sep94-7Dmr	fm	1	Ⓣ :221	:46	1:101	1:362	3↑ ⒻClm 75000	77	2	3	45	41¼	52¾	45¼	Valenzuela F H	LB 115 f	9.70	83-12	Baby O' Mine1172½ Venetian Fleet117nk Blue Tess1172½	Sav
18Aug94-8Dmr	fm	1 1/16	Ⓣ :24	:482	1:122	1:423	3↑ ⒻAlw 55396N3X	87	1	2	32	32	42½	44	Valenzuela F H	LB 117 f	23.20	89-07	PrivtePrsusion1162 FinImprssion1171 DncForVnny1191	Rail,
22Jly94-5Hol	fm	1 1/16	Ⓣ :24	:474	1:12	1:424	ⒻAlw 12500s	86	3	2	21	1hd	12	1¾	Valenzuela F H	LB 122	7.80	82-15	Northwest Storm122¾ Blue Sonata122½ Miss Juliet1221	Insi
26Jun94-7Hol	fm	1 1/16	Ⓣ :23	:464	1:11	1:413	+ⒻClm 70000	80	2	1	1hd	2hd	64¾	711	Stevens G L	LB 116	7.40	77-08	Fantastic Kim1161 Wild Again Miss122hd Liztoane113½	I
30May94-1Hol	fm	1 1/16	Ⓣ :24	:474	1:12	1:423	+ⒻClm 62500	80	4	2	21½	21	21½	22¾	Valenzuela F H	LB 116	3.20	80-11	Wild Again Miss1192¾ Northwest Storm1161¾ Misterioso1161	
15May94-9Hol	fm	1	Ⓣ :231	:47	1:111	1:353	ⒻClm 55000	83	4	5	57	55	33	22¾	Valenzuela F H	LB 116	12.90	83-14	Venturina1162¾ Northwest Storm1161 Liztoane115¾	Che
28Mar94-10YM	fst	1	:232	:47	1:104	1:363	ⒻMissYakima H27k	78	7	6	75¾	55	31	13	Allen M	LB 114	15.40	82-24	Northwest Storm1143 I. B. Forty116hd Good Lord Barbie118no	
11Oct93-8EP	fst	1⅛	:474	1:124	1:38	1:512	ⒻBC Oaks95k	55	5	2	41½	43	810	815½	Bayer J D	L 121 f	66.35	72-18	Astro Beauty121hd Donut Queen1211½ Dancing Writer1213	

WORKOUTS: Apr 27 SA 7f fst 1:273 H 2/3 Apr 20 SA 5f fst 1:012 Hg 20/47 Apr 10 SA 6f fst 1:141 H 10/19 Mar 31 SA 5f fst 1:022 H 43/53 Mar 25 SA 5f fst 1:014 H 57/85 Mar 19 SA 5f fst 1:023 H 53/62

Acceptable. If the mare had won on November 13, by these standards, she'd be unplayable. A loser by a head instead, she gets a rest. It's a fine distinction and close call. At a sweet price Northwest Storm lost by a nose on her comeback attempt against good turf horses at Hollywood Park.

Slewty
Own: Mobley Dixie
CHAPMAN T M (205 23 28 42 .11) $12,500
B. g. 4
Sire: Slewdledo (Seattle Slew)
Dam: Rushing Game (Such a Rush)
Br: Mobley Dixie & Ralph (Wash)
Tr: Roberts Tom (35 13 4 3 .37)
119

Lifetime Record:	10 3 1 0	$15,03		
1995	4 1 0 0	$3,755	Turf	0 0 0 0
1994	6 2 1 0	$11,280	Wet	2 1 0 0
GG	2 1 0 0	$3,575	Dist	1 1 0 0

29Apr95 2GG	wf	1 1/16	:23	:471	1:114	1:44	Clm 6500N2X	82	7	1	11	1½	11	13½	Carr D	LB 119 b	9.70	77-23	Slewty1193½ Wizer1193 Dudeicle1192½	F
16Apr95-7GG	fst	6f	:213	:44	:562	1:094	Clm 25000N2X	56	3	4	89	814	814	811	Lopez A D	LB 119	21.10	79-12	Lypheor Castle1172½ Wise And Bold1191 Star O' The West119½	
Lugged out backstretch																				
4Mar95-7YM	fst	1	:233	:473	1:122	1:373	Alw 7200NC	47	2	1	1hd	43	59½	513½	D'Amico D L	LB 116	7.80	63-24	NtiveRustler1152 RoylFrolic1152 JudgemntHour1144½	Got ou
[illegible]95-7YM	my	6f	:24	:482	1:011	1:142	AppleValleyH16k	64	6	1	13	22	37	37½	D'Amico D L	LB 116 b	11.30	64-31	Blustery Buck1146 Halo Passer1171½ Slewty1161½	E
Disqualified from purse money.																				
17Jly94-8YM	fst	6f	:222	:453	:574	1:102	ⓈAlw 10100N2X	39	9	1	44	87¼	816	814	Ward V M	LB 120 b	9.20	78-10	Irish Toast1132 Halo Passer1173 Mr Tew Socks117¾	
25May94-8YM	fst	5½f	:231	:473	1:00	1:063	Alw 10100N2X	58	5	2	21	31½	33	46¾	Ward V M	LB 120 b	4.30	75-23	StrongPursuit117no MgiclMountin1174¾ Comininlittlehot1202	
1May94-10Fon	fst	1	:23	:473	1:124	1:402	NebrskaDbyH32k	71	4	1	11	1hd	21	44½	Ziegler M G	LB 117 b	14.30	81-13	ShootTheJukebox121½ DocClum1133 ContinentlPrinc1191	S
9Apr94-9Fon	fst	6½f	:223	:472	1:13	1:194	Baxter H15k	54	2	3	14	11	21	21½	Hale D W	LB 115 b	6.90	87-12	ContinntlPrinc1161½ Slwty1151½ NtivLovSong1181½	Bothered
27Mar94-7Fon	fst	6f	:23	:464	1:00	1:123	Alw 5356N2L	70	1	3	1hd	11½	12	12	Ziegler M G	LB 116 b	*1.30	95-10	Slewty1162 Sugars Atthebottom1174½ Mister Breaker116½	
19Mar94-2Fon	fst	6½f	:22	:461	1:114	1:183	Md Sp Wt	60	6	1	1hd	1hd	1½	14	Ziegler M G	LB 120 b	14.70	95-04	Slewty1204 Tuscadaro1204½ Livin Big120½	Moved

WORKOUTS: •Apr 23 GG 3f fst :352 H 1/17 Apr 14 GG 4f fst :48 H 4/30 Mar 28 YM 5f fst :591 H 1/3 Feb 25 YM 5f fst 1:022 H 4/8

Not just acceptable, Slewty is sharp, and maybe a good thing. Horses swinging back after a big win in seven to fourteen days win more than their fair share of the starts. The quick return becomes a positive sign of trainer intentions. Horses swinging back in five days do even better.

On the other hand, if horses like Slewty run a lifetime top figure and come back in the normal two to three weeks, form becomes suspect, and so does the horse's ability to repeat. Figure analysts would predict a "bounce," but that's another topic.

I trust handicappers can make the distinction.

THE MIDLEVEL
THREE-YEAR-OLDS

The money was good and I liked the inventor, so I participated in a contest at Hollywood Park during 1995 in which the players claimed horses hypothetically. For $20, participants claimed ten horses, which became their stable. Players owned the horses for forty-nine racing days. Prize money was awarded for most money won (after recovering the claiming price) and for most wins. I bought five stables.

Events were proceeding swimmingly, and with two of the stables I had reached contention. Halfway along, while I languished in sixth place (money won), one of the contestants had jumped ahead of the runner-up by $11,000 and of me by $25,000.

Most of my claims were hard knockers. The horses might win repeatedly, boosting the win column. I also claimed seven 3YOs, in each instance grabbing an improving sort that might jump ahead in class and accumulate decent money.

Behind at the midpoint by $25,000, I was nevertheless confident of leaping to the lead and eventually earning the money-won pot. One of my 3YOs had been entered in a $70,000-added stakes at Golden Gate Fields. This filly looked like the pearl of the oyster. I was supremely confident she would win. So were the bettors in northern California. They backed the horse to 9–5, a co-favorite with a filly that had won five straight.

Examine the stakes conditions and the record of my improving 3YO:

8 Golden Gate Fields

1⅛ MILES. (Turf, chute). (1:41¹) 9th Running of THE SONGSTRESS BREEDERS' CUP. Purse $70,000 Added. Fillies, 3-year-olds. By subscription of $50 each to accompany the nomination. $250 to pass the entry box and

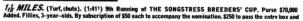

Turko's Turn											

In her third start of the 1995 season, Turko's Turn had exited an open stakes at Santa Anita, where she had demonstrated high speed at the pace call and had entered a $50,000 claiming race. She drew the number-one post at Hollywood Park that day, which meant Turko's Turn would be running against a severe negative rail bias, which would surely defeat her best effort. Against the rail bias, Turko's Turn ran fast and strongly, before tiring predictably in the stretch.

Even though I expected Turko's Turn to lose the $50,000 claiming race, I claimed her.

Favored for the first three races in her career, Turko's Turn had improved terrifically on her second try, as juvenile maidens should. Next she won a minor stakes at Pleasanton, in northern California, which runs for two weeks as part of a fair circuit that connects the meetings at Golden Gate Fields and Bay Meadows.

Turko's Turn followed the minor stakes with attempts in a Grade 2 event and two open stakes at Santa Anita, where she's pickled. But in her second start at three, Turko's Turn shows the telltale improvement.

That improvement should result in victory at the claiming level. But the rail bias interferes, shifting the emphasis to the next start, May 19. Now the filly is stretched to a mile and is shifted to the grass. If Turko's Turn has genuinely improved, she should defeat $62,500 claimers regardless.

Turko's Turn scampers wire-to-wire in a waltz.

Now the filly looks again like an improving sort en route to better days. Eligible to nonwinners twice allowances, Turko's Turn instead is aimed directly at a richer open stakes. It's on the grass, a surface she has obviously liked, and the purse is $70,000-added.

Following the $62,500 claiming romp, Turko's Turn has trained impressively, dispensing a best-of-morning six furlongs on June 5 in 1:12 ⅘, fastest of twenty-two workouts.

In the running of the Songstress Stakes, Turko's Turn pressed a fast pace, but nearing the quarter pole she stopped like a cheap speedster absolutely out of her element.

And that's why middling 3YOs qualify as the most difficult of all horses to comprehend. They are, as several handicappers have testified, consistently inconsistent. The outstanding implication for handicappers should be plain. If the case is ambiguous, do not accept a short price.

Revisiting Turko's Turn's performance in the Songstress, the record might be interpreted in another way. From January to June especially, and throughout the season generally, 3YOs moving from claiming to nonclaiming races represent high risks. That principle has proved less reliable in recent seasons, but 3YO claiming horses have presumptively convinced their management that a prosperous future is not on the horizon. Otherwise why present a young, unclassified racehorse showing some promise for sale?

The best protection for avoiding Turko's Turn's turnaround in the Songstress and the numerous similar situations that arise annually is to reject a short price. As favorites and low-priced contenders, discount these 3YOs. If Turko's Turn goes at 7–1 or thereabouts, that's different. Now the recent improvement can carry the cause.

Turko's Turn finished up the course and last in the Songstress, notwithstanding the pattern of recent improvement and my high hopes. Where should the horse be expected to win next? In a similar stakes? In a nonwinners' twice allowance race? In a claiming race?

The answer remains unclear, but probably she should not prevail in a similar stakes, unless the filly bled in the Songstress or offers another legitimate excuse for the pratfall.

In a nonwinners' twice other than allowance affair, Turko's Turn will be susceptible to any lightly raced improving 3YO of authentic talent that happens to be moving through its conditions. As handicappers appreciate, that occurs throughout the season, notably from January through September. If the impressively improving nonclaiming types are missing, Turko's Turn may grab another allowance purse. Handicappers must examine the speed figures and complete a careful pace analysis, consider the entire pattern of development, and make a close decision. Low odds, to repeat, are forbidden.

Where Turko's Turn will be acceptable, and probably belongs, is in claiming conditions similar to the kind she has already beaten. As the calendar year progresses, a greater number of middling 3YOs will be entered in the high-priced claiming races limited to threes, strengthening the competition.

In classifying 3YOs, not prematurely, handicappers benefit by relating recent races to the entire pattern of development. Turko's Turn, for example, may rebound from the Songstress debacle and impress anew. The filly has shown enough, and she was highly regarded in the beginning. The entire pattern of development remains inconclusive. Turko's Turn may be a decent horse, after all, or she may be the cheaper commodity. No one knows yet, not even her trainer and owner.

In that meticulous way, examine the even-money favorite in the Songstress. Where should Wish Of My Own be expected to win next?

Unlike Turko's Turn, Wish Of My Own reveals humble beginnings. On the other hand, recent races show rapid improvement while moving ahead in class. One element missing has been a hard-fought victory against nonclaiming 3YOs. The trio of recent nonclaiming wins have proved relatively facile, unmolested wire-to-wire jags on the grass.

Unable to secure the lead in the Songstress, Wish Of My Own proved no factor and never looked like a winner. She wears fronts. She remains unclassified.

After the requisite rest, I would expect Wish Of My Own to revisit the winner's circle in a high-priced claiming race, not in the stakes, and not in the advanced allowances. The Cal-bred filly certainly likes to win, but otherwise she looks quite ordinary.

The winner of the Songstress looked like this:

Both Ways 5—0
Own: Gogliano Frank J

B. f. 3 (Feb)
Sire: Siyah Kalem (Mr. Prospector)
Dam: Cucurucuru (Shirley's Champion)
Br: Thomas W. Bachman (Cal)
Tr: Puype Mike (49 7 7 13 .14)

117

	Lifetime Record : 12 4 1 1	$78,965
1995	2 0 0 0	$4,525	Turf	0 0 0 0	
1994	10 4 1 1	$74,340	Wet	1 1 0 0	$30,500
GG ①	0 0 0 0		Dist ①	0 0 0 0	

BAZE R A (507 150 107 78 .30)

Both Ways grabbed the lead, repelled Turko's Turn, and held. She had lost to Turko's Turn going short at Pleasanton in July, but she returned the favor in the Songstress.

Was Both Ways' victory predictable?

No surprise, it's another painstaking call. She had won the Lassie at Bay Meadows in December, but alone on the front in the mud. Quite impressive while moving ambitiously ahead at the conclusion of her juvenile season, Both Ways had disappointed twice when favored in similar stakes at three.

Now Both Ways is introduced to the grass, for which her pedigree is neither strong nor weak. In her favor, the two-sprint stretch-out pattern is best, Both Ways has already won at the route, and the barn has exercised the filly three times on the grass, the workouts sharp. Leading rider Russell Baze stays aboard.

As with Turko's Turn, the situation looks ambiguous. At a short price, no play. Both Ways went to the post a 5–1 shot, acceptable odds.

In choosing among Turko's Turn, Wish Of My Own, and Both Ways, handicappers grapple with resistance in every direction. The final arbiter must be price. At the odds, Turko's Turn and Wish Of My Own make no sense, a reality handicappers must accept. Both Ways is a possibility.

Beyond relating the recent races to the entire pattern of development, here are a few trusty guideposts for evaluating the midlevel 3YOs.

1. Remember, please, the horses will be consistently inconsistent.
   If the entire pattern has been positive, but the last race negative, depend upon the most recent win or strong performance.

Accept the horses at a class level one notch above or below that line.

2. A speed-figure top will often be followed by a relatively low figure.

    Midlevel 3YOs cannot be expected to repeat their top performances the next time. They often regress, but rebound a race or two later.

3. In evaluating speed, refer to the speed figures in the recent form cycle, not just the most recent race.

    A variation of the above guidelines, the speed figures a few races ago may be more representative of what the horse will do today. A rebound is more likely to occur if the latest speed figure looks unusually poor. The horse probably regressed, or merely disappointed, as many Turko Turns do.

4. Improving midlevel 3YOs can disappoint badly if they are rushed into advanced competition before the class rise makes sense, as from the first allowance win to a graded stakes, or from the nonwinners' twice allowance success to a Grade 1 or Grade 2 event.

    Midlevel 3YOs cannot tolerate huge leaps in class, as from claiming races to allowance races to the stakes (Turko's Turn), or even from claiming to allowance races, notably if the probable pace will be swifter or more intense.

5. In claiming races, speed figures and pace ratings should be emphasized. In nonclaiming races, the horses should fit the eligibility conditions snugly, regardless of their recent numerical ratings.

    In other words, speed and pace factors define the middling 3YOs reliably in claiming races. Their basic abilities, or class, define them much more effectively in nonclaiming circumstances.

6. Following a disappointing performance, do not necessarily expect another disappointment.

    Evaluate the horses based upon their recent good efforts, not the deep disappointment. Turko's Turn should not become a throwout next time, not in a claiming race, not in a nonwinners' twice allowance try, and not in a similar stakes race.

And that's why midlevel 3YOs are the most difficult horses to comprehend.

Did I already say as much?

Well, it bears repetition.

LEVERAGE

When the grass import Via Lombardia rallied from last to first to win Hollywood Park's 1995 Will Rogers Stakes (Gr. 3), the colt not only keyed a variety of interconnected wagers but also qualified as an outstanding illustration of one of the most dynamic concepts the game has ever produced.

It's leverage. A powerful investment tool that racetrack bettors have lacked, until now, leverage escalates the utility value of money, often in dramatic style. Exotic betting menus offering unprecedented choices are part and parcel of the new phenomenon.

Via Lombardia was 6–1, a nonfavorite that represented a surprisingly generous overlay. By my standards, Via Lombardia figured to overtake Mr Purple, the even-money favorite in the stretch of the one-mile grass stakes. The two were clearly best in the field of nine. I expected no more than 5–2 on the import. The past performances are presented on page 76.

Although generous odds help enormously, they are not required for leverage, but a nonfavorite is. When handicappers identify a nonfavorite as a key bet, the most important aspect of the betting opportunity has been satisfied. Just as integral, however, the circumstances of the race and the connecting races must be susceptible to effective handicapping.

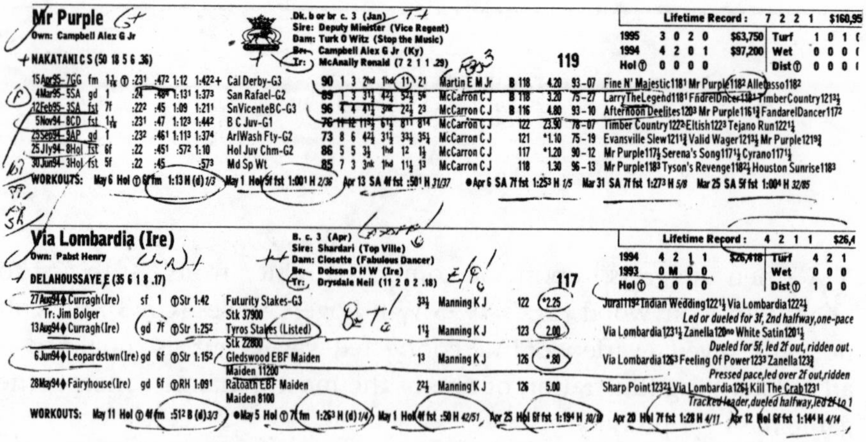

Mr Purple
Own: Campbell Alex G Jr
NAKATANI C S (50 18 5 6 .36)
Dk. b or br c. 3 (Jan)
Sire: Deputy Minister (Vice Regent)
Dam: Turk O Witz (Stop the Music)
Br: Campbell Alex G Jr (Ky)
Tr: McAnally Ronald (7 2 1 1 .29)
119

Lifetime Record:	7 2 2 1	$160,95		
1995	3 0 2 0	$63,750	Turf	1 0 1 (
1994	4 2 0 1	$97,200	Wet	0 0 0 (
Hol ①	0 0 0 0		Dist ①	0 0 0 (

15Apr95-7GG	fm	1 1/16 ①	:231	:472	1:12	1:422+	Cal Derby-G3	90	1	3	2hd	1hd	11	21	Martin E M Jr	B 118	4.20	93-07	Fine N' Majestic1181 Mr Purple1182 Alletasso1182
4Mar95-5SA	gd	1	:24	:484	1:131	1:373	San Rafael-G2	89	1	3	3½	4¼	5½	56	McCarron C J	B 118	3.20	75-27	LarryTheLegend1181 FndrelDncer1181 TimberCountry1213½
12Feb95-3SA	fst	7f	:222	:45	1:09	1:211	SnVicenteBC-G3	96	4	4	4½	3hd	2½	23	McCarron C J	B 116	4.80	93-10	Afternoon Deelites1203 Mr Purple1161¾ FandarelDancer1172
5Nov94-8CD	fst	1 1/16	:231	:47	1:123	1:442	B C Juv-G1	76	11	12	11½	6½	811	814	McCarron C J	122	23.90	78-07	Timber Country1222 Eltish1223 Tejano Run1221¼
25Sep94-9AP	gd	1	:232	:461	1:113	1:374	ArlWash Fty-G2	73	8	6	4½	3½	3½	35¼	McCarron C J	121	*1.10	75-19	Evansville Slew1211¾ Valid Wager1213½ Mr Purple1219¾
25Jly94-8Hol	fst	6f	:22	:451	:572	1:10	Hol Juv Chm-G2	86	5	5	3½	1hd	12	1½	McCarron C J	117	*1.20	90-12	Mr Purple117½ Serena's Song1171½ Cyrano1171½
30Jun94-3Hol	fst	5f	:22	:45		:573	Md Sp Wt	85	7	3	3nk	1hd	11½	13	McCarron C J	118	1.30	96-13	Mr Purple1183 Tyson's Revenge1182½ Houston Sunrise1183

WORKOUTS: May 6 Hol ① 6f fm 1:13 H (d) *1/3* May 1 Hol 5f fst 1:001 H *2/36* Apr 13 SA 4f fst :501 H *31/37* ●Apr 6 SA 7f fst 1:253 H *1/5* Mar 31 SA 7f fst 1:273 H *5/8* Mar 25 SA 5f fst 1:004 H *32/85*

Via Lombardia (Ire)
Own: Pabst Henry
DELAHOUSSAYE E (35 6 1 8 .17)
B. c. 3 (Apr)
Sire: Shardari (Top Ville)
Dam: Closette (Fabulous Dancer)
Br: Dobson D H W (Ire)
Tr: Drysdale Neil (11 2 0 2 .18)
117

Lifetime Record:	4 2 1 1	$26,4		
1994	4 2 1 1	$26,418	Turf	4 2 1
1993	0 M 0 0		Wet	0 0 0
Hol ①	0 0 0 0		Dist ①	1 0 0

27Aug94♦ Curragh(Ire) Tr: Jim Bolger	sf	1	①Str 1:42	Futurity Stakes-G3 Stk 37900	33½	Manning K J	122	*2.25	Jural1192 Indian Wedding1221½ Via Lombardia1222½	*Led or dueled for 3f, 2nd halfway,one-pace*
13Aug94♦ Curragh(Ire)	gd	7f	①Str 1:252	Tyros Stakes (Listed) Stk 22800	11½	Manning K J	123	2.00	Via Lombardia1231½ Zanella120no White Satin1201½	*Dueled for 5f, led 2f out, ridden out*
6Jun94♦ Leopardstwn(Ire)	gd	6f	①Str 1:152	Gledswood EBF Maiden Maiden 11200	13	Manning K J	126	*.80	Via Lombardia1263 Feeling Of Power1233 Zanella123¾	*Pressed pace,led over 2f out,ridden*
28May94♦ Fairyhouse(Ire)	gd	6f	①RH 1:091	Ratoath EBF Maiden Maiden 8100	22½	Manning K J	126	5.00	Sharp Point1232½ Via Lombardia126½ Kill The Crab1231	*Tracked leader,dueled halfway,led 2f to 1*

WORKOUTS: May 11 Hol ① 4f fm :512 B (d) *3/3* ●May 5 Hol ① 7f fm 1:263 H (d) *1/4* May 1 Hol 4f fst :50 H *42/51* Apr 25 Hol 6f fst 1:194 H *10/10* Apr 20 Hol 7f fst 1:28 H *4/11* Apr 12 Hol 6f fst 1:144 H *4/14*

In the Hollywood Park example, the track had introduced the "rolling doubles" in 1995. These doubles complemented the rolling triples (Pick 3s) already in place. That meant Via Lombardia might be keyed not only to win, but also in the exacta, trifecta, two doubles, and two Pick 3s. I took a piece of all seven pools. I also coupled Via Lombardia and Mr Purple in the quinella.

Examine the result chart:

The key bet to win ($200) returned $1400.

A $20 exacta ($35.40) with Via Lombardia on top returned $354.

Using three horses in the race preceding the Will Rogers, and two in the race following the Will Rogers, I caught both doubles and one of the Pick 3s. (Despite using three horses in a six-horse field, I had missed the seventh race, two legs before the Will Rogers.)

NINTH RACE
Hollywood
MAY 13, 1995

1 MILE. (Turf)(1.32^{3}) The 55th Running of THE WILL ROGERS BREEDERS' CUP HANDICAP. Purse $100,000 Added. ($75,000 added plus $25,000 from Breeders' Cup Fund). Grade III. 3-year-olds. By subscription of $100 each, which shall accompany the nomination, $750 additional to start, with $75,000 added and an additional $25,000 from the Breeders' Cup Fund for Cup nominees only. The host association's added monies to be divided 55% to the winner, 20% to second, 15% to third, 7.5% to fourth and 2.5% to fifth. Breeders' Cup monies also correspondingly divided providing a Breeders' Cup nominee has finished in an awarded position. All fees to the winner. Any Breeders'Cup monies not awarded will revert to the fund. Weights Sunday May 7. Starters to be named through the entry box by closing time of entries. This race will not be divided. Preference will be given in the following order: Highweights will be preferred under the following conditions, Breeders' Cup nominees will be preferred over Non-Breeders' Cup nominees assigned equal weights on the scale. Total earnings in 1995 will be used in determining the preference of horses with equal nominations status and equal weight assigned on the scale. All fees for entrants that fail to draw into this race will be cancelled. Trophies will be presented to the winning owner, trainer and jockey. Closed Wednesday, May 3 with 19 nominations.

Value of Race: $108,650 Winner $63,650; second $20,000; third $15,000; fourth $7,500; fifth $2,500. Mutuel Pool $368,249.30 Exacta Pool $245,079.00 Trifecta Pool $267,781.00 Quinella Pool $41,498.00

Last Raced	Horse	M/Eqt.	A.	Wt	PP	St	¼	½	¾	Str	Fin	Jockey	Odds $1
27Aug94 Cur^{3}	Via Lombardia-IR	B	3	117	4	9	9	9	9	4^{hd}	1$\frac{3}{4}$	Delahoussaye E	6.00
15Apr95 ^{7}GG^{2}	Mr Purple	B	3	119	3	4	4^{1}	4$\frac{1}{2}$	2^{hd}	1^{hd}	2$\frac{3}{4}$	Nakatani C S	1.10
15Apr95 ^{7}GG^{11}	Bee El Tee	LBbf	3	117	9	2	2$^{1\frac{1}{2}}$	2^{hd}	1$\frac{1}{2}$	2$^{1\frac{1}{2}}$	3$^{3\frac{1}{2}}$	Valenzuela P A	14.90
23Apr95 ^{8}Kee^{4}	Hidden Source	B	3	114	1	8	8^{2}	8^{hd}	8^{hd}	8^{4}	4^{hd}	Stevens G L	5.90
12Apr95 ^{8}SA^{2}	Oncefortheroad	LBb	3	115	7	6	5$^{1\frac{1}{2}}$	5^{2}	7$^{1\frac{1}{2}}$	7^{hd}	5no	Sorenson D	16.80
8Apr95 ^{1}SA^{4}	Judgement Day-IR	Bb	3	114	8	7	7^{hd}	7^{3}	5$\frac{1}{2}$	5^{hd}	6$\frac{1}{2}$	McCarron C J	5.50
12Apr95 ^{8}SA^{3}	Score Quick	LB	3	115	5	1	3$^{1\frac{1}{2}}$	3$\frac{1}{2}$	3$^{1\frac{1}{2}}$	3$^{1\frac{1}{2}}$	7$^{3\frac{1}{2}}$	Solis A	18.10
15Apr95 ^{7}GG^{3}	Alletasso	LBb	3	117	6	5	6^{1}	6^{hd}	4^{hd}	6$\frac{1}{2}$	8^{10}	Warren R J Jr	12.10
29Apr95 ^{4}Hol^{5}	Costly Frosty	Bf	3	111	2	3	1$\frac{1}{2}$	1^{hd}	6^{hd}	9	9	Almeida G F	36.80

OFF AT 5:42 Start Good. Won driving. Time, :23, :46^{3}, 1:10^{2}, 1:34 Course firm.

$2 Mutuel Prices:				
	4–VIA LOMBARDIA–IR	14.00	5.60	4.40
	3–MR PURPLE		3.00	2.60
	9–BEE EL TEE			6.00

$2 EXACTA 4–3 PAID $35.40 $2 TRIFECTA 4–3–9 PAID $306.00 $2 QUINELLA 3–4 PAID $15.20

B. c, (Apr), by Shardari–Closette, by Fabulous Dancer. Trainer Drysdale Neil. Bred by Dobson D H W (Ire).

VIA LOMBARDIA off a bit slowly, trailed off the rail early, moved outside HIDDEN SOURCE on the backstretch, continued outside that foe on the second turn, came widest into the stretch and finished strongly under right handed pressure to prove best. MR PURPLE was taken off the fence on the backstretch, bid four wide leaving the backstretch, raced three deep into the lane to gain the lead in midstretch but could not hold off the winner. BEE EL TEE cut to the inside into the first turn, dueled inside to midstretch and continued on willingly to the wire. HIDDEN SOURCE saved ground to the second turn, came off the rail on that bend, split foes in midstretch and finished with some interest. ONCEFORTHEROAD outside MR PURPLE early on the backstretch, inched forward five wide approaching the second turn, continued four wide through that turn and lacked the needed response in the stretch. JUDGEMENT DAY outside HIDDEN SOURCE on the first turn, continued outside ALLETASSO on the backstretch, raced between foes on the second turn and in midstretch and also lacked the needed late kick. SCORE QUICK forced out into the first turn, moved up between rivals and three deep into the second turn but weakened in the lane.

The eighth–ninth double paid $39.20. Three $10 doubles ($30) returned $197.

The ninth–tenth double paid $65.60. Two $10 doubles ($20) returned $328.

Playing a 3-3-1 combination ($3 each), I lost $27 on the seventh–eighth–ninth Pick 3.

Playing a 3-1-2 combination, I invested $18 in the eighth–ninth–tenth Pick 3, which struck for $209.10.

A $20 quinella ($15.20) returned $152

The exotic gross on a $135 investment was $1240, a net profit of $1105.

A similar bet to win ($135) would have netted $810. In this situation the exotics provided a 36 percent premium.

Of course I might have missed the exacta, the doubles, and the Pick 3. Or one, or two, of the exotics, a common mishap.

On the other hand, an 8–5 favorite won the eighth. I had covered the 7–1 second-finisher as well in the Pick 3. That horse, with Via Lombardia, with the 7–1 winner of the tenth race might have returned five-to-seven times as much in the winning Pick 3.

The profit extracted from the seven pools amounted to $3,105, which suggests the windfalls awaiting handicappers who practice the leverage suddenly available to them.

Several comments apply. First, leverage operates best when handicappers find key bets that are nonfavorites. Favorites can be leveraged in several pools, too, but too often favorites will be underlays in the exactas, doubles, and Pick 3s. Nonfavorites tend to be overlays in the exotics.

The bets to win are crucial. The win bet is part of a pattern that handicappers depend upon for predictable profits from season to season.

Leverage becomes a realistic proposition when the circumstances surrounding the key bets become ripe enough to exploit. In other words the exotic combinations have a greater probability of occurring than they normally do. As handicappers realize, exotic bets, all of them, are low-probability bets. Handicappers must recognize that specific combinations are likelier than usual to occur and that the profit potential looks abnormally high.

In the example, if Mr Purple should beat Via Lombardia, the quinella would exceed 50 percent of the exacta, as typically occurs in quinellas when overbet favorites finish first and a generous overlay finishes second.

In covering three horses in the race preceding the Will Rogers, I determined I had roughly an 80 percent chance to tab the winner. The two horses I covered in the race following the Will Rogers had a less likely probability of occurring, but my chances approached a 50 percent probability.

If the exacta, doubles, and Pick 3s had looked contentious or unpredictable, I would have backed Via Lombardia to win only. But the exotics looked predictable instead, and so therefore did the opportunity for leverage.

Following the races, a handicapping colleague inquired why I did not cover the trifecta in the Will Rogers, combining Via Lombardia and Mr Purple in the one-two holes and using the other seven horses to show. If the analysis of the race proved correct, he insisted, the trifecta was predictable, too, and the payoff might be generous.

A 14–1 shot finished third. The trifecta returned $306. The cost to play the trifecta by combining a 1-1-all twice would have been $28. That translated to 10–1.

I blew it. I should have played the trifecta, a wager I ignore too often because (a) my playing strategies have been weak, and (b) the payoffs in southern California are frequently too low. But in the example featuring Via Lombardia and Mr Purple, the trifecta makes sense, and if I could replay the wager, I would include the trifecta. The extra exotic wager would have enhanced my leverage, which is precisely the idea.

It's convenient to replay the fabulous opportunities for leverage that eluded my friend and bloodstock agent, Mike Loomer, Memorial Day, 1995, again at Hollywood Park, although Loomer expresses no regrets.

Loomer liked the generous winner of the Grade 1 feature, the Hollywood Turf Handicap, at ten furlongs on the grass, as a key bet. Earl of Barking not only won powerfully, but at 24–1 he paid $50.60. Loomer bet to win, and he also converted the Pick 3 encompassing the eighth–ninth–tenth. This paid $2658.30.

Loomer had bought the ten-horse eighth race and had combined those horses with Earl of Barking in the ninth to the single horse he favored in the tenth, which paid $7.80.

Fine.

But the opportunity for extensive leverage was fantastic, at a ridiculously low cost.

The $2 exacta of Earl of Barking on top of the favorite paid $263.60.

The eighth–ninth double paid $233.40. The favorite also won the eighth.

The ninth–tenth double paid $395.60. Loomer later conceded he should have collected that payoff. He liked both winners.

The $2 trifecta paid a whopping $1756, but Loomer confessed he would not have covered the winning combination.

Regardless, for an additional minor investment, say $24, Loomer would have pocketed an additional $892.60, which is a sweet windfall.

Leverage becomes the most potent weapon of all for good handicappers who are small bettors. When key bets to win that should be

nonfavorites have been isolated, handicappers should pause to consider the surrounding circumstances. Ponder the possibilities in each
exotic pool.

If the circumstances look inviting, risk the added investments. Be
assertive. Be confident.

If the handicapping has been effective, and the key horse wins, the
profits might be huge. If that happens a dozen times a season, imagine
the bottom line.

USING SPEED AND PACE FIGURES
IN COMBINATION

T he argument that speed figures are used to best advantage in combination with pace figures cannot be reduced to an assertion regarding the superiority of one or the other. Pace figures can supersede
speed figures, and speed figures can supersede pace figures, depending
upon a vast array of situational factors.

As a rule, pace figures take precedence in cheaper races (maiden-
claiming, low-level claiming, and claiming races limited to 3YOs)
where so many winners will be incapable of posting speed figures near
par. Speed figures take precedence in better races (high-priced claiming, advanced allowances, and major stakes) where so many winners
will be fully capable of posting pace figures above par.

Far more important, for the majority of unexceptional horses (mid-
level claiming, nonwinners' allowances, and numerous stakes) speed
and pace figures tend to be symmetrical. When the pace figure improves, the speed figure declines. When the speed figure improves, the
pace figure declines. These relationships were crystallized splendidly a
decade ago by researcher and handicapper Bill Quirin,* and few figure
handicappers who have played the game with Quirin-style speed and
pace figures even for a season will deny the basic dynamics of the
method.

Later comes *Beyer on Speed*, in which the inimitable Andrew Beyer
offers to handicappers first-person testimony on the principles and
practices of pace handicapping, in particular on the relationships between speed figures and pace figures.

By his own admission, Beyer has struggled with these relationships
for years. In his latest book Beyer's problems have not gone away, and

*William L. Quirin, *Thoroughbred Handicapping: State of the Art* (William Morrow, 1984,
chapters 9 and 10).

in his chapter "The Mathematics of Pace," handicappers cannot fail to feel the skepticism and equivocation with which the author surrounds not only his personal methods of making pace figures but also the alternative methods promoted effectively by others.

In essence Beyer has accepted the importance of pace handicapping and the principles of pace analysis, but he remains haunted by the apparent contradictions he finds in the numerical approaches to expressing the speed-pace relationships. He is especially rankled by the way pace figures appear to penalize certain horses unfairly, not because of relative abilities but because of running styles.

In Beyer's view pace figures will too often be unjust to stalkers, horses that run a couple of lengths behind the leaders during the early stages of races. In *Beyer on Speed*, he cites the following hypothetical situation:

Horse X opens a clear lead, runs a quarter mile in 22 ⅖ seconds, a half mile in 45 ⅕ seconds, and finishes six furlongs in 1:11.

Horse Y, who customarily stalks the pace, displays his usual style, sits three lengths behind the leader throughout the first half mile, and then rallies to finish within a nose of X.

This is presumably a good performance by Y, because it is not easy to catch a solitary front-runner.

Now the two horses are meeting each other again, and in pace analysis they will look like this on paper:

| Horse X | 22 ⅖ | 45 ⅕ | 1:11 |
| Horse Y | 23 | 45 ⅘ | 1:11 |

To handicappers using pace figures, they may look like this:

	Pace	Final
Horse X	100	92
Horse Y	87	92

Beyer concludes that by relying either on conventional speed and pace figures or on Sartin-style velocity ratings, Horse X will be rated the better horse, when actually the two horses are comparably talented. He judges this kind of pace analysis specious:

And this—in my view, at least—is where most pace-handicapping theory collapses into a heap of contradictions, illogic, and provincialism. Horse Y is viewed as an inferior horse just because he doesn't have a front-running style.

Although pace analysts would generally prefer Horse X in the illustration provided by Beyer (not if the track profile favored late pace), pace analysis utilizing pace figures does not favor front-runners, even lonely front-runners, at the expense of stalkers.

Pace analysis examines the relations among final times, fractional times, and running styles. The objective is to determine whether a particular horse can (a) set and maintain a rate of speed, or (b) track and overtake a rate of speed. In the illustration Horse Y loses, not because of his running style but because he runs too slowly for too long in relation to Horse X.

The irony, the overarching irony of Beyer's critique, is that modern pace handicapping has tended to shift the emphasis away from front-runners and toward running styles referred to as pressers and stalkers. The new methods reward position and beaten-lengths at the second call, for example, where off-pace horses will have reached striking position, and not the first call, where front-runners obviously dominate.

To appreciate the relationships better, and to show two variations of Beyer's illustration whereby the stalker should overtake the front-runner, let's arrange the fractional times of Horse X and Horse Y as follows:

	1st Fraction	2nd Fraction	3rd Fraction
Horse X	22 ⅖	22 ⅘	25 ⅘
Horse Y	23	22 ⅘	25 ⅕

In *Modern Pace Handicapping* (Morrow, 1991), author Tom Brohamer set down several principles of pace analysis relevant here and presumptively agreeable to Beyer:

1. Need-to-lead front-runners that cannot get the lead can be eliminated.

2. In sprints, the most important fraction usually will be the second. [Brohamer refers to the second fraction as "turn-time."*]
3. Off-pace horses, deep closers especially, will be disadvantaged severely unless they can complete the second fraction faster than the lead horse.
4. Pace standouts are typically horses that can dominate *two* of the pace segments, early, middle, and late.
5. Pace ratings (early, average, late) are best interpreted in relation to a track profile, i.e., the kinds of running styles that have been winning lately.

In Beyer's illustration Horse Y's inability to cut into Horse X's lead during the second fraction is the critical shortcoming. As Brohamer might indicate, Horse X has controlled two thirds of the race. Horse Y does not finish powerfully enough to catch up, which will be true of most stalkers and closers unable to gain on the lead during the second fraction.

Suppose Beyer's stalker ran three lengths behind Horse X at the first call and two lengths behind at the second call, a common scenario among stalkers in sprints. Horse Y still gains three lengths in the stretch.

Now the pace analysis looks like this:

	1st Call	2nd Call	Finish	Turn-time
Horse X	22 ⅖	45 ⅕	1:11	22 ⅘
Horse Y	23	45 ⅗	1:10 ⅘	22 ⅗

By running the first quarter mile in 23 seconds, the second quarter mile in 22 ⅗ seconds (instead of 22 ⅘), and the final quarter mile in the same 25 ⅕ seconds, Horse Y wins by a length, not by a nose.

Furthermore, to handicappers using pace figures (Quirin-style), the comparisons would look like this:

---

*Turn-time refers to the second fraction of sprints primarily and is calculated as the difference between the fractional times at the first and second calls, modified by lengths gained/lost.

	Pace Figure	Final Figure
Horse X	100	97
Horse Y	96	98

The front-runner boasts the higher pace figure by two lengths.* If the pace figures are added to the speed figures, Horse X gets 197 and Horse Y gets 194. Horse Y nevertheless wins. Pace analysis beats pace figures, as Beyer rightly insists. Regarding the numbers, pace analysts usually accept pace figures within two lengths of par or within two lengths of the lead horse.

Notice that Horse Y now controls two pace intervals, the second fraction and the third fraction. At the Del Mar meeting during the summer of 1993, where Beyer played for six weeks, sprinters that controlled the second and third fractions regularly won. Many were stalkers. In Beyer's illustration Horse Y controlled only the third fraction, and those sprinters regularly lose.

The illustration might be altered in another way, quite common, and advantageous to Horse Y:

Horse X (f)	22 ⅖	45 ⅕	1:11	22 ⅘ (T-T)
Horse Y (s)	23	45 ⅘	1:11	22 ⅘
Horse Z (f)	22 ⅕	45	1:11 ⅖	22 ⅘

If Horse X is a need-to-lead type, Horse Y wins. As Brohamer tells, need-to-lead front-runners that cannot get the lead can be eliminated.

Even if Horse X does not need to lead, and can press the pace of Horse Z without expiring, Horse Y probably wins. To recall, speed figures and pace figures tend to be symmetrical. When X presses Z's faster fractions, his final time should decline.

Notice, too, that Horse Y is now four lengths behind the early pace, not three. If Y stays within his customary three lengths of Z instead of four, won't Y's final time decline? Maybe, but a one-length difference early among stalkers should not translate to as much of a decline, if

---

*At the finish, one point equals one length; at the pace call, two points equals one length.

any, in final time as it does among front-runners and pressers. Multiple lengths, definitely; one length, not to worry.

In numerous situations, reliance on pace figures in combination with speed figures can clarify tactical advantages not nearly as precarious as in Beyer's illustration. When hidden advantages belong to horses having superior pace figures, but merely competitive speed figures, pace analysts identify overlays speed handicappers may not.

One of the sweetest opportunities of 1993 occurred at Hollywood Park in the $200,000-added Hollywood Oaks (Gr.1), at nine furlongs for 3YO fillies. Examine the Beyer Speed Figures shown below for the four fillies.

Likeable Style 4+N++
Own: Golden Eagle Farm
STEVENS G L (180 42 26 23 .23)

B. f. 3 (Jan)
Sire: Nijinsky II (Northern Dancer)
Dam: Personable Lady (No Robbery)
Br: Mabee Mr & Mrs John C (Ky)
Tr: Mandella Richard (88 17 16 15 .19)

105/92 105 SA
L 121

Lifetime Record:
1993 5 4 0 0 $259,350
1992 1 1 0 0 $15,950
Hol 1 1 0 0 $61,200

5Jun93-8Hol my 1 1/16 ⊗ :243 :491 1:141 1:461 ⒻHoneymoon H-G3 95 1 3 32 42 31 11¼ Delahoussaye E LB 122 *.70 70-32 Likeable Style1221¼ Adorydar1141¾ Vinis
15May93-8Hol fm 1 Ⓣ :233 :463 1:101 1:342 ⒻSenorita B CG3 97 2 6 62½ 52¾ 41½ 11 Desormeaux K J LB 121 2.80 93-09 Likeable Style1211 Adorydar113½ Icy Wa
7Mar93-8SA fst 1 1/16 :23 :471 1:11 1:424 ⒻS A Oaks-G1 86 1 7 76 78¼ 610 67½ Stevens G L B 117 *1.10 82-14 Eliza1174¾ Stalcreek1171 Dance For Van
13Feb93-8SA fst 1 :224 :463 1:104 1:363 ⒻLs Virgenes-G1 92 5 5 52¾ 31 1hd 13 Stevens G L B 117 *.90 87-15 Likeable Style1173 Incindress1171½ Blu
22Jan93-8SA gd 1 1/16 :234 :474 1:13 1:443 ⒻS Ysabela 75k 91 5 3 32 21 1hd 12 Stevens G L B 115 *.90 81-19 Likeable Style1152 Fit To Lead1176 Am
Off slowly, wide, ridden out
26Dec92-4SA fst 6f :212 :443 :57 1:093 ⒻMd Sp Wt 84 10 11 1210 65½ 42 11 Stevens G L B 117 7.10 88-09 Likeable Style1171 Aleyna's Love117no
WORKOUTS: ●Jly 6 Hol 5f fst :592 H 1/43 ●Jun 30 Hol 1 fst 1:384 H 1/4 Jun 23 Hol 6f fst 1:003 H 9/32 Jun 17 Hol 3f fst :353 B 8/33 May 31 Hol 5f fst 1:034 B 45/47 May 26 Hol

As a double-advantage horse on Beyer Speed (''double fig''), a Grade 1 stakes winner, and a media darling in southern California, Likeable Style went favored at 3–5. Users of speed and pace figures in combination knew better. Consider Likeable Style's speed-pace figures for her trio of stakes wins on the main track. Today's par, at both calls, is 105.

	Pace Figure	Final Figure	Beyer Speed
June 5	92	105	95
Feb 13	104	103	92
Jan 22	99	105	91

Recognizing Likeable Style as a conspicuous underlay, pace analysts turn their attention to the three fillies exiting the June 19th Princess Stakes (Gr. 2). All three show Beyer Speed Figures of 92. The speed figures are entirely misleading.

If handicappers would indeed ask, ''How was the figure earned?'' as Beyer urges in his text, one of the fillies becomes a stickout. To users of pace figures, the comparisons look like this:

	Pace Figures	Final Figures
Swazi's Moment	110	105
Fit To Lead	116	105
Passing Vice	106	105

The final figures correspond to the Beyer Speed Figures. But Fit To Lead stalked a terrifically fast pace for six furlongs (22 ⅗, 45 ⅖, 1:09 ⅖), grabbed the lead into the stretch, and held. Swazi's Moment and Passing Vice lagged comfortably behind the rapid fractions, and closed strongly. In a final time equating to par, neither closer got up.

If the probable pace of the Hollywood Oaks will permit Fit To Lead to lower her pace figure, her final figure should improve, perhaps by as many as five lengths. In any pace scenario, the closers cannot be expected to overtake Fit To Lead, and they might finish far back.

The odds at post time were:

| Likeable Style | 3–5 | Swazi's Moment | 7–1 |
| Fit To Lead | 8–1 | Passing Vice | 6–1 |

In this Grade 1 event, Fit To Lead stood apart on a pace analysis informed by pace figures and represented a wonderful overlay on which I enthusiastically not only invested a key bet to win but also coupled the filly in exacta boxes with three other nonfavorites.

As the result chart shows, Fit To Lead easily outran Likeable Style, Swazi's Moment, and Passing Vice this day, but she finished second nonetheless, six and a half lengths in front of the third horse.

EIGHTH RACE	1½ MILES. (1.46⁴) 48th Running of THE HOLLYWOOD OAKS. Grade L Purse $200,000 Added. Fillies

Hollywood
JULY 11, 1993

1½ MILES. (1.46⁴) 48th Running of THE HOLLYWOOD OAKS. Grade L Purse $200,000 Added. Fillies 3-year-olds. By subscription of $200 each which shall accompany the nomination, $2,000 additional to start, with $200,000 added, of which $40,000 to second, $30,000 to third, $15,000 to fourth and $5,000 to fifth. Weight, 121 lbs. Starters to be named through the entry box by closing time of entries. Hollywood Park reserves the right not to divide this race. Should this race not be divided and the number of entries exceed the starting gate capacity, preference will be given to those horses with the highest total earnings in 1993 and an also eligible list will be drawn. Failure to draw into this race at scratch time cancels all fees. A trophy will be presented to the winning Owner, Trainer and Jockey. Closed Wednesday, June 30 with 12 nominations.

Value of Race: $220,400 Winner $130,400; second $40,000; third $30,000; fourth $15,000; fifth $5,000. Mutuel Pool $347,249.00 Exacta Pool $308,725.00 Trifecta Pool $228,186.00

Last Raced	Horse	M/Eqt. A.Wt	PP	St	¼	½	¾	Str	Fin	Jockey	Odds $1
19Jun93 9Crc3	Hollywood Wildcat	LB	3 121	4	4	.2¹	2¹	.2²	1hd	11½	Delahoussaye E	16.60
19Jun93 8Hol1	Fit To Lead	LB	3 121	3	1·	1¹	1¹	1½	25	26½	McCarron C J	8.30
5Jun93 8Hol2	Adorydar	B	3 121	9	2	5½	4¹	3½	31½	3no	Almeida G F	5.80
19Jun93 8Hol3	Passing Vice	LB	3 121	8	5	9	7¹½	5¹	4hd	4½	Desormeaux K J	6.90
5Jun93 8Hol1	Likeable Style	LB	3 121	2	7	6²½	5hd	73	5hd	5²½	Stevens G L	0.70
20Jun93 9CD2	Added Asset		3 121	6	3	3²½	3²	4¹½	6²	6¹½	Valenzuela P A	28.40
19Jun93 8Hol2	Swazi's Moment	B	3 121	1	8	4hd	6¹	6hd	75	75½	Nakatani C S	7.50
5Jun93 8Hol4	Nortena	LBb	3 121	7	6	7¹½	9	9	83½	8¹³	Flores D R	66.40
1Jly93 1Hol3	Fondly Remembered	LBb	3 121	5	9	8¹	8hd	8hd	9	9	Pincay L Jr	63.60

OFF AT 5:22 Start Good. Won driving. Time, :22⁴, :46², 1:10³, 1:35³, 1:48² Track fast.

$2 Mutuel Prices:	4–HOLLYWOOD WILDCAT	35.20	12.40	6.40
	3–FIT TO LEAD		8.60	4.80
	9–ADORYDAR			4.40

$2 EXACTA 4–3 PAID $305.20 $2 TRIFECTA 4–3–9 PAID $2,171.00

Dk. b. or br. f, (Feb), by Kris S–Miss Wildcatter, by Mr Prospector. Trainer Drysdale Neil. Bred by Cowan Irving & Marjorie (Fla).

HOLLYWOOD WILDCAT, away in good fashion, sat just off FIT TO LEAD through the early stages while that opponent established the pace, engaged for the lead approaching the quarter pole, was not asked in earnest until inside the final furlong and drew clear in the last sixteenth under right handed pressure. FIT TO LEAD went to the front at once, established the pace through the early stages while going easily, resisted stubbornly after being taken on by HOLLYWOOD WILDCAT approaching the quarter pole to battle for command with that rival to the sixteenth marker, could not match that rival's response in the final sixteenth but was well in front of the others at the end. ADORYDAR, in contention early, got closer nearing the three-eighths pole, did not have the needed punch in the drive but eked out the show. PASSING VICE, made a steady move down the backstretch while wide, entered the stretch five wide and lacked the necessary response in the drive. LIKEABLE STYLE, patiently handled while being outrun early but not far back, failed to accelerate on the far turn when put to a drive and did not threaten in the stretch. ADDED ASSET, close up early, faltered. SWAZI'S MOMENT, also outrun early but not far back, did not have the needed response in the final quarter. NORTENA was four wide into the stretch. FONDLY REMEMBERED had no apparent mishap.

Although it relates not at all to speed and pace figures, the postscript of the Hollywood Oaks cannot go unremarked. The winner Hollywood Wildcat had shipped to Neil Drysdale's barn from Florida less than two weeks past. Her speed and pace figures were not competitive and she had not worked out since June 19, twenty-two days ago. Drysdale can be a formidable horseman, notably with Grade 1 objectives on the line. I never fail to evaluate Drysdale horses closely in Grade 1 stakes.

Hollywood Wildcat past performance chart

In the week preceding the Hollywood Oaks, however, Drysdale had been quoted as pointing his new filly toward Del Mar's grass stakes. Following Hollywood Wildcat's upset, Drysdale commented dryly, "I hadn't intended to enter the filly, but her sharp six-furlong workout last week changed my mind."

What "sharp" six-furlong workout?

The workout Drysdale referred to never appeared in the *Daily Racing Form,* as Hollywood Wildcat's past performances reveal. Private clockers missed it too. If the workout had been published, I would have covered Hollywood Wildcat in exactas with Fit To Lead, as undoubtedly would have other handicappers. The odds on the winner would not have been 16–1, but they would have been generous, and so would have the exacta. As it were, with Fit To Lead on the underside, the $2 Oaks exacta returned $305.20.

The incident has left a sour taste in my mouth. At the moment I grew terribly angry. An unfamiliar filly preparing for a Grade 1 stakes out of a Grade 1 stable at a flagship track trains impressively, and the workout is missed by all concerned.

In the aftermath southern California steward Pete Pedersen apologized in the *Los Angeles Times* to the betting public, advising handicappers that the industry's information systems are "not perfect." Thank you very much.

But I digress. In summarizing his stand on the state of the art of pace handicapping in *Beyer on Speed,* the nation's best-known speed handicapper acknowledged his capitulation to the principles underpinning pace figures, but withheld support of their practical applications.

"I'm just never satisfied with the way (pace figures) work in practice."

Too bad.

It's precisely the practical merits of pace figures to which so many handicappers, including me, have grown inexorably attached. In those applications contemporary figure handicappers will find the razor's edge, as the 1993 Hollywood Oaks and a multitude of other races clearly show.

One of the most impressive and indefatigable home-run swingers the pari-mutuel wagering game has ever produced, Beyer has lost the fat advantage he once attributed to his much-prized speed figures. Those days are gone. Beyer might have advanced instead with his customary confident vigor into a bright new era of figure handicapping, armed now with pace figures in combination with speed figures.

It works!

ROUTE-TO-SPRINT SPECIALS

Here is a gift to the growing number of handicappers who employ pace figures in combination with speed figures, and can relate the arithmetic to basic class distinctions. The situation involves good horses, either a stakes, classified allowance event, or maybe high-priced claiming races. It's a sprint, preferably a longer sprint.

The trick is to spot a classy horse having tactical speed and exiting a route where it earned a superior pace figure. The illustration below involves two of the types and qualifies as a particularly outstanding example.

It was the Hidden Light at Hollywood Park, $75,000-added, for fillies and mares, 3up, at six and one-half furlongs. Only five horses were entered. Two were uninteresting long shots. The records of the other three are presented. The numerical markings are Quirin-style speed and pace figures. The letter *S* refers to the speed figure that has been obtained by converting the pace figure in a route to a projected sprint figure. The conversion is elementary. Subtract three points from the pace figure of the route.

Study the past performances carefully. It's July 4. Par is 109.

92

Angi Go Own: Hartley Kenneth D
STEVENS G L (170 33 28 29 .19)
Ch. m. 5
Sire: Idaho's Majesty (His Majesty)
Dam: Angi Mo (Witmore)
Br: Hartley Kenneth D (Idaho)
Tr: Hofmans David (35 8 4 1 .23)
L 121
Lifetime Record: 29 15 8 3 $365,272
1995 4 1 2 0 $97,200 Turf 2 0 0 1
1994 10 3 3 2 $158,905 Wet 2 2 0 0
Hol 3 1 1 0 $82,200 Dist 3 2 0 0

28May95-9Hol fst 1 1/16 :22³ :45² 1:09⁴ 1:42² 3↑ Ⓕ Hawthorne H-G2 79 7 4 44½ 42 66 410¾ Stevens G L LB 117 b 5.80 78-13 Paseana122² Pirate's Revenge117¾ Top Rung117⁰ 4 wid
7May95-9Hol fst 7f :22 :44¹ 1:08² 1:21² 3↑ Ⓕ A Gleam H-G2 100 6 2 3¹ 32½ 21 11¾ Stevens G L LB 117 b 4.20 95-11 Angi Go1171¾ Desert Stormer118¹ Dancing Mirage115⁴ Clos
25Mar95-8SA fst 1 1/16 :23 :47² 1:11⁴ 1:42¹ Ⓕ Ⓡ SantaLucia H80k 98 6 2 2½ 2hd 1hd 2½ Valenzuela F H LB 118 b 8.20 83-20 Top Rung116½ Angi Go1183½ Borodislew119² Led, o
26Feb95-3SA fst 1 :22⁴ :46¹ 1:10 1:35⁴ Ⓕ Alw 60000N$mY 90 1 3 31½ 41½ 21½ 2⁴ Antley C W LB 121 b 3.20 86-16 Borodislew114⁴ Angi Go121⁵ Fit To Lead114½ R
30Sep94-12Fpx fst 1 1/16 :22² :45⁴ 1:11¹ 1:43 3↑ Ⓕ LsMadrinas H96k 94 3 3 34½ 31 2hd 1½ Valenzuela F H LB 116 b 8.70 95-07 Angi Go116½ Kelkyko114¾ Magical Maiden1221½
3Sep94-6Dmr fst 6½f :21⁴ :44 1:08² 1:14⁴ 3↑ Ⓕ Ⓡ JuneDarlingH66k 88 6 1 2½ 3³ 45½ 55¾ Stevens G L LB 116 b 6.20 91-06 Starolamo1162¾ Nijivision114nk Eliza120½
27Aug94-8Dmr fm 1 1/16 Ⓣ :25 :50 1:13⁴ 1:43² 3↑ Ⓕ Ⓡ Osunitas H80k 87 6 1 1¹ 1½ 2hd 44½ Black C A LB 116 b 3.40 84-11 Gold Splash121¾ Queens Court Queen118¹ Re Toss1192¾
8Aug94-8Dmr fst 1 :22⁴ :46 1:10 1:34³ 3↑ Ⓕ Bayakoa H66k 101 1 1 1hd 1hd 4¾ 31¼ Stevens G L LB 116 b 5.50 96-07 Exchange122¾ Glass Ceiling116½ Angi Go116¹
25Jun94-7Hol fm 1 1/16 Ⓣ :23⁴ :47³ 1:11 1:40³ + Ⓕ Alw 55000N$mY 94 1 3 3² 3² 3¹ 41½ Stevens G L LB 121 b 3.70 92-07 Ⓓ Miss Turkana115hd Queens Court Queen1141¼ Frenchman's Co
In very tight, took up sharply 7/8 Placed third through disqualification.
7May94-3Hol fst 1 1/16 :23¹ :46³ 1:11 1:41 Ⓕ Ⓡ Typecast61k 98 5 2 2¹ 2¹ 2¹ 21¾ Valenzuela P A LB 118 b *1.40 94-09 Potridee1141¾ Angi Go1181¾ Changed Tune114⁵
WORKOUTS: Jun 26 Hol 5f fst 1:01⁴ H 24/48 May 22 Hol 6f fst 1:12⁴ H 5/18 May 1 Hol 6f fst 1:13³ H 7/21 Apr 27 Hol 5f fst 1:03 H 42/51 Apr 21 Hol 6f fst 1:15³ H 13/14 Apr 11 SA 4f fst :50¹ H 18/27

Shapely Scrapper Own: Gann Edmund A
ANTLEY C W (190 24 29 18 .13)
Dk. b or br f. 4
Sire: Fit to Fight (Chieftain)
Dam: Awesome Promise (What Luck)
Br: Boone Hilary J Jr (Ky)
Tr: Frankel Robert (79 18 3 14 .23)
L 114
Lifetime Record: 15 4 5 1 $241,341
1995 2 0 0 1 $13,500 Turf 1 0 0 0
1994 8 2 2 0 $70,081 Wet 1 1 0 0
Hol 3 2 1 0 $53,300 Dist 1 0 0 0

23Apr95-3SA fst 6f :21² :44¹ :56⁴ 1:09¹ 3↑ Ⓕ Ⓡ TimeTo Leave60k 85 2 5 1hd 1hd 1hd 45¼ Nakatani C S LB 115 2.90 86-13 Nijivision115½ Eureka Lass1162½ Miss Bushett1152½ In
7Apr95-8SA fst 6f :21³ :44² :56³ 1:09² Ⓕ Ⓡ Very Subtle60k 88 4 2 2hd 2hd 1hd 32¼ Flores D R LB 115 3.40 87-12 BallerinaGal1161¼ Nijivision1151¼ ShpelyScrpper115hd Dueled, out
28Dec94-8SA fst 7f :22¹ :44³ 1:09 1:21⁴ Ⓕ La Brea-G2 82 4 4 3¹ 2¹ 2¹ 55¾ Antley C W LB 117 27.80 87-10 Top Rung115¾ Klassy Kim119¹ Twice The Vice119² W
26Nov94-7Hol fst 7f :22² :45³ 1:10¹ 1:23² 3↑ Ⓕ Alw 41000N3X 90 5 2 1hd 1½ 1⁶ 13½ Antley C W LB 114 3.30 87-15 Shapely Scrapper1143½ Kelkyko1182¼ Eureka Lass116¹ Kep
19Oct94-3SA fst 7f :22² :45¹ 1:09⁴ 1:22³ 3↑ Ⓕ Alw 49000N3X 81 4 3 2hd 2hd 1² 2¾ Nakatani C S LB 113 4.90 88-15 MalibuLight118¾ ShpelyScrpper113¹ PhoenicinMiss116⁴ Overt
25Aug94-8Dmr fst 6½f :21⁴ :44¹ 1:08³ 1:15 Ⓕ CERF60k 66 3 4 4¹ 43½ 4⁶ 411½ Delahoussaye E LB 116 5.60 84-13 Phone Chatter117¹ Airistar120½ Klassy Kim115¹⁰ (
16Jly94-7Bel fm 1 Ⓣ :22³ :45¹ 1:08⁴ 1:33¹ 3↑ Ⓕ Alw 34000N3X 59 5 3 3² 41½ 64½ 619¾ Velazquez J R 111 11.40 76-06 Dayflower1195½ Silky Feather117nk Light And Love114½
18Jun94-7Bel fst 6f :22¹ :45² :57 1:09 Ⓕ Prioress-G2 69 3 2 43½ 51½ 5⁵ 512¼ Bailey J D 121 4.70 84-10 Penny'sReshoot1162¼ HeavenlyPrize121⁶ BeckysShirt1141½ Save
29May94-7Hol fst 6f :21³ :44⁴ :56⁴ 1:09³ 3↑ Ⓕ Alw 41000N2X 87 7 2 4³ 3¹ 2hd 2hd Gonzalez S Jr LB 109 2.50 92-09 Ⓓ SilentLord116hd ShpelyScrpper109no Ms.Somthing1162¾ 5 wide
Placed first through disqualification.
15May94-7Hol fst 7f :21⁴ :44¹ 1:08² 1:21¹ 3↑ Ⓕ Alw 41000N2X 88 1 4 11½ 11½ 1½ 23½ Valenzuela F H LB 113 *1.60 94-10 PrivatePersuasion1143½ ShpelyScrpper113² Freezelin119¾ No m
WORKOUTS: Jun 29 Hol 3f fst :35⁴ H 2/23 ● Jun 22 Hol 5f fst :58³ B 1/28 ● Jun 16 Hol 6f fst 1:13 H 1/4 Jun 8 Hol 6f fst 1:01¹ H 18/48 Jun 1 Hol 5f fst :59⁴ H 4/41 May 22 Hol 6f fst 1:12² H 3/18

Borodislew is a Grade 3 stakes winner at seven furlongs at Longchamps, near Paris. She was a 3YO beating older horses that day.

The mare has won twice in the states, the most recent a stylish win in a classified mile at Santa Anita.

Five weeks ago Borodislew set a rapid pace, a sprinter's pace actually, in the Grade 2 Hawthorne Stakes won by champion Paseana. The six-furlong pace figure of the race was 116. The projected sprint figure is 113, which is four lengths faster-than-par for today. Borodislew set the sizzling pace in the Hawthorne. She earned that super pace figure.

On February 26, at Santa Anita, in the classified event won by Borodislew at a mile, the pace was again swift. I dug for the pace figure. For the race it was a 115. Using a one-to-one beaten-lengths adjustment, which Quirin recommends, Borodislew's pace figure is 113. The projected speed figure is 110, one length faster-than-par for today's long sprint.

Not unimportantly, on February 26, Borodislew's speed figure was 110, superior to par by two lengths for the classified mile. The mare had delivered a faster-than-par pace figure in combination with a faster-than-par speed figure against good horses going long. I like that.

With a pair of pace figures at the route converting to irresistible speed figures at a sprint and a pace-setting style last out, I quickly knew it would take quite an argument to pull me away from Borodislew in the Hidden Light. I realized as well the odds might be seductive, the mare's advantage nicely hidden, which makes the route-to-sprint figure play one of my favorites.

Angi Go exited the Hawthorne, too, beaten two lengths at the pace call of the Grade 2 stakes. Her projected speed figure today was an impressive 111, two lengths faster-than-par. In addition, Angi Go had become a Grade 2 winner May 7 at seven furlongs, recording her highest Beyer ever. She was two-for-three at today's sprint distance. She was simply a marvel of consistency.

What I did not like was Angi Go's lackluster finish in the Hawthorne. Borodislew's excuse for the tail-off was the rapid pace she blazed. Angi Go had relaxed behind that pace. She had moved at the six-furlong call, gaining ground, but quickly faded.

Borodislew had worked out repeatedly in the five weeks since the Hawthorne, Angi Go just once. I assigned a form edge to Borodislew.

I knew, too, Angi Go would be overbet in the long sprint, which she definitely was.

Shapely Scrapper had achieved no stature for today's test. The filly remained a non–stakes winner whose easy win on November 26 had been rated two lengths slower-than-par. She was capable of high-speed figures, but her speed-pace combinations were persistently fast-early slow-late. Shapely Scrapper preferred an average-to-slow come-home fraction, which she would not encounter here. I eliminated Shapely Scrapper with haste.

The bettors did not. Overbetting trainer Bobby Frankel, they sent Shapely Scrapper to her predictable demise at 9–5, a severely overrated second choice.

The odds before post provided the final persuasive detail:

Borodislew 5–1

Angi Go 4–5

Shapely Scrapper 9–5

With enthusiasm I took Borodislew to win and an exacta coupling Borodislew atop Angi Go. The result chart is a convincing testament to the power of superb pace figures in routes, when good horses having tactical speed switch to sprints.

THIRD RACE

Hollywood
JULY 4, 1995

6½ FURLONGS. (1.13¹) 1st Running of THE TERLINGUA. Purse $75,000 Added. Fillies and mares, 4-year-olds and upward. Weight, 121 lbs. ($100 to start.) Non-winners of $35,000 other than closed, claiming or starter in 1995, allowed 3 lbs. Non-winners of $25,000 other than closed, claiming or starter since December 1, 5 lbs. Non-winners of $25,000 other than closed, claiming or starter since August 1, 7 lbs.

Value of Race: $75,500 Winner $41,750; second $15,000; third $11,250; fourth $5,625; fifth $1,875. Mutuel Pool $336,949.40 Exacta Pool $292,068.00 Quinella Pool $42,098.00 Minus Show Pool $1,414.97

Last Raced	Horse	M/Eqt. A.Wt	PP	St	¼	½	Str	Fin	Jockey	Odds $1
28May95 ·9Hol6	Borodislew	LB 5 118	1	4	3hd	42	1¹	1¹½	McCarron C J	5.00
28May95 9Hol4	Angi Go	LBb 5 121	3	2	1hd	1¹	2²	2³½	Stevens G L	0.70
13May95 3Hol3	Airistar	LBb 4 118	5	1	2½	2½	3½	3¹	Solis A	7.70
15Jun95 8Hol5	That'll Be Fine	LBf 4 115	2	5	5	5	5	4½	Nakatani C S	14.10
23Apr95 3SA4	Shapely Scrapper	LB 4 114	4	3	4¹½	3½	4½	5	Antley C W	2.60

OFF AT 2:19 Start Good. Won driving. Time, :21⁴, :44, 1:08, 1:14² Track fast.

$2 Mutuel Prices:	1–BORODISLEW	12.00	3.40	2.10
	3–ANGI GO		2.40	2.10
	5–AIRISTAR			2.10

$2 EXACTA 1–3 PAID $24.00 $2 QUINELLA 1–3 PAID $8.40

B. m, by Seattle Slew–Breath Taking, by Nureyev. Trainer Inda Eduardo. Bred by Janus Bloodstock Inc (Ky).

BORODISLEW saved ground just behind the early pace, came through inside ANGI GO leaving the turn to gain the lead into the stretch and proved best under strong handling. ANGI GO sped to the early lead inside AIRISTAR, held a short lead off the rail until nearing the stretch, could not match the winner while drifting out in the drive but was best of the rest. AIRISTAR forced the pace outside ANGI GO for a half mile, came between rivals into the stretch and weakened. THAT'LL BE FINE had a rail trip. SHAPELY SCRAPPER outside the winner on the backstretch, raced four wide on the turn and into the stretch and weakened.

Owners— 1, 505 Farms; 2, Hartley Kenneth D; 3, Gallup Frank E; 4, Buss Jerry; 5, Gann Edmund A

Trainers— 1, Inda Eduardo; 2, Hofmans David; 3, Cenicola Lewis A; 4, Buss Jim; 5, Frankel Robert

Overweight: That'll Be Fine (1).

Postscript. The route-to-sprint special pops up at major tracks perhaps a dozen times a season. With full-card simulcasting from multiple tracks, the opportunity has been multiplied by four or five. In most situations the odds will be as generous or higher than they were on Borodislew in a five-horse field. That makes it special.

TRIP HANDICAPPING

M y complaint about trip handicapping can be summarized succinctly. It's not fundamental. The method does not deal directly
with the basic abilities of horses. The implication of that position is
equally stark. Trip handicappers best be careful how they apply their
handiwork. Trip handicappers can suffer the fatal mistake of confusing
the incidental and the fundamental. Many do.

Figure handicappers who depend upon trips to interpret speed figures probably commit the grossest errors. Aware the horses have experienced troubled trips, they inflate inferior figures. Convinced
impressive winners have benefited from perfect trips, they discount
superior figures.

The logical extension of the pattern finds figure analysts supposing
that lower-figure contenders will defeat higher-figure contenders. More
often than not, the high-figure horses will win regardless. Troubled
trips do not alter the equation sufficiently. The fastest horses predom-
inate.

When Andrew Beyer played full-time at Del Mar in 1993, a number
of his bets, too many in my judgment, were predicated upon trip playbacks. A couple of other horses in the race may have looked better on
cold dope, but the troubled trips carried the cause. Figure handicappers
routinely evaluate trips in relation to speed figures. The danger involves awarding the trips a priority against the figures. The odds may
be higher, but the win percentage will be lower. It's a risky trade-off.

I refer to Beyer deliberately. Not only does Andy personify the figure analyst who relies upon the influences of trips to interpret speed
figures, but he's also sustained a considerable success at the game for
a long, long run. Early in 1993, at Gulfstream Park, Beyer touted me
onto a long shot in the final race on Florida Derby day.

"Competitive fig, bad trip last out, has the inside" was Beyer's terse
synopsis of the situation. When I saw the horse on the tote at 35–1,
naturally I bet. The long shot promptly won by four and paid $77.

As I recall, the long shot's speed figure (77) was third best in the field. The favorite showed an 82, another horse a 79. Without a doubt the troubled, hidden trip had played a prominent role in Beyer's thinking, in the outcome, and notably in the payoff. Just an excellent play, well executed. I do not envy the trip handicappers who attempt to mimic the upset day in and day out.

First, not many figure analysts or trip handicappers would have been shrewd enough to execute that play at Gulfstream Park. The danger increases when the speed figures are somewhat lower, the odds significantly lower, and the trips not as well camouflaged, which will typically be the case. Now the trip horses will not win as frequently, and when they do, they will not pay nearly as well.

When speed handicappers rely upon trips to interpret speed figures, too often in my experience they end by betting on trip playbacks that are not talented enough to win. The reason is that trip handicapping does not assess the comparative abilities of horses well enough. The method can be subverted; the extrapolation from bad trips to the winner's circle becomes a weak connection. Intended to clarify speed figures, and purportedly to strengthen them, overreliance on trip data produces an opposite effect. Misapprehended trips muddle the situation, and they can weaken the figure analysis.

A tenable correction postpones trip handicapping until a more fundamental analysis has been conducted. Handicappers will have closely evaluated the horses on speed (unadjusted for trips), class, pace, and form. The main contention has been isolated. Interesting overlays have been spotted. Now trips can be superimposed, either strengthening the basic analysis or weakening it.

In this scenario not only is trip handicapping secondary, it's also analytical, not mathematical. Numerous figure handicappers adjust speed figures by adding and subtracting points, based upon wide trips and troubled trips. Trip data are essentially qualitative, however, and extremely difficult to quantify with accuracy. Highly practiced speed and trip specialists might be capable of performing these tricks, but ordinary handicappers cannot. Handicappers are urged to treat trip data analytically, not mathematically.

An alternative to manipulating trip data as an aspect of speed handicapping views trips as an adjunct to form analysis. Trip data can be seen as a vindication of dubious form. If the last running line appears dubious, inexplicable, or contradictory, the explanation may reside in a troubled trip. Other running lines warrant the same inspection for problem trips. Handicappers can excuse the race, or discount it. The tactic will be especially appropriate when evaluating 3YOs, who typically experience a number of excusable trips as they mature, maneuver through eligibility conditions, and generally obtain the competitive seasoning they lack. Do not confuse the bad trips with bad form.

In a recent stakes at Hollywood Park, two splendid fillies went co-favored in the Grade 1 Hollywood Oaks at nine furlongs. The situation crystallizes several problems inherent in trip handicapping:

Both fillies were exiting troubled lines. Sleep Easy had stumbled at the start, before disappointing at 8–5. Bello Cielo had overcome serious mishaps to win. Bello Cielo's trouble proved so severe at two key points in the June 4th allowance race, she would be knocked down to 4–5 as the betting in the Oaks began.

Examine the Beyer Speed Figures. Sleep Easy had run faster than Bello Cielo ever had twice. She qualified as a "double-fig." Apparently the Hollywood bettors felt the bad trip Bello Cielo had been forced to overcome was so problematic, she might have finished faster by lengths in a trouble-free run. Perhaps, but at the paltry price, why bet on it? Trip handicappers fall into that booby trap incessantly.

My personal analysis of the 1995 Hollywood Oaks took a different direction and is worth pursuing, considering what actually happened. Excepting Bello Cielo, the fillies in the Oaks had shown early speed, but each of their pace figures had been suspect, below par. When 3YOs will be pressed to run faster than normal on a contested pace, prior speed figures will regularly drop.

Unclear to me was Sleep Easy's running style at the route. Would the Frankel filly take the lead, press the lead, or relax behind the lead? In her single route try, Sleep Easy had stumbled out of the gate. From the number-one hole in the Oaks, I imagined Sleep Easy would set or force the early pace.

By that analysis Bello Cielo would lag behind an uncomfortably fast pace. If the front of the field tired, the closer would rally to win.

The gates opened.

Bello Cielo took back off the early pace, but so did Sleep Easy. Already my analysis was worthless.

Around the clubhouse turn, Bello Cielo went inexplicably wide, and turning into the backstretch, she rushed to the front and pressed the front-runners while four wide. I was relieved the odds had prevented the bet.

As the fillies scampered down the backstretch, three of them were forcing the pace, and Sleep Easy ran relaxed in a solo position approximately four lengths in arrears.

Bello Cielo faded early. Sleep Easy rallied from behind and went on to win in a drive.

Sleep Easy experienced a perfect trip. Bello Cielo experienced a horrible trip. When the two fillies return to action, the speed figures and trip data will look like this:

Beyer Speed/Top Four					Trip Data/Last Two
Sleep Easy	90	88	94	95	Perfect trip last
					Stumbled 2nd back
Bello Cielo	83	90	84	82	Horrid trip last
					Overcame severely troubled
					trip in second back to win

If Sleep Easy goes at 4–5 and Bello Cielo is 5–2, what should handicappers do?

Too many speed handicappers and trip handicappers would support Bello Cielo at 5–2, citing the speed figure of the second line back and the pair of awful trips. Those handicappers have a splendid chance of tearing up their tickets. Even if they win, the mutuel will not compensate them adequately.

Sleep Easy is simply faster and shapes up as a probable winner based on the fundamentals. The bad trips may redeem Bello Cielo eventually, but the filly is not a play against Sleep Easy now unless the odds drift up to about 8–1 or thereabouts. It's a crucial comparison for trip fanciers to comprehend.

Another complaint about trip handicappers regards the common situations that regularly qualify as troubled or bad. The routinized comments that horses have been bumped at the start or have raced wide or have steadied or checked or have lugged in or out are frequently not as problematic as handicappers are led to imagine. The mishaps happen all the time.

Only a few trips are routinely ruinous. If route horses have been swept wide on the clubhouse turn while being used, that's a severe problem, particularly for front-runners, pressers, and stalkers. Now the wide trip has been accompanied by a premature loss of energy. The energy loss, not the ground lost, represents the crux of a wide trip. If horses have lost obvious and unreasonable degrees of energy early in the race, that's a difficult trip to overcome. Few of them will finish well.

Yet off-pace horses will be routinely wide, not necessarily because the trip has been troubled, but due to running style. If closers have swung wide while under the jockey's control, not squandering inordinate amounts of energy, the exertion is minimal and the disadvantage is probably minor. Assuming the wide horses might have run faster, thereby improving their speed figures, may prove more harmful than helpful.

A bad trip curiously underestimated by many has occurred anytime horses have been used prematurely, including the several situations at the route where horses can be seen running rank on or near the lead. The outstanding example that cannot be averted occurs when horses break tardily and are subsequently rushed to the front. Sprint or route, few of them endure.

Handicappers can alert themselves to rank or restrained horses by watching the jockey's grip against the horse's stride. The hold will be tight, and the stride will be strong, maybe rapid. Neither horse nor rider will appear relaxed. If handicappers notice the hard hold, they should record the trip. The situation is virtually ruinous on grass and at the route.

Similarly, if off-pace horses have been forced to take up in the late stages after their rally has begun, breaking momentum, that's obviously a troubled trip that will be difficult to overcome. But it also focuses trip handicappers on what matters most when horses have been steadied, checked, blocked, or taken up. The horses should regain stride quickly and begin to gain ground anew. If they do not, the incidents are best dismissed. The trouble cannot be interpreted in any meaningful way. The troubled horses may improve next out, but just as likely they may not. Trip handicappers bungle these situations by overestimating the consequences of the trouble.

Another caution trip handicappers too often disregard involves the odds. Troubled trips that have been noticeable are notoriously overbet. Bello Cielo takes her place in a staggeringly long line of trip playbacks that have been bet too much for the wrong reasons and have disappointed as well. For some reason handicappers like to back horses returning from problem starts, as if the inside information demands action. Why bother?

Finally, I deplore the trip notation. The descriptive phrases that appear in the *Daily Racing Form* never satisfy, and many of them will be more misleading than helpful. Trip notes circulated in newsletters and by other information services will be more descriptive perhaps, and more beneficial, but all of it leaves much to be desired. The descriptions will typically be limited to a small segment of the race, and worse, no indication is provided as to how handicappers should interpret the mishaps.

What does the trouble mean? That is the operative question, and it usually goes unanswered. Without the interpretations, the scantily clad descriptions of trouble lack context, coherence, and therefore meaning.

An alternative to present procedure would describe key horses' trips in their entirety, certainly for winners and close runners-up, using notation at each stage of the race. The notation would begin at the gate, include the clubhouse turn, when relevant, continue down the backstretch, around the far turn, entering the stretch, and in the stretch. The notation might look like this:

Slo-2, 5ft, 4B, 4T, 3E, out-NF

Or like this:

Pop, Rail-BTE, WL-MS

The first horse is a router that broke slowly by two lengths, ran five-wide around the clubhouse turn, four-wide down the backstretch and on the far turn, three-wide entering the stretch, and lugged out near the finish. Now, that's a wide trip!

The second horse is a sprinter that popped the gate and ran on the rail into the stretch. In midstretch the horse was running on the wrong lead.

Numerous trip handicappers buy videotapes of the races at stiff rates and watch them repeatedly. I do not recommend this practice to casual handicappers. Casual handicappers can watch video race replays, maybe more than once, but it's not the same. It's convenient to realize later that the horse going wide was in the six-path, instead of the three-path. If a horse appeared wide entering the stretch, it's nice to recall whether the horse also ran wide down the backstretch and around the far turn.

On and on, the myriad of circumstances that trip handicapping entails, but that nonexpert trip handicappers regularly miss. Trip notation should save the day.

A practical alternative to trip notation that encompasses the race in its entirety, preferably for several finishers in a field, might be a reliance on a few interpretive symbols. Trip analysts at the *Daily Racing Form* and at sister publications would interpret the trouble, mishaps, and situations they observe, and determine whether the races should be excused. They might also report whether trips have been error-free.

Three symbols would cover a multitude of possibilities:

X Legitimate excuse (the horse should be expected to improve in its next effort)

Xl Had an excuse, and probably would have won otherwise

P Perfect trip

Handicappers would benefit more by the appearance of an X than by insubstantial phrases such as "raced wide," "bumped at the start," "steadied on the turn," "lugged in," "blocked at the 1/4 pole," and so many other comments that cannot be interpreted reliably. No X, no P, reflects an insignificant trip.

Perhaps most important of all, trip handicappers should keep in mind what outrageous experience has taught them ad nauseam. The racing game is characterized by a tremendous error factor. Horses encounter trouble, jockeys make mistakes, and accidents happen. Virtually every race, every day. Trip data can be seriously overstated and overrated. Because trips repeat themselves constantly and reflect only the circumstances of races, unaware handicappers can be easily and repeatedly misled.

Troubled trips deserve the handicapper's attention, demand the handicapper's attention. A cautious interpretation is highly recommended, at least much of the time. If other contenders in the race look superior on the hard evidence, they probably are. Bad trips, even when translated to improved performances, are not automatically converted to winning trips. Best playbacks arise when problem trips can be linked to the fastest horses.

Before getting trapped in trips, handicappers benefit by examining horses' speed and relative class and by completing a pace analysis. If a few horses shape up as particularly strong at that juncture, trip playbacks should look equal to the task at fair-to-generous odds to warrant a bet.

THE CADDY

Watching John Daly line up a crucial putt in the final round of the 1995 British Open, I experienced a flash of insight, one of those thunderbolts that come zigzagging out of the sky, as to how handicappers might double or triple their annual profits. Daly's caddy was kneeling alongside, his head looking over Daly's shoulder, the caddy helping the golfer to line up the putt.

Eureka! It came to me.

Good handicappers need good caddies.

Someone to help them line up the bets. After all, it is the dawn of full-card simulcasting. Not a day goes by that handicappers do not confront an array of bets as elliptical and curvaceous as golf shots. If the leading golfers in the world want the assistance, so should handicappers. After handicappers have completed the race analysis, and after setting an odds line, the helpers come into play.

The handicapper explains the intended action, and the caddy reacts.

Maybe the handicapper has overlooked a juicy overlay. Perhaps the third-rated contender at an attractive price represents the best bet. Maybe the trifecta makes sense, but the handicapper hasn't noticed the possibilities.

Maybe the overbet favorite represents an excellent bet to place, while the second choice should be bet to win.

If the handicapper likes an underlay and an overlay in the same race, the caddy might remind the player to use the overlay on top of the underlay in the exacta and combine the two of them in quinellas.

How about the Pick 3 and the Pick 6? The racetrack caddy might help enormously in structuring those tickets.

With full-card simulcasting running rampant, handicappers typically pay attention to multiple tracks having multitudinous betting opportunities. A sharp caddy looking over the bettor's shoulder can enhance the final score.

The day at the races has changed. It's a decision-making game now. Each playable race at each track on the simulcast program contains a wild array of potential bets. Doubles, exactas, quinellas, trifectas, Pick 3s, and win-place-show combinations. Errors of omission have increased terrifically. So have basic misplays. Missing overlays. Bungling combinations. Betting too little. Risking too much.

Handicappers can use a helping hand. The professional golf caddy becomes an apt metaphor. But who will play the handicapper's helper?

The ideal assistant would be a trusted colleague. Unfortunately the colleague will be concentrating on playing the game. Helping a colleague identify and structure bets will be a distraction, if not an imposition.

At the same time, the handicapper's helper needs to possess a relatively sophisticated comprehension of handicapping and wagering. Not just anybody qualifies. How should the helpers be compensated? A percentage (10 percent) of the successful bets determined in collaboration? A flat fee for services?

I don't know.

Maybe the thunderbolt of insight remains impractical. Perhaps the helpers would create more problems than they would solve. The complications would probably be several and severe. Arguments would erupt. Colleagues would no longer be friends. Everybody knows the less lonesome it gets, the less successful it gets.

Maybe the idea of a handicapper's helper is just a bad idea. How would it work?

But I can't forget the careful collaborations where the leading golfers in the world elicit the feedback of their caddies in tournaments. I still like that idea.

How to translate the teamwork successfully to Thoroughbred racing and make it succeed for the handicapper as well as the handicapper's helper?

FALSE FAVORITES

A mong regulars at the nation's racetracks, nothing so spices the daily program as the prospect of clobbering the favorites. The inclination grows with experience. Practiced handicappers realize that success correlates with value. Although several do, favorites are seldom perceived as offering value.

The trick is to recognize which favorites might be bet, which are best ignored, and which should be bet against. Any favorite the handicapper prefers at a legitimate price might be bet. Any overbet favorite the handicapper prefers is an underlay, and must be abandoned. Frequently so must that race.

The worst mistake is betting too much too often on false favorites, which too many handicappers do persistently. Because the false favorites will have attracted the largest portion of the win-pool, added-value might be found elsewhere. Whenever that value coincides with a strong opinion, handicappers have isolated one of the best bets at the track. Win-bets can be bolstered by smart investments in the exacta, trifecta, Pick 3, and maybe other pools. The extra leverage favors the player tremendously.

Let's begin with a false favorite highly reliable in its tendency toward losing, but which too many handicappers typically fail to recognize. It's April 3. The fifth at Santa Anita was for allowance horses, nonwinners twice other than maiden or claiming. The 6–5 favorite looked like this:

Timbalier finished fourth. Handicappers might have expected that. Why?

Whenever a horse wins a race and stays away from the races for two months, that constitutes a negative pattern. The presumption that something adverse has prevented the horse from racing should hold. The presumption the horse has lost at least some conditioning should hold.

Supporting evidence is frequently apparent, and should be regarded as pertinent. Timbalier shows just four workouts since February 4, notably a gap in his training pattern from March 7 until March 25. A low-percentage trainer adds to the probability a false favorite will disappoint, and that an alternate choice might pay better than it should. Trainer Speckert, though he's handled several prominent stakes horses, consistently wins with fewer than 10 percent of his starters.

Against Timbalier, I backed the second choice, who won at 3–1. Remember this. If horses have won impressively more than six weeks ago, and have been unraced since, the reason should be clear and convincing. If it's not, and the horse has been favored, an opposing bet makes sense.

On the same afternoon Timbalier blew, I had spotted a second false favorite. Now the opposing bet did not turn out so well. Review the race conditions and the well-known favorite I regarded as false:

7 **Santa Anita Park**

1 MILE. (Turf). (1:32³) ALLOWANCE. Purse $60,000. Fillies and mares, 4–year–olds and upward which are non–winners of $25,000 other than closed or claiming at one mile or over since December 1. Weight, 120 lbs. Non–winners of such a race since October 1, allowed 3 lbs. Of such a race since August 1, 5 lbs. Such a race since June 1, 7 lbs.

At 4–5, Possibly Perfect scooted wire-to-wire unmolested, winning in hand.

For years I have benefited by ignoring legitimate Grade 1 stakes winners when they return from layoffs under classified allowance conditions. The horses are invariably overbet, as was Possibly Perfect. They are also typically short of form and not exactly hell-bent to win.

Stables do not indulge all-out efforts to win classified races with Grade 1 and Grade 2 stakes stars. So the best horses might be expected to lose. If they meet classified types in top form and particularly well suited to today's probable pace, distance, and footing, they regularly do lose. Class bows to form, in combination with situational factors.

On this front, times have changed. An oversupply of stakes races has rendered the classified allowance event practically extinct. When graded stakes stars do return under classified conditions, the decline in the competitive quality of nonclaiming races has generally meant that many will be destined to win regardless. The others are simply no match.

In addition, due to simulcast revenues, classified allowance purses at major tracks have been generously increased. Possibly Perfect competed for a $60,000 purse, grabbing a fat $33,000 for winning. The horses may not be fully extended, or even well intended, but the barn will hardly be immune to the size of the purse. They try a bit harder.

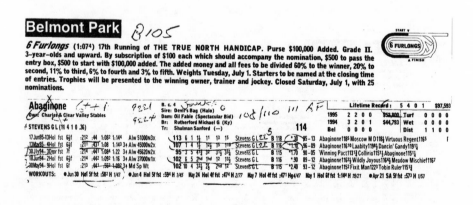

The colt above was entered in the race above. He went at 4–5 in New York, 3–5 in the simulcast to southern California. Why?

Because he showed the highest speed figures, superb pace figures, rapid turn-times, and a sizzling workout for a high-percentage stable. Abaginone finished up the course.

Anytime a developing colt exits a nonwinners' allowance race and enters a Grade 1 or Grade 2 stakes, the presumption should be the horse will probably lose. The horse must look best on speed, pace, and form to counterbalance that presumption. Other factors should be positive as well. The lower the odds, even more the requirement that all the proper credentials be in order.

Abaginone represented a risk on form. Whenever a good horse returns from a lengthy layoff and wins two in a row, that horse faces a "bounce" next time. Less than 5 percent of horses returning from long layoffs win three races in a row. If the comebackers have not bounced after the first win, they will probably disappoint after the second. I would have discounted Abaginone in a Grade 2 sprint for that reason alone.

In the 1995 True North Handicap, three other horses possessed not only high early speed but also the ability to complete the second fraction in less than twenty-three seconds. Two of those horses had won Grade 3 sprints. Challenging legitimate stakes horses, Abaginone figured to be severely pressed for four furlongs at least. If he survived that contest, Abaginone would be challenged strongly by off-pace contenders in the long Belmont stretch he had never experienced.

Abaginone might be talented enough, but why would anybody bet on it? At 3–5, betting amounts to pari-mutuel suicide.

Below Grade 2 presents a different scenario. Now, the impressively brilliant winner of an advanced nonwinners' allowance race (NW3X4X) has every right to succeed. The smaller the purse, the better. Open stakes, even Grade 3 stakes may be within their grasp, but not the Grade 1 and Grade 2 kind. If favored there, they represent false favorites. The majority of them will lose, and several will finish out of the money, à la Abaginone.

Unfortunately I could not disentangle the 1995 True North Handicap, despite spending forty minutes in the attempt. In the simulcast of the stakes to southern California, when the odds-on local shipper faded, the upset winner paid $61.40 and the trifecta rocked the tote at $16,000-plus.

In the age of exotic wagering, false favorites are sometimes not without their considerable charms.

Here's a brief laundry list of familiar phonies that pop up again and again as choices of the crowd:

1. Claiming horses dropping in class following a win
2. High-figure horses that won last out with a speed figure that sticks out, when other speed figures in the record have been invariably lower
3. Last year's champions, near-champions, and division leaders whose speed figures have declined by three lengths or more
4. Following a big win in a claiming race limited to 3YOs, any 3YO entered today in an allowance or stakes, especially during the first eight months of the year
5. Any 3YO or 4YO moving from a lower level to a graded stakes with a pace figure more than two lengths below par for today's class

A convenient way to become acquainted with these impostors is to spend two weeks hunting for them among the past performances. With the multiple tracks of full-card simulcasting on the daily menu, the shopping will be easy.

It's useful to conclude a discussion of false favorites with a caution. A sucker bet at the track finds handicappers betting against favorites they detest, but without a strong opinion otherwise. Spreading among nonfavorites in the exotic pools often makes sense, but serious bets to win do not. Lacking an opinion as to which nonfavorite should beat the favorite, pass the race.

In my formative years as a handicapper, a friend and colleague approached every card by slamming the favorites he longed to upset. He bet against the overbet favorites aggressively, usually without a convincing alternative. As far as I recall, he never enjoyed a winning season.

REMEMBER, PLEASE,
MY ADMONITIONS TO YOU

Do not form any opinions about the races until all the evidence
has been collected and considered.

Do not discuss the races among yourselves.

Don't let anybody dissuade you about your selections.

Do not let anybody push you onto horses.

Do not consult with insiders.

Do not change your mind with less than two minutes to go in
the betting.

Do not bet on horses you really do not like.

Do not bet on the underlays.

Do not forget to back the overlays you liked the night before.

Do not chase your losses.

Do not run low on money before the races you like best arrive.

Do not play the races on scared money.

Do play the overlays having a legitimate chance to win.

Do keep copious records.

Do bet more when winning and less when losing.

Do play to your strengths and avoid your weaknesses.

Do continue to play when you're winning.

Do trust your instincts and take the risks that pay.

Do play to win.

Do keep a separate, sizable bankroll for playing the races.

Do improve your knowledge and skill continuously.

Do crush the races every chance you get.

Do read the good books (including all the books by James
Quinn).

Do not bet long shots to place and show.
Do not play baseballs in the exactas and trifectas.
Do not forget to plan your wagers.
Do not play pairs of long shots in the exactas.
Do not use favorites on top of other low-priced contenders.
Do not bet a large amount on the losers and a small amount on the winners.
Do not lose your cool during losing runs.
Do not fraternize with losers.
Do not play the Pick 6 without a carryover.
Do not bet on low-percentage jockeys and low-percentage trainers in nonclaiming races.

Do play the races as often as your schedule permits.
Do not forget to respect the game.
Do not look back.

Del Mar

8

1 mile

start & finish

ONE MILE. WINDY SANDS STAKES. 1
Year Olds and Upward which are non-wi
subscription of $50 each, which shall ac
entry box, with $60,000 Added, of whic
fourth and $1,500 to fifth. Weights Mond
entry box, by the closing time of entries. "
closed Saturday, August 10 by 12:00 Noon

LETTHEBIGH...

3yo (May) gelding, gray
Trainer: Bob ...
Owner: Mich...

Poster ($35,000)

Right Jig

Wet:
Turf:
Dist:

111 Co...

8Jun91	6Bel	ft									nously	119	5.4
													5
2?May91	8Bel	ft									...	107.b	13.2
			Gr.1 Metropolitan Handicap										6
26Apr91	3Hol	ft	3	Stk71050	71	21.50	44.10	108.70	121.30	20	3 3² 3²₁	N⁴ 17½ E Delahoussay	122 Bb	1
			Harry Henson Stakes										
11Apr91	6GG	ft	3	Stk53700	81	21.90	45.30	57.50	1.10.30	87	3⁴₅ 4³ 4½ 2₄	14 C Nakatani	122 Bb	0.4
			PLEASANT SMILE										87m
28Mar91	8SA	ft	3	Stk58000	6½|	21.30	44.10	108.70	1.18.10	28	7 2₅ 2ᴺ	1½ E Delahoussay	117 Bb	1.8

HORSEMEN AND HANDICAPPERS

Handicappers who make the mistake of fraternizing with horsemen will regret it eventually, and at a serious cost. After two decades plus of playing the races, I can assert with confidence that horsemen know as much about the art of handicapping as handicappers do about training the horses.

The reality should be evident to all interested observers. Charles Whittingham liked to bet on his hot ones but, when occasionally questioned about the bottom line, never failed to scoff at the contrariness of the breed and the impossibility of beating the game. The pain of a long legacy of losers has been painstakingly obvious.

Bobby Frankel hasn't made a bet in twenty years.

Once upon a time, for a season, your correspondent had occasion to carry bets for the great Laz Barrera. At Santa Anita in 1981, Laz went one for fourteen, an 8–5 shot trained by Whittingham. The Hall of Fame trainer never once collected on his stable's horses, despite devout convictions the horses would not lose.

The culture of the racetrack devotes an enormous energy to the mystique of inside information. Nothing so characterizes a day at the races among the regulars as somebody's secondhand whispered tip that trainer so-and-so likes his horse—quite a lot. When the horse blows at 5–2, the trainer's explanation is equally facile. He (the horse) didn't like the track. The jockey botched the ride. The trip was regrettable. As revealed by postrace exams, the horse was bothered by a throat virus.

After a half-dozen seasons of self-delusion, the excuses continue, but the betting stops. Nobody mentions that playing the horses is a game dominated not by certainties but by probabilities, and that the best players will be wrong much more often than correct. Horsemen become an easy prey for the probabilities that dominate this game.

Recently I encountered my friends Lou and Ruth Eilken at Hollywood Park. The couple had traveled a long way to watch the debut of their maiden colt, trained by Ron McAnally. Lou is the former director

of racing at Canterbury Downs and former racing secretary at Santa
Anita. Not surprisingly, he's a fine handicapper who could make ends
meet at any racetrack. Ruth also likes to play and she likes to know
what the insiders think.

Shortly after our chat began, Ruth Eilken advised me that McAnally
really liked his horse in the feature. "Do you like the horse?" she asked,
seeking reinforcement. I did not.

At least twice in the conversation Ruth Eilken reiterated the trainer's fondness for his horse in the feature, saying she intended to bet a
sizable amount on it.

"How much is McAnally betting?" I asked.

Mrs. Eilken did not know.

I recommend the rejoinder to anyone at the races who comes into
contact with trainers who "really like" their horses on that day's program. Ask the horsemen how much they intend to bet. If the horses
qualify as really good things, those really good things translate into
really good betting opportunities. It's easy money, like stealing. Or is
it? How much is the trainer willing to risk on his opinion?

The answer, I suspect, is not very much, and probably nothing. As
noted, veteran horsemen have long since stopped betting on their
opinions, but few of them have stopped giving them.

The same cold water might be thrown on the passionate opinions
dispensed by other insiders. If a jockey's agent insists he really likes his
chances in the ninth, ask the agent how much he's betting. The same
line can be applied to stable foremen, assistant trainers, clockers, vets,
and exercise riders. Owners are exempt. However subjective and ridiculous their opinions and tips, owners will wager serious money on
hope.

Happily I have been spared this nonsense. On my second season
at the races I bought a box at Hollywood Park. That provided access to
inside information. The flow began immediately. Every day we were
handed secondhand opinions on ready, well-spotted horses that could
be traced to horsemen.

My partner that season was Don Menaguale, a CPA. Early on, the
two of us decided to document the inside information. Of the first one
hundred tips, ninety-four lost. Random selection would have performed as well. We stopped keeping score.

Betting aside, one of the most fascinating aspects of the racetrack experience concerns the analytical differences between handicappers and horsemen. The two groups pursue success as if separated by a great divide. Horsemen betray an inordinate taste for jockeys, weight, and post position, factors handicappers routinely regard as incidental.

Hardly a stakes race passes that some prominent horseman is not prone to notice that the winner was giving the others six pounds. If a 3YO defeats older handicap horses by a neck during summer, members from the losing camp will be certain to announce the younger horse was getting eleven pounds or such on the scale. Abundant, repeatedly replicated research has shown that weight differences and weight shifts of any degree cannot account for race outcomes. Horsemen are obviously not convinced.

Horsemen's preoccupation with post positions cannot be assigned to any rational force of handicapping, and it reaches farcical proportions during the Triple Crown and Breeders' Cup weeks. If handicappers are duped by these discussions, they deserve their fate.

In a blast of fresh air, when trainer Bill Mott drew the far outside with Cigar in the 1995 Massachusetts Handicap at Suffolk Downs, a bonus of half a million at stake, he pointed out the post position would not mean anything.

"I never mind the outside when I have a decent run to the first turn," observed Mott, and no handicapper could have stated the case more succinctly. Mott's observation generalizes well to the Kentucky Derby, the Breeders' Cup Classic, and all other races characterized by that decent run to the clubhouse turn. And contrary to the popular belief, the rail does not spell defeat.

Of the salient differences between handicappers and horsemen, none approaches their distinctive views of running times. Time doesn't mean a thing, assert numerous horsemen, who have become too familiar with fast horses that suddenly stop and fade when they confront better horses. Horsemen prefer class to speed.

Time is critical to handicappers, although they quickly concede that adjusted times and the associated speed figures are much more important than actual times. If speed is the primary attribute of the racehorses, and it is, time reflects speed, and it's crucial for handicappers to know which horses have run the fastest in the past.

In fact studies reveal a perfect positive correlation between speed and class. Better horses run faster. The relationships hold firm at every racetrack, large, medium, and small. The fastest horses may not be the best, as horsemen appreciate, but the best horses are the fastest, which handicappers understand, but many horsemen do not.

The fundamental handicapping factors on which horsemen and handicappers converge are class and form. Both camps recognize the factors as fundamentally important, though many handicappers claim to be dubious of class. When horsemen reveal they like their horses, they usually mean their horses are coming to the races in positive form. But even when trainers know their horses' current form to be sharp, they have not evaluated the competition closely, have not conducted a pace analysis, and have not even considered the several other factors of handicapping that might apply.

In other words, horsemen who know their own horses reasonably well can be astonishingly weak in comprehending performance.

The acute differences between the camps on the handicapping factors is one reason handicappers cannot anticipate support in their efforts from horsemen. Another reason relates to horsemen and the media. Nothing could be further removed from the handicapping purpose than the prerace and postrace interviews with jockeys and trainers. Regardless of the circumstances, the jockey and trainer are guaranteed to say nothing that might alienate the owner. The owner pays the bills, and supplies the horses that generate the trainer's income. The owner can remove the horses from the barn tomorrow, and many of them will.

When speaking to the media, the agenda of the trainer consists of pleasing or placating the owner with whatever positive spin appears to be convenient or appropriate. Thus the hackneyed clichés, pitiful excuses, and generally vacuous comments that dominate the exchanges.

On this front, the media, broadcast and print, persist as extraordinarily naive. Deadlines and television spots or not, if the intent is to understand performance and clarify horses' abilities and preferences, the interviews with horsemen would benefit from a full-dress makeover. Instead of eliciting opinions that will be entirely subjective and self-serving, turf writers might present trainers with objective evidence of a good, bad, or indifferent performance and solicit a reaction. If evaded, they might even press the point. They might also appreciate the crucial relations among jockeys, trainers, and owners, and thereby arrange the interviews more intelligently.

Ironically some of the most astute contemporary racing analysts have been women, whose number among handicappers has remained artificially low. In the simulcast of the 1995 Peter Pan from Belmont Park, comely blond analyst Jan Rushton in the walking ring nabbed trainer Nick Zito, whose Suave Prospect was favored at even-money.

"Nick, you were on record as saying Suave Prospect needed a rest following the Kentucky Derby," began Rushton. "You were intending to skip the Belmont Stakes, and suddenly Suave Prospect shows up in the Peter Pan. Why the sudden change?"

Zito seemed rather stunned at the question. He grimaced, hesitated, and finally offered an unpersuasive explanation. Zito trotted out the cliché about the horse having to tell the trainer how he really feels. Suave Prospect was eating up and doing well. Zito now saw no reason not to run.

When the analyst pressed the matter with a couple of additional pointed questions, Zito walked away from the interview in disgust.

Handicappers had been well served on that occasion. At even-money, Suave Prospect offered his backers a mild run on the far turn and finished haplessly up the course.

An outstanding illustration of the media's benign neglect of handicappers sprang to life after Thunder Gulch had won the 1995 Kentucky Derby and paid boxcars, when he should have been 4–1, or 6–1, or maybe 8–1, but not 24–1. D. Wayne Lukas is prized by turf writers and broadcasters alike, at least for his media relations. But the media revealed how little they had come to understand the colorful trainer during Derby week of 1995, the most important days of the season.

A week before the 1995 Derby, as all remember, Lukas announced he would enter the brilliant filly Serena's Song against the colts. Lukas would be starting three contenders in the Derby, Serena's Song, Timber Country, and Thunder Gulch. Lukas preferred his 2YO champion Timber Country, but that colt had disappointed in three preliminaries at Santa Anita, prompting the filly's late entry.

From the moment the filly's entry was announced, the media focused relentlessly on Lukas and the relative merits of the filly vis-à-vis the colts, notably Timber Country. Lukas himself had focused just as relentlessly on the two horses, shaping the media coverage. Thunder Gulch was virtually ignored.

Thunder Gulch had squandered the Blue Grass Stakes (Gr. 1) at 6–5, but at 2–1 had won the Florida Derby (Gr. 1). The neglected Lukas horse was not only a dual qualifier on dosage and the Experimental Handicap rankings, but he had also recorded competitive speed figures and the speed handicappers had relished his chances. Why was the colt so disrespectfully dismissed during Derby week?

It's understandable, even obvious, why Lukas discounted Thunder Gulch, but the media can offer no acceptable excuse.

Timber Country was owned by William T. Young, of Overbrook Farm, of Texas, and Lukas's leading owner. Serena's Song was owned by Bob and Beverly Lewis, of southern California, and for whom Lukas trains approximately one hundred horses. The two clients had resuscitated Lukas's financial career and also represented his financial future.

Thunder Gulch was owned by Michael Tabor, a European, who had sent the colt to Lukas during the late fall of its juvenile campaign. Lukas trained exactly one horse for Tabor.

Hundreds of media reps who follow Lukas continually managed to miss the essence of this remarkable man during Derby week. While the media were missing the entire ballgame, Lukas was promoting not Timber Country and Serena's Song but the interests of William T. Young and Bob Lewis.

In the meantime Thunder Gulch, an authentic contender, had been shuffled to the background. The national Derby audience, not to mention thousands of casual handicappers not especially familiar with Thunder Gulch, deserved better.

Omissions of this kind are indulged weekly, as trainers genuflect to owners and the media miss the beat. Interestingly, as Thunder Gulch was winning the Kentucky Derby with authority, fulfilling lifetime goals, Wayne Lukas reportedly sat silent and unemotional, as if uninvolved, in William Young's box.

When the Derby had ended, before leaving Young's box, Lukas discussed Timber Country's eventful trip in detail, not even mentioning Thunder Gulch, as if the winner did not matter. He next attempted to find Bob Lewis to reassure the owner about Serena's Song. Only then did Lukas depart for the winner's circle. In a heightened microcosm of the Derby week's proceedings, even in winning the most important race of the year, the race that Lukas adores above all else, Thunder Gulch was discounted in favor of the trainer's truly important clients.

If handicappers want to comprehend horsemen at a primitive level, let them contemplate Wayne Lukas's behavior at the 1995 Kentucky Derby. It speaks volumes. The media that listened and capitulated while Lukas prattled on about Serena's Song and Timber Country, but not Thunder Gulch, might reconsider the situation as well. If turf writers and broadcasters intend to assist racing's customers in evaluating performance, they do not reach the high mark by soliciting the opinions of jockeys and trainers. The prerace and postrace interviews are essentially a waste of time. Handicappers will be better served by tuning out.

So handicappers and horsemen struggle along their separate paths at the races. The casual customers who wish they could know what the insiders know should know instead that inside information becomes their worst nightmare. If newcomers are intrigued, but new and unformed as handicappers, depending upon horsemen for cues and direction can set them back a number of years. As noted at the top, the financial penalty will be severe.

Handicappers should play their game as astutely and aggressively as their knowledge and skill allow, and forget about the half-baked opinions of horsemen.

TREVOR'S CALL

It was a $50,000 claiming sprint, 4up, at Hollywood Park last week, and I was alive for a healthy Pick 3 to a pair of 5–2 co-favorites, Appendix Joe and Utmost. The horses had barely found their stride out of the gate and were headed toward the half-mile pole when loud and clear came Trevor Denman's opening call of Utmost, an off-pace closer.

"Utmost has his ears pinned and has dropped back next to last. He's just not interested today." Not another race caller in the country would have offered that observation.

I gave up on Utmost. The 5–2 shot never moved up, not passing a single opponent.

After more than a decade of listening to them, I am still more than occasionally astonished by the sheer intelligence of Trevor Denman's calls. The above incident is a marvel to me, that a track announcer would know before the horses had traveled a furlong that a co-favorite would not win; would not even run. Only one race caller could have made that call, and several others of comparable insight, and it's Trevor Denman, who calls the circuit in southern California and is sorely missed when he's absent even a day.

Another incident that amazed me jumps to mind. It happened during Oak Tree at Santa Anita in 1994. The horses' names elude me, but as the field in a route approached the top of the stretch, the leaders still rounding the curve of the far turn, the horse Denman announced as the horse to beat was running last. That horse soon circled the field, leveled anew, and drew away.

On watching the replay, I could detect no rapid acceleration or unusual movement at the moment Trevor had dubbed the horse the probable winner. In my defense, I have been playing the races for only two and one-half decades and have not yet evolved as much of a trip analyst. Denman spots the telltale clues I miss in a split second, and he is not often misguided. In further defense, I have never heard another track announcer call a horse positioned last on the far turn as the horse to beat. It's quite a gift.

And so, of the manifold attributes that set Denman's race calls apart, it's the substance, or intelligence, of his commentary that rings so meticulously true with practiced handicappers. Not only does Denman comprehend a good performance when he sees it, as opposed to a mere winning performance, but he also recognizes quickly and surely when favorites and contenders are not doing enough, a phrase he frequently employs, to the chagrin of handicappers holding tickets on the horses.

Imagine holding a $200 win-ticket on the day's best bet at 7–2. The horses are rounding the far turn, or turning into the stretch. Trevor calls your good thing, and says,

". . . not doing enough in this one," or

". . . not responding," or

". . . having to be asked to keep up," or

". . . has to do better," or

". . . is being asked the question, but not answering," or

". . . not finding . . ."

It's disconcerting, too, to have your horse clearly in front in the stretch, but Trevor makes it equally clear the horse is tiring, or lugging out, or shortening stride, or not changing leads.

To be fair, handicappers also experience an opposite effect with key horses and best bets. At the same critical junctures, with your horse absolutely in contention, Trevor says,

". . . has not been asked yet," or

". . . he's well within himself," or

". . . running effortlessly," or

". . . moving up strongly on the outside," or

". . . here's the danger," or

". . . this is the horse to beat," or

". . . finding more," or

". . . just cruising,"

Or my favorite phrase, usually released at an earlier stage of a route race,

". . . he's just loving it out there . . ."

Denman also provides deeply appreciated sustenance to trip handicappers whose horses may be trapped or blocked but otherwise look full of run. If Trevor raises his pitch slightly and says the unfortunate horse is crying out desperately for room, trip handicappers can take heart. If the horse eventually finds room, it regularly surges forward and frequently wins.

Earlier in the races, Denman relentlessly picks up both positive signals and danger signs and relays them to the bettors. Horses have their ears pricked, or the ears are flicking, signaling alertness, or they have grabbed the bit, or they're pulling hard (against the jockey's rating), or they're out there where they like to be (front-runners who need the lead), or they're running easily, or they're relaxed, or they're racing wide, or maybe the saddle slipped, or the jockey's feet have left the stirrups, or the pace is a good one for this distance.

He misses virtually nothing. It's a marvelous, colorful, amazingly detailed call. Not only has the bettor's day at the races been greatly enhanced, but also the trip handicapper's purpose has been greatly abetted. Trip handicappers of southern California owe Denman a special nod. He's their sidekick, and a best friend at the races.

After his powers of anticipation have focused and intensified the race-watching experience for the bettors, Denman does not desert them at the finish line. He describes the stretch drive with enthusiasm and he calls short heads, noses, even fingernails, and he's rarely wrong. If Trevor says the race has been too close to call, it is, and the photo will be almost imperceptible. A dead-heat is plausible.

As accurate as Denman's call can be at the wire, once at Santa Anita, on the grass, I backed a 19–1 shot that Trevor called a winner, when the horse had actually finished third, beaten more than a length in the official chart. While lengths in front, the horse had drifted to the far outside in the final sixteenth. Trevor recognized the drifting out and the two horses rallying toward the inside, but he called my guy the winner. I was not concerned when the photo sign flashed.

When the official numbers went up, I could hardly believe my misfortune. What's the chance of Trevor Denman calling a third-place finisher the winner? Is that a tough beat?

Denman salutes and compliments jockeys generously, not only the patented rides, such as Delahoussaye's close, Pincay's rugged finish, and Pat Valenzuela darting out of the gate, but the talented rides delivered by journeymen and minor riders. A few days ago, in a stakes at Hollywood Park's odd distance of seven-and-one-half furlongs, Chris Antley gave a

3YO named Pumpkin House a splendid, weaving, well-timed ride from far back early and Denman saluted horse and rider at every pole.

On pace, Denman likes to relate the rate of speed to the distance. "A good pace for this distance," he will note, notably going long on the grass. If a front-runner is running away with the jockey, Denman calls it. If the pace has been inordinately slow, he notes that.

In years long gone by, some handicappers complained that Denman's pace calls alerted jockeys unduly, giving an unfair advantage to certain riders and horses. Nothing was done, thankfully. First, the pace calls are subjective, interpretive, and may be wrong. In practice, few jockeys hear the calls, fewer still react, and without as many as two race outcomes a season being altered, the pace calls help the audience appreciate the competition, which is the basic idea.

The intelligent substance of Denman's calls should not obscure the style, which is so utterly good that any comparisons with others are essentially unwarranted. What criteria do handicappers consider material? Diction. Pacing. Rhythm. Articulation. Vocabulary. Syntax. Phrasing. Accuracy. Denman gets high marks on all counts.

When Denman arrived from South Africa, not a few handicappers criticized his accent. Whether by acculturation or adaptation, nobody remains critical. The voice is firm, vibrant, crystal clear, and pleasant. Denman's calls suffer no silences, no stumbles, no mumbles, no awkward gaps, and no inappropriate words or phrases. He covers every horse front to rear, and most horses repeatedly, with close attention to the betting favorites. Midrace moves and late maneuvers are captured virtually without omission. In the stretch, every horse in contention is called, and so are fast-closing horses.

At times Denman anticipates that hard-charging closers will rally to win, only to have the horses flatten out in the upper or middle stretch. Only then do Denman's calls register as fallible, after all.

Comparisons with colleagues do not really apply, but in certain circumstances the undiluted advantages supplied by Trevor's call cannot be denied.

In the running of the 1995 Kentucky Derby, the bulky nineteen-horse field had not yet reached the clubhouse turn when Mike Battaglia's futile call came sharply and disturbingly into focus. There's no softer way to put it, the call was awful. Not more than four or five horses had been mentioned, and no one watching without wide-angled binoculars could have gathered anything but the vaguest idea where any contender was, from the speed horses, to the favorites, to the others. Matters did not improve. In deep stretch, the order of succession remained a mystery, presumably even to Battaglia. A truly forgettable call.

The most overrated caller in the country, in my judgment, has been Dave Johnson, the announcer Denman removed after one year at Santa Anita, now at The Meadowlands, and who somehow manages to sign contracts by which he calls numerous national telecasts. It's regrettable casting.

From the early days Johnson's calls have consistently resounded with an artificial sheen, as if delivered by someone who knows less about the subject than he pretends. With his powers of anticipation poor, and his description of close-driving finishes weak and frequently nonspecific, Johnson's schtick registers to the practiced handicapper as vain, smug, and supercilious.

With his contrived, cloying cry every time of "down the stretch they come," Johnson can be relegated to the dubious category of journeyman race callers who intend to advance their reputations and careers by confusing substance with slogans. Phil Georgeoff performed the same trick forever at the Chicago tracks with "here they come spinning out of the turn." It's artifice more than signature.

By comparison, Trevor Denman's "moving like a winner," and his fast-closing "freight trains" are not only invoked selectively, they are inevitably apt, touching off the call like a dessert topping.

New York's Tom Durkin is solid, if nondescript, but the best of the others is the new young caller at Golden Gate Fields, Alan Buchdahl. Buchdahl is crisp, clear, and accurate, and he knows the game well. His powers of anticipation remain in process, with the same deep closers that occasionally flatten on Denman his main problem. Buchdahl anticipates they are coming on strongly, but often they are not.

Perhaps race calling is not an American art. Denman was imported by Santa Anita from South Africa. Hollywood Park imported the intelligent and underrated Michael Wrona from Australia. European callers as a group sound far superior to the American product.

If my observations are correct, in the past couple of seasons the quality and color of Denman's incomparable calls have improved even more. It's been wonderful to experience the races from Trevor's point of view, and it's getting better all the time.

THE RACING TIMES
AND THE *DAILY RACING FORM*

A rare blow for the horse player landed flush against the *Daily Racing Form* in 1991 with the unprecedented publication of a rival national newspaper, *The Racing Times*. The new kid presented racing's customers with new past-performance records, and they were bigger and better.

Not only that, for the first time in the history of the game, racegoers had now gained access to information describing a horse's speed, in the form of professional speed figures. For various technical reasons the data on speed provided by the *Daily Racing Form*, its running times and speed ratings, could not inform racing's customers how fast the horses had run in the past, but the Beyer Speed Figures did. The speed figures would assist handicappers in comparing horses that had competed on different racing days, at different distances, even at different racetracks, comparisons the *Form*'s data items not only obscured but had also distorted. It was a giant step for the customer, and should have been a great leap forward.

There was much more.

Racegoers were provided with summary data describing horses' performances at today's track and distance, on the grass, and on wet tracks. Below the ten races portrayed, *The Racing Times* presented the horse's top Beyer Speed Figure in the past two seasons, its lifetime top on the dirt or grass, depending upon today's surface, its top on wet surfaces, and its top at today's distance. Nice!

Racing dates separated by layoffs of thirty days or longer were underlined.

The exact conditions of eligibility were notated, a contribution that represented a tremendous boost to class handicappers. Purse sizes of allowance races and ungraded stakes were printed.

Running times were recorded in hundredths (decimals) instead of fifths (fractions), a numerical change that annoyed many customers accustomed to the familiar fifths of a second, but which improved the accuracy of handicappers interested in estimating the true speed of horses.

Under the first three finishers a trip handicapping line was inserted toward the right-hand margin, as needed, using English words and phrases. For the first time ever, a useful brand of trip handicapping had sneaked its way into the past performances.

For the first time too, symbols designating Lasix and front wraps were included. Do handicappers want that information?

The workout line was extended from the traditional three or four workouts to six, more for first-starters, and eventually workouts were ranked according to speed at the distance, such as third fastest of forty-six workouts that morning.

For foreign horses, the imports, the gradings, and the purse values of stakes were provided and so were tag lines that described running styles and perhaps the quality of the horses' performances.

Editor-in-chief Steve Crist understood absolutely that the paper's primary audience consisted of racegoers, handicappers, and bettors, and not owners, breeders, horsemen, and track officials. He hired turf writers who were authentic handicappers, such that the reportage, analysis, and handicapping were superior to the *Form*'s. The substance, tone, and comprehensive coverage of the new paper represented a serious improvement.

Crist introduced a daily opinion page, and finally racing's customers might be provoked by critical thinking, constructive criticism, intelligent analysis, and competing opinions, pro and con, soft and hard, right and wrong, on their sport and game.

The Racing Times became a breakthrough moment, exciting, stimulating, and genuinely helpful, a change from the status quo that was desperately needed and long, long overdue. It lasted one dazzling year.

With the publication of the Beyer Speed Figures and the several additional progressive changes in the past performances, with a credible big-name editor (Crist had covered horse racing for ten years for *The New York Times*), and with professional handicappers and turf writers that should be more appealing to racing's core customers, *The Racing Times* had assumed that the paper would capture 40 percent of the market within a year. It captured 18 percent instead.

Postmortems can be unseemly, as people who are hurt, disappointed, and angry point the finger of blame, and the premature demise of *The Racing Times* did not escape the usual recriminations. People pointed at other people, and everyone enumerated the critical mistakes that should have been avoided or corrected.

None of that mattered very much. The demise of *The Racing Times* was related less to the paper itself than to the industry and market it had intended to serve. To say that a majority of racetracks and racegoers were not prepared for *The Racing Times,* and therefore were unable to benefit from its innovative changes, understates a terrible truth. A better product will not make a difference to people who do not know how to use it.

Of the great game of handicapping and about playing the races, the market as a whole is depressingly uneducated, and that more than anything else explains the failure of *The Racing Times.*

Two incidents I experienced dramatize the situation exceedingly well.

Months before the paper hit the streets, *The Racing Times* conducted focus groups. These invited handicappers and turf writers to express opinions, concerns, and recommendations. The one I attended in Los Angeles was conducted by Scott Finley, general manager of the paper, a serious horse player and a good friend.

Roughly thirty people participated. Early in the proceedings I suggested the paper's price should undercut the *Form's* $2.50. I suggested $1.50, at least as an introductory price for the initial six months. The paper would promote the lower price heavily, and advise the market as to when the price would be increased, and by how much.

Finley did not entertain the suggestion. He stated that the decision on price had already been made. It would be the same as the price of the *Daily Racing Form* ($2.50). In explanation Finley reported the paper's management was confident its product would be of significantly higher quality than the *Daily Racing Form,* and would be perceived that way by the market. A lower price was thought to cheapen the product unnecessarily and to be a bad idea.

If memory serves, nobody else in the focus group supported a lower price either, which stunned me. I dropped the matter.

Flash-forward nine months, and *The Racing Times* is sinking in troubles, especially on the West Coast, where sales that were anticipated to be strong have been surprisingly weak. Steve Crist is on the line and telling me the paper's western edition would soon be changed from a broad form to a tabloid, similar in size to the *Daily Racing Form*.

Would I be willing to conduct a few seminars in southern California on using *The Racing Times*?

I agreed enthusiastically, and mentioned something to Crist about imagining that the inclusion of professional speed figures would capture 40 percent of the market.

In a firm, exasperated tone, Crist replied, "These people [racegoers] do not even know what a speed figure is."

That's right, and that's why *The Racing Times* perished. Not only do racegoers not know how to interpret and use speed figures, but also too many cannot interpret and use effectively the other changes *The Racing Times* introduced, including the eligibility conditions, running times in hundredths of a second, equipment and medication, and even the trip notes.

In the focus group, curiously, nobody suggested that the customers might be unable to benefit from the high-quality innovations. It was assumed that the greater quality of the paper and its past-performance tables would be experienced that way. To the degree that the assumption proved incorrect, a lower price might have encouraged racegoers to try the product for a time.

It's a consolation of sorts to *The Racing Times* and its staff, as well as a credit to its customers, that racegoers who did try the new paper for a time, perhaps thirty days, remained loyal customers. They could not return to the *Daily Racing Form*. If *The Racing Times* could have persevered for five years, no doubt it would have replaced the *Daily Racing Form* as the leader in the marketplace.

And as a lasting testament to the quality and depth of the paper's mission, handicappers need only inspect the issues covering the Breeders' Cup event day of 1991. Throughout that week, and on Cup Day in particular, *The Racing Times* knocked the *Daily Racing Form* out of the water. The coverage was fabulous.

As *The Racing Times* staggered before the impending knockout, the *Daily Racing Form*, through its corporate parent, purchased the paper and its assets, notably the software and the database containing the new data items. During the next couple of years several of the rival paper's data items were introduced to the *Daily Racing Form*'s past performances, including the Beyer Speed Figures. Spurred to improve itself, the *Daily Racing Form* had begun to do exactly that. It's a more professional paper today than ever, dramatically improved in comparison to what it was before *The Racing Times*.

The competition had benefited racegoers and handicappers alike in no small ways. It's instructive to review the past performances of the *Daily Racing Form* in 1989 and their past performances of 1995. Consider the examples provided below and on page 132.

The *Daily Racing Form* also followed its competitor's advance in the hiring of talented handicappers as turf writers and analysts. Where previously *Form* users too often suffered from the slants of second- and third class handicappers, today they benefit from the excellent handicapping and analysis of Dave Litfin, in New York; Steve Klein, in Kentucky; Brad Free, in Los Angeles; and many others.

The "Closer Look" feature that accompanies the past performances of the western edition is wonderful, a vibrant expert's sound bite that can bring the past performances to life, and must be a tremendous practical assist to casual handicappers. When maidens, first-starters, and newcomers to turf racing are the menu, the trainer stats and sire stats the *Form* handicappers supply can take even regular, practiced handicappers to the heart of the matter.

Editorial content has improved dramatically, as has the scope and quality of the reportage, and on Sundays the *Form* publishes its own unprecedented opinion page, plus letters to the editor. Critical thinking is now permitted, and unfavorable opinions may see the light of day. It's progress.

Daily Racing Form 1989

The Racing Times 1991

OLE MARCONI

(data table — past performance chart for OLE MARCONI, $10,000, Sire: Hot Oil, by Damascus; Dam: Marcos Two B., by Negrum; Bred in IL by Jean Cole; Career record and race lines)

Daily Racing Form 1995

Mighty Forum (GB)

(data table — past performance chart for Mighty Forum (GB), B. c. 4, Sire: Presidium*GB (General Assembly); Dam: Mighty Flash (Roife); Lifetime Record: 11 4 0 0 $104,201)

All is far from satisfactory, however, with the *Daily Racing Form*. After a couple of years characterized by progressive change, by the midpoint of 1994 the changes had suddenly ended and the progress had stopped. Economic determinism had no doubt reared its ugly head. An end to progress and change can only be considered distressing in the age of information and full-card simulcasting.

Handicappers now play multiple tracks, at least two that present familiar horses, and selected races from other unfamiliar circuits. The players' overarching ache is for information (not data) that they can analyze quickly to make decisions. Further revision and amplification of the past-performance tables will be inevitable. Information reports, electronically generated and distributed, will be mandatory. If the *Daily Racing Form* does not supply the desired changes, somebody else, à la *The Racing Times*, eventually will.

An overdue change that has not been forthcoming despite the ac-

cessibility of *The Racing Times'* database concerns the accurate recording of running times. Numerous figure handicappers prefer their own
speed figures to the Beyer Speed Figures, and many others use speed
and pace figures in combination. Accurate data are crucial, and the
Daily Racing Form falls down badly on the timing scale.

Consider the 1995 Santa Anita Derby. Won by Larry The Legend,
the mile time and nine-furlong time were recorded on the tote board
at Santa Anita in hundredths of seconds and later in the result chart
and past-performance tables of the *Daily Racing Form* in fifths of a second. Examine the difference:

	One Mile	Final Time
Santa Anita	1:34.97	1:47.99
Daily Racing Form	1:34⁴	1:47⁴

How fast did Larry The Legend run? The colt ran at least two
lengths slower than the *Daily Racing Form* reported he had.

Regardless of actual times, the *Daily Racing Form* rounds the hundredths of a second downward, to the nearest fifth of a second.

The Santa Anita Derby did not go 1:34 ⅘ to the mile call. It went
1:35 flat. Larry The Legend did not run 1:47 ⅘. He ran 1:48.

The difference equals two lengths. Is two lengths important to
handicappers making speed and pace ratings?

The Racing Times would have reported the actual times as they were
recorded at the racetrack.

The thousands of high-tech handicappers entering data supplied
by the *Daily Racing Form* into computer programs have been misled.
Garbage in, garbage out. The hackneyed cliché is not inappropriate
here.

Figure handicappers at Santa Anita or at simulcast sites making the
same speed and pace ratings would have an enviable edge, provided
they recorded the more precise data supplied by the tote board.

These variations occur every racing day at tracks that record the
running times in hundredths of a second. The *Daily Racing Form*'s
rounding protocol means the sport's official repository of information
can be inaccurate by two to three lengths in any race. The industry

tolerates the misinformation, as it has for half a century. The inaccurate records accumulate, sadly and unnecessarily.

Why hasn't the *Daily Racing Form* switched to the more precise format, bought for a princely sum four years ago?

And where are the Beyer Speed Pars? Handicappers attempting to interpret the Beyer Speed Figures have a right to know how fast the typical winner of this kind of race should be expected to run. A par figure astride the conditions of eligibility would suffice.

And a valuable contribution, indeed a monumental change, would replace the traditional but impractical misleading column of *Form* speed ratings and track variants with a Beyer par for each race in the record and a track variant that actually reflected that day's track-surface speed. The new information (98-F2) would fit snugly, requiring no additional space.

Why not?

If the explanations begin and end with tradition, or some patronizing, condescending assertion about the unwillingness to change of racetracks or of racing's customers, the future is bleak.

With full-card simulcasting the dominating aspect of that future, and on-line electronic services a growth sector, it's inconvenient and even unacceptable that the progress and innovation provoked by *The Racing Times* has apparently been halted. Only two national databases of the past performances exist, and the *Daily Racing Form* is number one.

More optimistically, a change at the *Daily Racing Form* not directly related to the past performances, but tracing to *The Racing Times* as well, is an emphasis on customer education. It's called the Partners Program, a joint venture between the *Form* and the tracks. The racetracks become a distributor of the *Form*, and the two collaborate on a program of fan education.

At Santa Anita in 1995, three half-hour television programs were developed (*On Class, Speed and Pace,* and *Form*), featuring the *Form*'s Brad Free and Los Angeles handicapper Jeff Siegel. In regard to scripts, talent, and delivery, the programs were excellent.

It recalled to mind Steve Crist's exasperated observation that racing's customers do not even know what a speed figure is. Until the industry decides to take that problem seriously, and correct the problem, the rest is spinning wheels.

MY ARGUMENT WITH BARRY

A day at the races with Barry Meadow can be fascinating, provocative, and even fun, although two days would be difficult, and three days virtually impossible.

On the bright side, Barry is a comedian. He's funny enough to host the shows at the comedy clubs, which he does regularly throughout Los Angeles, Orange, and San Diego counties. I have not attended the show, but at the races Barry becomes the performer, constantly on, full of quips and clever enough to take the experience of the moment and convert it to a wry, ironic, exaggerated slice of the racetrack.

My favorite of his shticks is "The Obvious Selection." No matter what happens on the track, Barry can explain in persuasive detail why the outcome might be considered obvious. Suppose the 1995 Kentucky Derby had been won by Lake George instead of Thunder Gulch.

Barry would explain why the colt was "The Obvious Selection." In an elevated pitch and staccato rhythm, he might say,

"Lightly-raced colt is beautifully bred for the classic distance. Has a Northern Dancer father and Secretariat mother. Last three races show improving Beyers. Working out sharply at Churchill Downs. Graduated from maiden win to third-place finish in a Gr. 2 stakes at Santa Anita. Beaten just three lengths that day by pre-Derby favorite Afternoon Deelites. Beaten just one length by Derby favorite Timber Country.

"Lightly-raced, well-bred improving sort could be any kind. Gets off the Santa Anita rail and has every right to surprise at a price.

"Can't blame anybody for thinking Lake George is The Obvious Selection."

Some of Barry's explanations prove hilarious, particularly to handicappers painstakingly revisiting the record and believing the horse makes no sense. The horses never look that far-fetched once Barry's done. The routine mimics an undeniable fact of racetrack life. No matter the outcome, somebody has bet on it, and usually it's somebody sitting nearby. To those holding negotiable tickets, the horse may not have qualified as "The Obvious Selection," but they looked good enough to be backed.

When Barry's not being funny, he's being skeptical. The comedian is also a skeptic. This is Barry's darker side. Barry enjoys nothing so much as challenging others, unless it's challenging the very assumptions on which some generally accepted view is based. In playing the quarrelsome skeptic, Barry adapts the roles of scientist, mathematician, statistician, and researcher, each of which he implements well, and he's particularly harsh on the presumptions of writers and researchers, attacking their sample sizes, probability estimates, measurements (data), and the conclusions flowing from any of the above he judges to be bogus.

In a recent discussion on the possibility of identifying winning handicappers, Barry would not accept a sample of one hundred bets, or two hundred, or three hundred, even repeated twice, as conclusive. At dinner he will spar with mathematician Dick Mitchell about math and probabilities until midnight.

Years ago Barry disapproved of the formulas used by William Ziemba to develop the Dr. Z. approach to beating the races with place and show betting. He sent a paper on the topic to the renowned Edward Thorp, who had written the introduction to Ziemba's text.

In the company of Meadow and Mitchell, I subsequently went to hear Thorp lecture on markets and games at UC Irvine. During the question-and-answer segment, someone asked Thorp about the Dr. Z. system, and whether it worked, the only question that night about horse racing.

Thorp defended the system as sound. He then mentioned he had received a paper from a Barry Meadow (who might be in the audience) challenging the validity of the Dr. Z. formulas. Thorp noted he had reviewed Barry's paper and had found the arguments well developed and valid. But, Thorp added, Barry's complaints did not alter the results sufficiently to justify any revision. For once Barry stood chastised. With Thorp as a fountainhead to follow, I often feel the same way after an extended jousting with Barry.

The most notorious of these bouts occurred across lunch at Santa Anita during the winter season of 1995. An overzealous advocate of Pick 3 wagering at the time, I had anticipated Barry's presence so that I might engage him in a discussion (argument) of my brilliant strategy for beating the Pick 3. I expected a debate but, convinced of the integrity of my arguments, I also imagined a final corroboration. I knew, too, that holes in the strategy would be ripped wide open by Barry's astute comprehension of matters pari-mutuel, which is not readily excelled.

What followed was a two-hour tug-of-war.

I began with the proposition that the Pick 3 represents the first exotic wager that gives the bettors a reasonable probability of winning large amounts on a regular schedule. Handicappers who can isolate a race's contenders extend themselves a 50 to 80 percent chance of hitting each leg of the three-race wager. This reality might be converted to fantastic hitting possibilities. I presented Barry with a summary and chart of the day's Pick 3 combinations.

My strategy places a race's main contention and overlays into A and B columns and assigns a probability (of winning) value to each contender. Each contender's probability of winning is added. The sum equals the bettor's probability of winning that leg.

On June 11, at Hollywood Park, the first race, two horses were used, with Lady Sorolla assigned a 15 percent chance of winning and the favorite Prospero De Oro assigned a 40 percent chance of winning.

The two horses represented a 55 percent chance of surviving the first race.

Three horses in the second race represented a 73 percent chance of winning. Two horses in the next race gave me a 50 percent chance of winning the third.

If the probabilities of winning each race are multiplied together, that product equals the probability of hitting the Pick 3.

For races one, two, three, that meant $0.55 \times 0.73 \times 0.50$, which

amounts to a 20 percent chance of hitting the Pick 3. The odds are
4–1 against, which handicappers will recognize as favorable odds of
winning a three-race serial wager.

With mixed success, basically positive, I had persevered with variations of this strategy for eighteen months. The trick is to afford your-
self a 50 percent or greater chance of winning each leg. That means
the handicapper has a 12.5 percent chance (or greater) of winning the
Pick 3. The odds will be 7–1 or lower; nice.

By comparison, the odds of hitting the Pick 6 with a pair of singles
combined with the contenders of the other four legs are abysmally low.
The Pick 6 makes no sense, unless a gigantic carryover pool is sitting
there, free money representing a potentially huge payoff.

Once the Pick 3 combinations have been set, the odds of winning
the wager can be compared to the number of combinations, bet sizes,
cost, and probable payoffs. If an attractive overlay looms, make the play.
The probability of actually winning, as we have seen, is reassuring.

The discussion flowed and ebbed until I pressed my main point on
Barry. In playing the "rolling" Pick 3s, I argued, the whole will be
greater than the sum of its parts. That is, key-bet singles excepted,
handicappers must use all the contenders in each leg. The coverage is
intended to render the probability of winning unusually high, without
surrendering value ridiculously. The Pick 3 in southern California pays
so generously so often that overlays abound in the natural course of
events. The underlay combinations that win are too few to erode profits seriously enough to matter. Only the occasional roll of favorites
throughout the card interferes with the strategy.

Barry disagreed. He insisted it would be better to combine each
contender in leg one with each contender in the other two, multiply
those probabilities, and eliminate any of the combinations that would
be expected to return as an underlay. In the June 11th example, Barry
might combine the favorite in the first race, for instance, with a contender in the second and third, as follows:

Prospero De Oro (0.40) × Roo Tale (0.20) × Slewsi (0.25) =
0.02.

The combination has a 2 percent chance of occurring. The odds
against winning translate to 49–1. A $3 wager at Hollywood Park, Bar-

ry's Pick 3 must pay $150 (50 × $3) for that combination to be a fair bet. If handicappers estimate the payoff as greater than $150, they might bet; if the probable payoff is less than $150, they should eliminate that combination. And so forth, with each combination of contenders in the three races.

In that way, Barry argued, handicappers eliminate the probable underlays but still tap into the overlay combinations. The probability of winning the three races, or rolling the Pick 3s, drops, maybe severely, but presumably the profits long-haul should rise.

The two of us debated the merits of the two positions relentlessly. I would not relinquish the notion that the whole would exceed the sum of its parts because (a) the Pick 3 payoffs have been surprisingly generous, even when two favorites have won; and (b) bettors would "roll" many more combination bets successfully, cashing overlays more frequently, even if the intervening underlays were bet.

To make matters more concrete, let's apply the alternative strategies to the fourth, fifth, and sixth sequence at Hollywood Park on June 11.

Using two of six horses in the fourth, I had estimated a 65 percent chance of winning. With three of the twelve horses in the fifth, I imagined a 63 percent chance of getting that one. Using three of eight horses in the sixth, I had another 63 percent chance of winning that leg.

My chance of hitting the Pick 3 could be estimated at $0.65 \times 0.63 \times 0.63$, or 25 percent. The odds against cashing, a mild 3–1. What do handicappers think of 3–1 odds when betting an exotic wager that often pays extremely well?

The sixth was The Californian (Gr. 1), a $250,000-added nine-furlong preliminary to Hollywood Park's signature stakes, the $750,000-added Hollywood Gold Cup. The favorite would be the popular gelding Best Pal, a horse I deliberately did not include. Now seven, Best Pal had been inconsistent and therefore unreliable for the past three seasons. My line was 4–1. I knew Best Pal would run as a serious underlay. He went favored at 3–2. Barry would approve.

My Pick 3 covered eighteen combinations. The A and B contenders are secondary to this discussion, except that I usually bet $5 tickets on the A combinations, $1 tickets on the B combinations, and the standard $3 ticket on any A-B combinations. Four A combinations ($20), one B combination ($1), and 13 A-B combinations amounted to a $62 investment.

At 3–1 odds against, the break-even point would be $248. The Pick 3 returned no less than $605.40, quite a healthy overlay.

Using Barry's strategy, I might not have scored. Employing the same probability estimates:

Ashtabula (0.25) × Welcome Day (0.15) × Concern (0.28) = 0.01, or odds of 99–1 against winning

A $3 ticket (one combination) would need a fair return of $300. Even though Best Pal would be seriously overbet, the key consideration, with Concern and Ashtabula as firm second choices in races six and four, I might have passed on this particular combination, which won. No doubt I would have combined Ashtabula with Tossofthecoin and Let's Be Curious in the sixth, confident the payoff would overcompensate me for the reduced probability of winning. I would not have felt as confident about the generosity of the second choices in combination. I might have abstained.

Using the morning lines and his own betting lines to estimate the risks and rewards, Barry might be quick to assert he would have played. I don't know. My estimates of the probable payoffs were less technical, more intuitive, and therefore not as precise. I'm less comfortable at times with evaluating the sum of the parts.

Barry and I volleyed back and forth on the strengths and weaknesses of the strategies repeatedly. I described a number of refinements I had discovered to bolster the approach. I emphasized a goal is to stay alive, to continue the roll. Losing a race interrupts the flow of events unpleasantly. Losing the fourth or seventh races, in particular, sacrifices five races in the nine-race roll. As I advised Barry, I'll cover shaky favorites I might not otherwise tolerate to stay in the roll. I sometimes accept an odds-on favorite that has been seriously overbet in the fourth or seventh.

Barry remained unmoved and insistent about eliminating the specific combinations that will underpay. He described numerous simulations that I discounted in favor of my whole-and-parts paradigm. Barry demanded proof. I recounted my experience, which Barry rejected.

Dick Mitchell joined us at the lunch table and he became a paragon of patience as the discussion proceeded rather fruitlessly. After approximately two hours, anxious now to prevail, I softened my stance to concede that whether the Pick 3 combinations in their entirety were actually greater or less than the sum of the parts, like so many parimutuel relationships, was ultimately an empirical question. Handicappers would be forced to experiment for a couple of seasons and examine the data.

Following the long debate, Barry was equally exasperated with me. In a rare grudging concession, he turned to Mitchell, the authentic mathematician.

"Dick, you've been listening to this," said Barry. "Which of us is right?"

"Well, Jim's saying if you combine all the contenders in each leg and limit play to the overlay situations, you'll win.

"Barry's saying if you combine each contender with each other contender, and eliminate the probable underlay combinations, you'll win.

"You're both correct."

REFORM

Certain irregularities, falsehoods, and assaults against the people at the races cry out for reform. But reform is slow, or it's nonexistent. Instead of correcting the problems that do serious and irreparable damage to the bettors, track managers have been more or less content with announcements, solemnly prepared and delivered, that the four-horse in the seventh race will be two pounds overweight.

What do the lawyers say? The certified public accountants, what do they advise? The International Association of State Racing Commissioners, what does that august body think?

Is there a chief executive officer or a track president whose sense of decorum, fair play, and justice is not offended and aroused by the list of grievances to be submitted? Or has contempt for the bettors become so deeply, irretrievably entrenched that no matter the egregiousness of the neglect or offense, the customers can just drop dead.

The list of grievances is topped, as it should be, by a number of pari-mutuel betting irregularities that defy the imagination. Entitled to a truly run race and a fair shake, too often the bettors receive neither. It's convenient to keep in mind, too, that, except for the horses themselves, the bettors pay for everything, from the regulatory body's taxes, to the executives' salaries, to the horsemen's purses.

BETTING IRREGULARITIES

On opening day during Oak Tree at Santa Anita, 1994, an announcement suddenly comes over the public address system while the horses are warming up for the fifth race:

"Ladies and gentlemen, there is a late scratch in today's eighth race. Scratch Number Nine. Number Nine has been scratched from the eighth race."

Except that a totalizator operator misinterpreted the message. He thought No. 9 had been scratched from the fifth race. So even as No.

142

9 in the fifth (Caesour) was warming up on the track, the tote operator removed No. 9 from the odds board.

Between the eight- and five-minute marks prior to the race, No. 9 was officially off the board for approximately two and one-half minutes. When the error was recognized, No. 9 was reinstated on the tote. No announcement was made!

During the off-on interim, the biggest bettor at Santa Anita walked to the window and asked for $10,000 to win on No. 9. He was told No. 9 was scratched. So he bet the same amount on No. 7.

After making his wager, the High Roller walked to the bar and ordered a drink. He never became aware that No. 9 had not been scratched after all, was indeed running, and was now bettable.

Naturally, Caesour, No. 9, won. A 3–1 contender on the morning line, the horse paid $11 even, or 9–2.

Not personally involved in the wagering, I was certain all bets would be canceled and all monies returned to the bettors. No announcement; nothing!

The next afternoon I heard about the High Roller's fate, but could hardly believe the story. The snafu had cost the bettor $45,000 in profit, not to mention the $10,000 he had sacrificed on No. 7.

A few days later I encountered the High Roller, a personal acquaintance. I could not resist.

"Is it true you attempted to bet ten thousand dollars on Caesour on opening day and were informed by the teller the horse had been scratched? That you bet the same money on the seven instead, went to the bar, and were never advised your horse had not been scratched?"

"It's a true story," said the High Roller, "except for the amount. I wanted to bet ten thousand five hundred dollars."

"That's an incredible experience. You lost more than fifty-five thousand dollars. How do you feel about this incident?"

The man turned sideways, cocked his head, threw up his arms, and replied with resignation, "They could have made an announcement!"

In the aftermath the usual accounts were published, followed by the inevitable palliative that the California Horse Racing Board was investigating. The *Daily Racing Form* published the following account (Oct. 8, 1994):

Phantom horse is a winner

SANTA ANITA PARK, Calif. – The Oak Tree Racing Association set a dubious opening-day record of sorts Wednesday when a horse, believed to be scratched for two and a half minutes, reappeared on the tote board and won the fifth race.

 Many fans were angered over the incident, an apparent human error, when Caesour won a $47,000 allowance race transferred from the turf to the main track. The horse's number, 9, went blank on the board from roughly eight to five minutes before the race was run, leading many bettors to presume the horse must have been scratched, although he was in the post parade and no such announcement was made.

"The mistake was due to a tote operator error," said George Haines II, director of the pari-mutuel department. "Number nine was inadvertently scratched in the fifth race instead of number nine in the eighth race. The number was off the board for two and a half minutes before the error was discovered at the same time by the tote room and the stewards."

Caesour, 3-1 in the morning line, paid $11 to win. The California Horse Racing Board is investigating. *--Steve Schuelein*

When questioned, Santa Anita management regretted the error, but emphasized the track could not take responsibility for any wagering mishaps.

Why not? Whose responsibility was it? The bettors'? Of course not. Or the track's?

It was the track's mistake, however inadvertent, and the track's responsibility was definite, acute, and to the bettors. Nobody can possibly imagine otherwise. When an announcement was not forthcoming, and the betting period not extended, which sensible decision makers would have arranged, all bets should have been canceled and all monies returned to the bettors. Or No. 9 should have been scratched.

A few weeks later I asked the High Roller if his gigantic bet had been returned. "Of course not." He sighed, not happily. Any Las Vegas casino would have treated him with greater respect.

The outcome of the Racing Board's investigation eludes me. Perhaps the tote operator was sanctioned. Track management might have been sanctioned and fined severely, but were they?

In the end, as usual, the bettors suffered.

Earlier in 1994 at Santa Anita, in the San Antonio Stakes, the track's major prep to the million-dollar Santa Anita Handicap, and a terrific betting event featuring a gateful of outstanding handicap horses, a shipper from northern California named Slew of Damascus broke through the starting gate, ran off, and was scratched.

After a brief delay the gates were sprung and the field was dispatched. The 8–5 favorite, Best Pal, finished out of the money.

The next afternoon I received a distress call from Bill Arsenault, a Beverly Hills CPA who bets substantial amounts on the horses. Arsenault likes the Pick 6, especially the carryovers, of which a six-figure amount had graced the exotic pool on the day of the San Antonio Stakes.

"Were you at the track yesterday?" Bill began.

I was.

"I absolutely loved Slew of Damascus in the San Antonio," he continued. "I singled the horse in the Pick Six and the Pick Three for substantial money."

"I hated Best Pal. . . . I'm so pissed. That goddamned rule [bleep] . . . You won't see me at Santa Anita for a long time. . . ."

The blasphemous rule that ruined Arsenault holds that late scratches in Pick 6 and Pick 3 wagering will automatically be transferred to the betting favorite. It's a stupid, larcenous, contemptuous regulation that buries the serial bettors under favorites they detest.

Slew of Damascus was 10–1. Not only that, Arsenault's bets had been predicated, to a significant degree, upon Best Pal's paltry odds. He was betting against the favorite, which he ends up backing inadvertently, due to track error. Through no fault or intent of his own, Arsenault's money is shifted to a horse he doesn't want. He has no control.

What irritated Arsenault most (me, too) was that horses had been breaking through Santa Anita's starting gate at an alarming rate (virtually every other day) for the past several seasons. He cursed the track and its starting crew.

Occasionally a track executive will be pinned on the despicable unfairness of the scratch rule by one of his regular customers. It's even-money the executive will exacerbate the matter and alienate his customer further by offering a reaction amazingly naive, such as, "Well, you get the favorite, and those favorites win one out of three. Nobody ever yells when the favorites win."

The idea that racing's customers have the right to play the horses they like, or that a bettor's purpose might be to bet against an overbet favorite such as Best Pal, without being penalized, not only has been lost but also gets devalued by the very executives entrusted to provide the adequate protections.

If a late scratch occurs at the gate, on the track, in the paddock, or for any reason, what should be done in regard to serial bets that have already been placed? Should racing customers ask a class of grade-school children what would be fair, and compare those responses to the typical comments of track executives?

To be sure, all bets involving the scratched horses should be returned to the bettors. Or consolation payoffs should be calculated, as is done with daily doubles. Can any adult of the slightest maturity, intelligence, or worldliness believe otherwise? Why is it so difficult for track management to do the right thing?

When his bets in the Pick 6 and Pick 3 pools were transferred to Best Pal, Bill Arsenault lost $2,000. He would prefer to have his pockets picked. But, other than Arsenault, who cares?

In a partial exercise of racetrack reform, this despicable regulation, which had sat undisturbed on California's books for years, was amended during spring 1995 at Hollywood Park. In Pick 6 wagering, bet cards now allow bettors to select an alternate horse in each leg, in anticipation of late scratches. If bettors fail to identify an alternate, and late scratches occur, the money is still shifted to the favorite.

Why isn't the money returned to the bettors, where it belongs?

Even so, as this is composed, if late scratches occur, Pick 3 bettors are still expected to suffer the larcenous indignity of having their money transferred to the favorites they usually despise. Why Pick 6 bettors have been protected, but Pick 3 bettors ignored, has been assigned to complications with the software. Reform is on the way, apparently, as soon as the computer programs can be developed. In the meantime it's legal larceny, but that's okay. Who cares?

Another injustice occurs in Pick 3 wagering whenever dead-heats occur. Regardless of odds or the number of combination tickets sold on each horse, Pick 3 bets are pooled and divided equally, not proportionately. A bettor backing a 6–1 shot gets paid an amount equal to the bettor backing a 9–5 favorite, even though far fewer tickets have been sold encompassing the 6–1 shot. Is that pari-mutuel wagering? The bettor holding the tickets on the 6–1 horse has been cheated.

It happened to me on a recent Sunday at Hollywood Park. I was fortunate enough to complete a Pick 3 in the eighth race to a 6–1 overlay, but unfortunate enough to touch the wire at the exact moment the 9–5 favorite touched. The payoffs were blatantly unfair:

		Odds
6th Race	Cee Ghee (5)	1.00–1
7th Race	Constant Craving (4)	8.80–1
8th Race	Journalism (4)	1.90–1
	Seahawk Gold (1)	6.90–1
	Pick 3 5-4-1	$184.80
	Pick 3 5-4-4	$184.80

Compare the Pick 3 payoffs with the exactas coupling the dead-heat winners Journalism and Seahawk Gold:

Exacta 4-1	$16.00	
1-4	$20.00	

The 25 percent difference reflects the fact that more combinations were sold coupling Journalism on top of Seahawk Gold. The exacta payoffs are accurate. The same dualities exist in the Pick 3 pools. Why the bogus payoffs?

But other than the bettors being fleeced, who cares?

When horses break through the starting gate prior to a race's start, their chances of winning nose-dive to ground zero. Instead of the horse being scratched automatically, and the bets refunded, the horses are quickly reloaded, and sent to their demise. The helpless bettors are again expected to suffer the consequences.

A five-minute delay would ameliorate the problem, but that is considered unfair to the horses already loaded, and it would be annoying to the impatient bettors who have placed their money on the other horses. No delay, or a short artificial delay, is standard operating procedure. That the circumstance is highly unfair to the backers of the horse breaking through the gate is never seriously contemplated.

Once more the tracks refuse to take responsibility for their actions, preferring to jab the bettors in the pocketbook. Horses that break through the starting gate should be scratched. If the race is a stakes, and owners want their horses to run regardless, fine. Let the breakers run as nonwagering interests and give the bettors their money back. Is that a novel notion?

The betting irregularities are unacceptable and indefensible. Any track executive who does not believe that reform is mandatory, or that serial bets nullified by late scratches should not be refunded, does not belong at the racetrack.

One additional comment on the desired pari-mutuel reforms. A certain kind of track executive, somewhat defunct in the aforementioned attributes of maturity, intelligence, and worldliness, imagines that money refunded, however appropriate and just, amounts to revenue lost.

The opposite is closer to the truth. Refunded bets are almost immediately and entirely churned. More importantly, the new bets have a far greater chance of becoming successful. That stimulates a greater churn.

Much more importantly, the bettor has been properly served. That bettor is a more satisfied customer. He returns more often, bets more, and contributes significantly more action to the churn. Goodwill grows. When Santa Anita took Bill Arsenault's $2,000 worth of bets and stuck them on Best Pal in the 1994 San Antonio Stakes, the track lost Arsenault, a good customer, for the season, and maybe longer.

If horses break through the gates, but are reloaded as quickly as possible, and sent to a premature fate, the bets having not been refunded, nobody wins, including the track. The customer is pissed, rightfully so, and feels abused. Many have not come back.

THE STEWARDS

What can handicappers say about the stewards? Nothing positive, unfortunately. In more than two decades of playing the races, I have
never heard a regular handicapper praise, commend, or endorse the
performance of the stewards. That's a felonious indictment.

The criticism has not been contained to moments of heat and pas-
sion, while the inquiry sign is flashing and the bettors nervously await
the stewards' ruling. It's leveled in quiet, measured, rational conversations as well, at restaurants, at parties, at meetings, in seminars. Not
only handicappers level the worst charges. Owners, trainers, jockeys,
and racetrack officials consistently complain about the stewards. It's
no overstatement to assert that virtually no one having a legitimate
point of view believes racing's stewards are doing a good job.

In southern California, when the inquiry sign flashes, and regardless of the incident, no one, and I mean not anybody, knows what the
stewards will do until they do it. That's because the same incidents
have been treated so inconsistently from time to time and from situation to situation. For the same and similar incidents, some horses are
punished and some horses are cleared. The constant variation and contradiction applies to jockey tactics as well. The inconsistency is so rampant, and so deeply embedded in the collective psyche at the racetrack,
that the bettors' only pragmatic reaction to the inquiry sign is to keep
their fingers crossed.

Certain disqualifications just enrage the bettors. The kind that
have been systematically ignored. Recently at Hollywood Park the inquiry sign flashed and the bettors' attention was directed to the run
toward the clubhouse turn. Replays showed no bumping and no perceptible movement that tightened traffic, no bearing out, and no
crossing over. The winner was nevertheless disqualified for coming
over and taking another horse's path. As long as eight weeks later a
handicapper assured me it was the worst call he had ever seen.

What disgusts handicappers is that so many similar incidents are
rarely even reviewed. Anybody who has played the game for a time
not only knows that but also can recall several similar incidents that
have caused much more trouble, yet winners were allowed to stand.

At one Oak Tree meeting several years ago inquiries that were not called by the stewards were called by jockeys Shoemaker, Pincay, McCarron, Delahoussaye, and other leaders. Is that a case of negligence?

In recent seasons in southern California a rash of inquiries have involved horses and jockeys attempting to come between horses in the late stages. To a degree, the incidents tend to feed off one another. The stewards have tended to disqualify one of the lead horses for bearing in or coming out, presumptively blocking the charging horse's path, and causing the oncomer interference that was judged to have robbed the horse of his rightful position. The counterpoint holds that the rallying horse had no rightful path to begin with. Horse and jockey thereby caused their own trouble by attempting to find a hole that was simply not there.

The most notorious incident of this kind occurred in the million-dollar 1993 Santa Anita Handicap (Gr. 1), won ostensibly by The Wicked North by seven open lengths in a brilliant display. The inquiry sign flashed.

The replay showed jockey Alex Solis on a D. Wayne Lukas long shot attempting to come between The Wicked North and a horse on the rail path in the upper stretch. Coming off the far turn, and now changing leads, The Wicked North had moved barely, almost imperceptibly to the inside, just as Solis and the Lukas long shot had attempted to shoot between horses. Not enough room could be found, and Solis took up.

When the Lukas long shot was nodded out of third at the wire, the stewards ruled that the incident in the upper stretch had cost Lukas third place. They blamed The Wicked North and jockey Kent Desormeaux, and took the winner down. Desormeaux was enraged and so was practically everybody else, not merely the bettors backing The Wicked North, but just about anybody having a well-modulated sense of fair play. The angry citizens were correct. This was a desperately weak call, reflecting not only a lack of competence but astonishingly poor judgment.

The ruling cost The Wicked North, who was not yet a Grade 1 winner, and who had seemingly come off the far turn and changed leads in a natural movement similar to practically every rallying horse in any race, the winner's share of a million-dollar purse (55 percent), the Grade 1 title, his well-deserved stature as the leading handicap horse in America, and several million dollars in breeding value.

In a remarkable show of calm and restraint, trainer David Bernstein bit the bullet and said, "We'll get them next time."

An incensed Kent Desormeaux insisted that his horse could not have moved more than "three inches," that any movement that occurred was natural and barely perceptible, that jockey Solis should not have been there in the first place and would not have been except for the million-dollar purse, and that by any rational standard the order of finish should have been allowed to stand.

If Solis and the Lukas long shot had finished third instead of fourth, the stewards would not have made the change, ruling instead the incident had not affected the order of finish. The supposition that the incident had altered the order of finish, in my judgment, is absurd and readily countermanded. Suppose the Lukas horse had driven between horses successfully, struggled with The Wicked North until the sixteenth pole, and tired badly from the effort, now finishing seventh? By that account the incident might have aided the horse's actual finish. It's hypothetical, but the point to be stressed is that no steward can infer from an incident in the upper stretch how the stretch drive and order of finish were affected. That's supposition.

I had placed no bets on the Santa Anita Handicap, but the incident took me back fifteen years to the ninth race one day at Del Mar, a similar incident in the upper stretch, but a different outcome, and my first bad brush with the stewards' rulings. My good thing held a small advantage when a horse rallying off the far turn came out two lanes and bumped him off stride. My guy regained his stride in a few jumps but now was forced to chase after the other horse, who had gained a half-length advantage. They ran together to the wire. My horse lost by a head. The inquiry sign flashed.

The replay showed the bumping incident clearly. To my surprise, and chagrin, the stewards allowed the finish to stand. They ruled the incident did not affect the order of finish. I was as incensed as Desormeaux on The Wicked North. My horse had been 8–1. How could the stewards say the incident, an obvious foul, did not affect the order of finish? How did they know that? It was a head! I thought the ruling patently stupid. I remember walking around in small semicircles as the crowd left the premises, as if searching for justice, or validation, or maybe support. That was long, long ago. I have long since learned not to agonize about the stewards' rulings, regardless of their merit or disrepute.

The inconsistent rulings, the contradictory judgments, the occasional glaring example of incompetence (at Saratoga several seasons ago the stewards actually disqualified the wrong horse), all the countless misgivings can be traced to a lack of training, certification, and supervised experience.

In southern California, as matters stand, fouls might occur and be officially observed, but the stewards might allow the finish to stand. When this happens, which is regularly, one of three explanations are typically presented to the bettors:

1.   The incident did not warrant a disqualification.
2.   The incident did not affect the order of finish.
3.   Both horses contributed to the incident.

Only the first explanation merits support, although the public interest would surely be much better served if in place of the vague, nondescript statement that sounds suspiciously like a cop-out, the stewards described the incident in some detail and characterized it as minor, inadvertent, unclear, or some combination of the above. The stewards need sufficient flexibility to distinguish between flagrant fouls, serious fouls, and minor infractions. The solution cannot be a set of rigid rules to be applied technically to all incidents at all times.

The second explanation requires inferences the stewards are not capable of drawing, except perhaps in a small number of obvious situations near the finish line that would gather a large agreeable consensus. In truth the stewards cannot judge with any acceptable degree of probability whether the bumping, or blocking, or coming over, or bearing out did or did not alter the order of finish.

If the lead horse in the stretch drifts out by a lane or two, and without bumping it or blocking its path intimidates another horse, causing that horse to slow its run or to refuse to try harder, has that incident affected the order of finish? Maybe, and maybe not. Is that a foul? Either it is or it isn't. Apply the relevant standards. It's presumptuous for stewards to imagine they can tell whether the several and various incidents that occur have altered the order of finish. That's supposition. The sport would serve its public well by stopping the practice.

The third explanation is facile, only occasionally true, and often a cop-out. When two or more horses are bumping, invariably one of them has instigated the bumping match. The other horse has been hit, crowded, knocked off stride, or pushed in or out, and reacts, sometimes shifting its position and bumping back. The instigator has been at fault, not both horses, just as surely as I am at fault if, without warning, I punch you in the face and you slug me back.

As almost everybody criticizes the stewards, and rather harshly, it's curious why no meaningful efforts at reform have been waged. In a nutshell it's inertia, neglect, and a lack of concern on the part of institutional forces, who have no regard for the plight of the bettors.

But owners also suffer the consequences of the stewards' rulings, sometimes severely, and this group, the so-called kings, does matter. It's hardly a coincidence that stewards' rulings are contested only when owners have become so upset by the experience of unfairness that they are motivated to go to court. If a bungled decision has deprived a bettor of a Pick 6, so what? But if the same decision has deprived the owner of a stakes race having relatively high prestige and consequence, that's a cause for taking action. The incidence of court proceedings has been kept low, not because owners do not become as furious as bettors but because stewards' inquiries occur less frequently in major stakes races and ambiguous disqualifications even less frequently.

By large consensus the Kentucky Derby is the roughest race in America. The jockeys say so, and anyone watching on television can testify that the typical run to the clubhouse turn amounts to a stampede and a rodeo ride. The race and ride remain rugged all the way. In the history of the hallowed race, there has been exactly one disqualification, and that did not involve the winner, the second horse, or the third horse. I have watched the race closely twenty-five times and do not recall even a second inquiry. Is it perhaps because any major change in the order of finish that mattered to owners' economic lives would be reviewed in a court of law?

A meaningful effort at reform might be happening now. As a result of squabbles with trainers about representation on a variety of issues, horse owners in southern California formed their own organization in 1993, the Thoroughbred Owners of California (TOC). A leading item

on the TOC's agenda has been the training, certification, and assign-
ment of stewards. All handicappers should rejoice.

The deficiencies of the current practice are easily enumerated and,
assuming a willingness to act, just as easily corrected. They are as follows:

- Stewards are not qualified to perform their duties.
- Adequate training and certification programs do not exist.
- Standards for guiding stewards' rulings as to disqualifications
  either do not exist or are inadequately formulated.
- Public accountability as to individual stewards' decisions and
  judgments is lacking.

Jockeys obviously have a basis in experience for becoming racetrack stewards, but many of the other political appointments are ridiculous. Several appointees will be despairingly dense about
Thoroughbred racing, completely unfamiliar and inexperienced with
the sport, not to mention the game. Some may not know what a furlong or an exacta is. Several do not have a clue about observing a horse
race intelligently. Meaningful reform gets under way by appointing as
stewards people with some basis in experience for performing the role.

Training and certification programs should follow the appointments. These would have a curriculum, a sequence of instruction, and
standards for completion. A tenure track of two to three years might
be part of the certification process. Tenure would extend a number of
years, not a lifetime. During the probationary period the candidates'
work would be supervised and reviewed, and appointees might be ro-
tated among several tracks on the circuit or within the region. Tenure
would be earned, not bestowed.

Finally, public accountability is essential. Bettors have a right to
become aware of the decisions of individual stewards regarding disqualifications or no change. Unanimous decisions and split decisions
would become public knowledge and so would the voting records of
each steward. Public accountability would mean individual stewards
would accumulate public reputations, just as referees and umpires do,
which is healthy procedure.

An institution that accepts the public's money as wagers on its
events, but will not accept public accountability regarding official de-

cisions that affect the distribution of that money, does not deserve the public's trust or respect, and will not receive it.

Stewards' decisions impact the redistribution of millions of dollars of the public's wagering dollars year after year. The current climate of disrepute and disrespect for those official decisions should be intolerable to anyone who cares, and can be changed.

The bettors care, but they are powerless to act, except by withholding their wagers. No estimates exist as to how many customers and how many wagering dollars a tortured history of inept stewards' decisions has cost the game, but the numbers cannot be insignificant.

SMALL FIELDS

If betting irregularities and stewards' rulings qualify as institutional problems begging reform, other nagging problems are merely administrative. The requisite reforms might be administered quickly, almost overnight, so to speak, assuming the will to change. The worst of these by a wide margin is the preponderance of small fields, notably in nonclaiming races, especially the richer stakes.

Almost everyone who is not an owner or trainer cites small fields as a nasty problem having a severely negative impact on the sport, so why hasn't the situation been solved? Because the best solution would require a reduction in racing days and stakes races, and that conflicts, at least presumptively so, with the economic interests of racetracks and horse owners.

The economic conflict is much more imagined than real. A reduction in racing days and races would serve everyone's long-term financial interests because it would improve the long-term health of the sport. In other words, less is more. Too bad so many people reside in the short term.

Although the distaste for small fields has grown pervasive, how many racing people really appreciate how debilitating the problem has become? The two most dire consequences of the phenomenon have not been much discussed.

One, the small fields present the bettors with too many underlays.

Racetrack executives should understand once and for all time that their customers do not lose too much money and will not be forced to quit the game because they play too many races (full-card simulcasting has begun to demonstrate the point convincingly), or too many exotics. They lose too much and too often because they play too many underlays.

Underlays are overbet horses. The horses' chances are not as good as the odds suggest, setting the table for an unfair payoff. Even when the underlays win, the bettors lose, a reality apparently difficult for many to grasp. Small fields have increased the supply of underlays at most tracks tremendously, and that more than anything else has been a disastrous development for racing's customers.

Second, small fields have cheapened the sport to the point where too many overnight races are bad races and a Grade 1 stakes title may not mean anything special.

With so many racing days and so many stakes races available to horsemen, the oversupply of races has been accompanied by a corresponding decline in the quality of the competition. Even Grade 1 races go begging, if a superstar or clear-cut division leader has been entered.

On the day before the 1995 Belmont Stakes, which itself was a sorry rendition resulting in the slowest running time in a quarter century, Belmont Park's Grade 1 Mother Goose Stakes, second leg of New York's Triple Tiara for 3YO fillies, featured Serena's Song and six plugs. So Serena's Song went to the gate at 1–20, won by making the course, and paid $2.10. Is anybody cheering?

Trainer Wayne Lukas implored racing fans to travel to Belmont Park and watch his star filly perform, but nobody cared. It happens now at every major track (Churchill Downs and Gulfstream Park excepted) several times a season. If track officials are willing to pay that price for an oversupply of racing days and so many stakes opportunities, that's too big a price to pay.

Consider southern California, where the best stakes racing and some of the most intense overnight racing occur. The program during winter at Santa Anita has declined to the point that many of the cards are no longer recognizable as major-league racing. Hollywood Park and Del Mar have been injured almost as badly. Several of the weekday cards are just awful.

The situation can be readily reversed. If Santa Anita and Hollywood Park eliminated five racing days each and Del Mar eliminated two, the reduction amounts to 180 races. That eliminates 150 cheaper races and a few superfluous stakes. Fields would be fuller, quality better. No revenue would be sacrificed, as full-card simulcasting would supplant the live racing on dark days and purse monies would be redistributed. A deteriorating situation would improve.

If the reforms impressed, and further reductions were entertained, the situation should improve even more, perhaps dramatically. Fuller fields. Better races. Grateful customers.

In any event, where small fields remain problematic, the future depends absolutely on an intelligent mix of live racing and full-card simulcasting, notably less of the former and more of the latter.

In the meantime, other readily available incentives might be used to improve the size and quality of the nonclaiming fields, certainly the major stakes. In spring of 1995, Maryland officials announced that a purse supplement of 40 percent would be attached to any race having nine horses or more. Purse supplements represent one incentive for enhancing field size.

Why shouldn't the purses of stakes races be indexed according to the size of the field? The standard field size might be defined as eight. A field of seven competes for a smaller purse, a field of six for an even smaller purse, a field of five still smaller. A field of nine competes for a greater purse, a field of ten for an even greater purse, and eleven or twelve still greater.

A helpless victim of the small fields and the proliferation of stakes has been the allowance race. A stakes alternative somewhere else or even the presence of an authentically talented horse among the entries means the allowance race either will not fill or will fill with six starters, one or two probably entered at the urging of the racing secretary, and one of which might be scratched late in the morning of race day. It's a pitiful situation.

At many tracks, for ages 3up, perhaps an allowance win or equivalent should be prerequisite to entry in a graded stakes. Maybe 3YOs should be required to win two allowance races (or equivalents) before they may enter a Grade 1 or Grade 2 event.

If horsemen refuse these innovations, perhaps all but a core of allowance races should be eliminated altogether. Stakes races have overwhelmed the allowances already. Too many of the races do not fill. Why not institutionalize the general practice of rushing horses into stakes? Stakes racing has been standard fare among better horses in

Europe. Allowance races appear infrequently there. Should U.S. racing adapt that practice?

Racing's annihilation of the small field has been too long overdue. Its consequences have wreaked misery, and they could become ruinous. Bettors despise small, noncompetitive fields, and at last racetracks do too. Enlightened trainers and owners might support the eradication of small fields. Like the advent of simulcasting, cross-track betting, and full-card simulcasting, innovations horsemen instinctively distrusted, the elimination of the small field will enhance horsemen's financial interests much more than horsemen themselves realize.

What good does it do a journeyman trainer to grab a minor share of a nonclaiming purse in a five-horse field while risking the long-term health of the sport?

LATE SCRATCHES

Exactly one racing day before the bet cards allowing Pick 6 bettors to select an alternate in each leg took effect at Hollywood Park, with a splendid carryover spicing the pool, approximately five late scratches were announced after the Pick 6 betting had begun. Bobby Frankel scratched his horse in the first leg approximately five minutes before that race was scheduled to be run. No delay.

In close pursuit of the small fields, the most detestable facet of contemporary racing is late scratches. These come in bundles. They have been permitted wholesale for practical reasons, and horsemen have been poised and pleased to abuse the privilege. Once more the bettors are left to endure the consequences.

The euphemism is conditional entries. Horsemen are permitted to scratch out late from a field they have entered, provided they have identified a future race they intend to enter instead. It's a nonsensical arrangement that does not work as intended and, in its practical effects, condones the habit of horsemen to do exactly as they please whenever they want.

If trainers do not like the post position, they scratch.

If they do not like the probable pace, they scratch.

If they do not want to compete against another horse in the field, they scratch.

The idea that horsemen have picked a similar or comparable spot, and will run back soon, is a romantic interlude. They may, and they may not. Stakes races have become a favorite prey. Horsemen who decide they do not care to run just do not run.

Racing secretaries capitulate, as if on cue. Any reflection that numerous customers may have ventured to the track to bet on a particular contender, or to watch an appealing stakes competition, never occurs to them. Any reference that the track's regular handicappers may have spent hours studying the past performances and conducting pace analyses will be met with a smirk.

At Saratoga, in 1994, the persistent rains and the experimental elimination of also-eligible lists resulted in a torrent of late scratches that simply ruined the meet, at least for many loyal handicappers who patronize the spa as if it were a shrine. The late scratches were so plentiful and so brazenly imposed on the faithful that not a few veteran handicappers, including Andrew Beyer, swore they would not return to Saratoga.

In southern California several trainers practice the late-declaration game admirably, but a special award has to be reserved for Bobby Frankel. He's the most notorious late scratcher in the country, and Frankel enters lots of horses. In Frankel's defense he's simply playing the hand he has been given, and his reputation for manipulating his horses and the condition books has been well deserved. Frankel also cares about himself and his owners, and let the bettors be damned, an understandable if lamentable attitude.

The racing officials having considerable responsibility for the integrity of the entries can be provided no similar defense. In the spirit of reform, one can imagine a scene in the racing office at Santa Anita during opening week:

The first time Frankel wants to scratch out late because he feels like it, the director of racing tells Bobby how much they enjoy having him at Santa Anita and how much his stable means to the attractiveness of the program, but reminds him they would also like to have him stabled in New York or in Kentucky. Regardless, Frankel's not about to scratch out late again on some limp pretense.

Bobby would hate the experience with a vengeance, and the confrontation between Frankel and the director of racing would escalate to a personal and public crescendo, but the late scratches would cease. Other common violators would fall compliantly into line.

In any event, the abundant late scratches have to stop. If horses have been entered, they are intended to race, and can be withdrawn only on a veterinarian's legitimate excuse. If conditional entries are used, fine. Final scratches must nonetheless be declared prior to the printing of the official program. Horsemen can beat that deadline.

It's a simple reform, having the extra-added attraction that it's wonderfully consistent with the rules of racing.

THE SIMULCASTS

In the final days before the conclusion of its 1995 winter season, Santa Anita simulcast a couple of minor weekday stakes, one a day, from Keeneland and from the Racing Festival of the South at Oaklawn Park. Very good. Except that the simulcasts were scheduled between the second and third races on the local cards and were weighted down with a half-hour interval between each race.

Fifteen minutes would have been slightly too long. Thirty minutes downtime—an hour elapsed between the second and third—became an unadulterated drag. In the sections nearest to me, nobody, not anybody I saw, was preoccupied with studying the simulcast past performances or hurrying to bet. People were just waiting. Many were unmistakably bored.

That's not the idea. A positive advantage of simulcasting is a reduction in downtime. As simulcasts proliferate and full-card simulcasting takes its foothold, many tracks struggle with the video presentations on the schedule. To be steadfastly avoided are inordinate delays. Twelve minutes or thereabouts between races will be enough. Concurrent races, as in Las Vegas race books, are not particularly bothersome. Handicappers who want to bet on simulcast races will be prepared to do so. Casual customers do not care enough, and the great majority do not wish to be invited to wait an extra half hour so that races they would just as soon disregard can be accommodated.

Another consideration for simulcast bettors is seating and work space. As full-card simulcasting evolves to dominate a day at the races, the handicapper's need for comfortable seating and work space has intensified.

Hollywood Park has planned for a simulcasting future as well or better than any major track. Ample seating with work space has been provided in every section of the plant. The Player's Club in the club-house qualifies as a model environment. Grandstanders can find seating with work space, as can customers on the aprons, both in the grandstand and in the clubhouse areas.

A tour of Hollywood Park on an extensive simulcast day finds the seats filled and the customers at work. It's a refreshing sight. Simulcast handicappers also like to check the horses and the odds and probables. On both counts, Santa Anita's production in-house soars, although the race analysis leaves a lot to be desired and an exacta matrix board is overdue.

Several other tracks provide impressively strong analysis, not infrequently conducted by women, most impressively by Jenny Ohrenstein at Philadelphia Park, and by Jan Rushton in New York.

The television production and analysis are equally important to simulcast bettors, who will be unfamiliar with the horses, the trainers, and the track surfaces. As racetracks in the late nineties and beyond will be competing for bettors primarily on the quality of their signals and racing programs, it will pay to allocate the necessary resources to both.

THE NYRA REFORMS

The most interesting reform movement in modern racing began when Kenny Noe was installed as NYRA's president in 1994 and was accelerated later that year when Steven Crist was named director of communications and development, a job description that has been defined by more than a half-dozen hats.

Noe undertook an unprecedented corporate restructuring with perennial critic Crist, and Crist undertook to develop and implement a program of change that had as its primary audience the bettors.

The NYRA reformers, it must be acknowledged, began with the same and not-to-be-underestimated advantage as the proven baseball manager who takes over a formerly impressive division leader now in disarray and spiraling toward the cellar. Events cannot get much worse.

As Noe and Crist prepared to launch, a deteriorating situation at the NYRA tracks presented them with so many obstacles that any efforts at reform might be too late:

- The state legislature and the NYRA had been at war for years.
- Crowds at Belmont Park during spring and fall had dwindled to between six thousand and seven thousand live ones.
- Savvy New York handicappers had preferred the simulcast programs at the Meadowlands, in New Jersey.
- The NYRA's simulcast policy had to be considered the worst in the nation, surpassing California's passivity and neglect.
- Some long-term loyal stables had begun to depart for Kentucky, and several others were thinking about it.
- Stakes horses in the East and Middle Atlantic States that formerly looked to New York for added-money opportunities were increasingly looking toward Kentucky and Florida.
- Small, unattractive fields were multiplying in kind and number.
- The New York label no longer meant quality racing, most notably to simulcast bettors throughout the country.
- New York betting pools could not be co-mingled with the betting in Las Vegas and Atlantic City.
- Worst of all, New York City OTB Corporation still was there, in all its ugly personifications.

From these depths some improvement was practically guaranteed. Nonetheless expectations were exceeded. In the seven months between December 1994 and June 1995, the following reforms were implemented:

- Free parking and discounted admission were offered to customers during the winter season.
- Home betting was introduced on Long Island and at New York City OTB.
- A five-day race week replaced an onerous six-day race week.
- The take-out on straight wagers was reduced by 2 percent, but the take-out on exotic wagers was increased by 3 percent, a dubious trade-off that will cost the bettors millions, which the NYRA insists it needs immediately for capital improvements.
- Simulcast wagers in Las Vegas and Atlantic City were co-mingled at last with the New York pools.
- A program of fan education was introduced.
- Lasix was approved.
- Prices of hot dogs, beer, sodas, and other concessions were reduced dramatically.
- Full-card simulcasting from Gulfstream Park replaced the ab-

breviated five-race program from Florida in 1994; Santa Anita was also imported during winter, a first.

The take-out trade-off aside, that's a gaggle of reforms that will benefit the bettors and was characterized most of all by its speed. Because the NYRA does not own or manage its OTB sites (other corporations do), New York is unique, and normally cannot serve as a model for other states and tracks, but maybe the rapid delivery of so many critical reforms can be an inspiration for change.

Other tracks and jurisdictions can implement major and several reforms in rapid succession if the racing associations choose to get things done. If the state of racing in New York has begun to improve, that should be an added incentive toward reforms that benefit racing's customers and bettors. It's crucial that the new NYRA succeed.

Finally, the granddaddy of all postmodern reforms will be the one only innovative, progressive, and gutsy racetracks would have the courage to try. It's a remedy for the times, perhaps for all times. Full-card simulcasting, whereby multiple tracks are accepted simultaneously, represents the ideal situation.

Stimulate the churn aggressively and excessively. Reduce the take-out on all pari-mutuel wagers to 12 percent, maybe as low as 10 percent.

The traditional churn encompassing nine races a day is passé. The churn can now encompass forty races a day, maybe more, and innumerable wagers repeating themselves all day, all night. If 90 percent of each pool were returned to the bettors each time, what would the resulting revenues be?

The track that is willing to find out will be very pleasantly surprised.

GULFSTREAM PARK AND
CHURCHILL DOWNS

A nd the new leaders are . . . Gulfstream Park and Churchill Downs! How about that!

In less than ten years since New York and southern California handicappers were locked in fruitless argument as to which circuit presents the best racing, and management teams on both coasts assumed it was they, neither does. The best racing now occurs at Gulfstream Park in winter and Churchill Downs during spring and fall. It's not a close call. Those two middle-class racing centers have drawn away from the competition by a wide margin, not to be overtaken anytime soon.

It's instructive to consider how it happened, and why. The new order has been no fluke.

First, and most decisively, the intelligent use of satellite technology. While most tracks from the mid 1980s to the early 1990s were preoccupied with preserving a dwindling on-track attendance, a noble but nearsighted purpose, Gulfstream and Churchill realized, either by design, or intuitively, that the future would depend primarily upon off-track handle.

On-track attendance is hardly unimportant, and demands constant vigilance, but it is no longer the near future. Major tracks that allocated the lion's share of resources to retaining their on-site attendance base have been out of step with the times. They have paid a dangerous price. Belmont Park and Santa Anita Park have paid the dearest.

Gulfstream Park and Churchill Downs concentrated instead on distributing their product to simulcast sites via satellite technology, and not haphazardly, but systematically.

Fastening on the advantage provided by Florida's winter dates, which they had secured at no small pain, as well as on the seasonal presence of the leading New York stables, Gulfstream sent its signal to the Meadowlands, which relayed the entire Gulfstream card. New York bettors preferred the Gulfstream simulcast, denied to them by the NYRA, to Aqueduct's winter racing. Millions of wagering dollars began to leave New York, headed to Gulfstream Park via the Meadowlands. In short time Big Apple bettors were accounting for a giant percentage of Gulfstream's out-of-state handle.

If New York bettors relished their simulcast so avidly, Gulfstream management reasoned, maybe other assorted bettors would too. The signal was marketed aggressively to various simulcast centers in the East and Middle Atlantic states especially, markets that favored New York racing and that had also shipped a number of local horses to Florida for the winter.

More and better horses, horsemen, and stables were strongly attracted to Florida for the winter. Fields filled, with many of the races overflowing. Handicappers everywhere relished that. The cycle intensified, the signal being beamed to additional simulcast sites. Revenues grew, purses bulged, more stables desired a piece of the action, and Gulfstream's program was suddenly a soaring success.

Meanwhile, in Kentucky, Churchill Downs was busy erecting a network of OTB parlors, self-owned, that would soon become the envy of everybody else. A few of the Kentucky-owned simulcast sites crossed state lines. The signal went out. As the network grew, simulcast handles increased, and increased, and increased, the host track retaining a significant share.

Churchill Downs recognized its future. The track-owned OTB network was expanded farther, and the signal was sent simultaneously out-of-state to racing circuits closely aligned with Kentucky racing. As off-track handles surged, purses were raised significantly, and the winning cycle had begun. Stables in Chicago, Louisiana, Arkansas, and other central racing states were much impressed. Several were attracted irresistibly to Kentucky's fabulous purses.

Better horses began migrating to Churchill Downs. Kentucky racing improved dramatically, and the fields were jammed. Ever greater expansion of the simulcast product followed, and simulcast bettors liked what they saw. I know; I was one of them on my occasional visits East.

The racing program continued to improve, and so did the Churchill purses. Eventually Churchill was distributing $300,000 a day to horsemen. Stables as far away as New York were impressed, and a few abruptly departed for Kentucky. Certain southern California horsemen liked what they saw from afar, too. A couple of southern California stables and many of that area's second-string stakes horses began to make appearances at Churchill Downs.

Bettors increasingly chagrined by the small fields and declining quality on their tracks began to notice Churchill's dynamite program. Word of mouth among handicappers was wonderful. The Gulfstream and Churchill signals were fast becoming the most popular in the country. Full fields. First cabin, competitive races. A fantastic array of overlays. Bonanza exotic payoffs daily. Fun, challenging, bettable race cards all the time, weekdays as well as weekends.

A second reason Gulfstream and Churchill have risen has been a devotion to improving their overnight programs and purses.

Interestingly, neither Gulfstream nor Churchill is renowned for its feature races, though Gulfstream presents the Florida Derby, and the half-million Gulfstream Park Handicap, both Grade 1s, plus other appealing stakes, and Churchill can never be disassociated from its Kentucky Derby (Gr. 1), not to mention the Kentucky Oaks (Gr. 1).

While other tracks competed for horses with big-ticket stakes features, Gulfstream and Churchill have boosted the overnight purses at every turn. Horses, horsemen, and stables converged on the money. As a result, the claiming races, the nonwinners' allowance series, the classified allowance conditions, and the grass races at the two tracks have presented simulcast handicappers with the deepest, most competitive overnight racing anywhere.

In further consequence, mutuel payoffs have been wonderful, few underlays clutter the card, and exotic payoffs will be extravagant as a matter of course. Not many small fields and miserly payoffs can be found at the new flagship tracks.

Compared with the full fields, competitive races, and attractive mutuels at Gulfstream and Churchill, the New York and southern California brand names no longer mean quality to the bettors, a frustrating fact of life the simulcast directors in New York and Los Angeles have increasingly been forced to concede and confront. Not everyone is scrambling to receive the New York and southern California races anymore.

A third and not unimportant reason Gulfstream and Churchill have prospered attaches to a sensible mix of live racing and simulcasting. The two tracks conduct a not-excessive number of live racing programs, although Churchill has sought to expand its dates. Gulfstream's fifty-five-day January–March season and Churchill's late-summer vacation bridging its summer and fall seasons permit horses that prepare for the meetings to compete in sharp form from beginning to end. In 1994 Gulfstream Park did something else refreshingly smart. The track lowered the take on straight wagers by one percent. Revenues increased dramatically. Not certain whether the stimulus could be traced to the reduced take or to the expanded simulcasting, or both, in 1995 Gulfstream lowered the take-out by another one percent. Revenues again increased dramatically.

In the age of full-card simulcasting, a key to the financial vault will be the churn. The lower the take, the greater the churn. With bettors at dozens to hundreds of simulcast sites now participating in the churn, every race, every day, the synergism can be fantastic, and unprecedented, as Gulfstream and Churchill have learned.

Racetracks that set sails to maximize the churn through expanded simulcasting and a lowered take-out will be richly rewarded. All that is needed is a racing program attractive to the bettors top to bottom, which does not mean five-horse fields in the featured races and a depressing array of bad races choking the life out of the overnight programs.

Not to be underestimated, Gulfstream Park and Churchill Downs have been aided and abetted in their new prosperity, not deliberately, by the passivity and mismanagement in New York and southern California. If the competition among racetracks in the nineties and into the twenty-first century is hinged to the appeal of their simulcast signals, the majors on both coasts have fallen haplessly behind the times, both in the quality of signals they send and in the number of signals they take.

The presupposition by New York and southern California executives that their tracks present the finest racing, and that therefore other less fortunate markets should be willing to pay a premium to obtain the signals, has turned to a haunting refrain. Not only has the assumption proved arrogant and unexamined, it has proved increasingly untrue.

If directors of simulcasting in New York and southern California have experienced problems in extending or renewing their simulcast contracts, notably at the premium rates, the reason is that the quality of the product on the racetrack has been slipping away before their eyes. Sad but true, simulcast bettors no longer view the racing programs from New York and southern California as top-of-the-line. They prefer Gulfstream Park and Churchill Downs, as well as other programs instead. The flagship tracks on both coasts would be wise to improve the quality of their simulcast product as a first priority, which means full fields in the fanciful stakes and attractive competitive overnight races.

At the midpoint of the decade, too, prospects in New York and southern California for effective change did not appear especially bright. The NYRA has been strangled by the relentless presence of the Manhattan OTB Corporation, and other regional OTB corporations, and southern California is burdened by an elaborate ridiculous intertrack wagering network, the SOUTHWINC, as it is awkwardly known. Both entities have evolved as political monsters. Both stand staunchly in the path of the necessary, meaningful changes.

In the meantime Gulfstream Park and Churchill Downs will continue to sail along, strengthening their front-running positions with expanded simulcasting, richer purses, and better racing. Many thousands of new and grateful bettors will jump aboard. Handicappers everywhere will now look forward with enthusiasm to the openings of Gulfstream Park and Churchill Downs, as they once looked forward to the opening day at the local racetrack.

In the brand-new world of satellite racing and full-card simulcasting, numerous tracks having unappetizing signals will be suffering. Yet two midsize tracks that ranked nowhere near the mountaintop only a decade ago will be shining brightly.

Well done.

THE MARKETING EFFORT

Santa Anita has its own program of
handicapping events, and we let the rest of
that world go by.

—ALAN F. BALCH
December 1982

It was a beautiful Sunday, spring of 1981, and I remember the Lakers were playing the Celtics in the NBA play-offs at the Forum, next door to Hollywood Park. First post then was 2:00 P.M. Eager to arrive slightly earlier than normal (I must have liked the first), I had departed my spot in Brentwood at 1:00 sharp. The drive covered some fifteen miles. I arrived at my box at 2:20 P.M.

On Florence, near Prairie, two miles away from the track, traffic suddenly stopped. Gridlock. It was backed up as far as the eye could see, and so were the cars in the opposite direction. I swung out, took another direction, but was stopped again. And a third time.

It was not the accident I had originally imagined, and it could not have been the basketball game, capacity of 17,505. What's happening, anyway? By circuitous routes through Inglewood's side streets I steadily approached the track, but on this day would be forced to park a mile away and walk.

Having missed the first, when I finally sat down, I gazed about, and there it was, unlike any crowd I had ever seen at the races, a mob scene. Neighbors in the box area let the cat out of the bag. This was "tote bag" day, the first ever. Hollywood Park was giving tote bags to its first forty thousand customers. The attendance would level at slightly in excess of eighty thousand people.

As I listened to the repetitive announcements apologizing profusely to some forty thousand distraught, beleaguered souls who did not receive a tote bag, I realized that a new dawn had just risen. The era of the giveaway. The promotion struck me as a good thing, actually,

169

and maybe something wonderful. Knowing nothing about marketing, I intuitively imagined the giveaway might be racing's marketing miracle, a cheap, easy lure that would bring the masses to the races.

Once the tracks had motivated large numbers of people to come, all that was needed were ways to get a decent percentage of them to come back, become loyal customers, that kind of thing. I was supremely confident I knew how to do that. Show those customers who exhibited an interest in playing the races how to play the game. The great game of handicapping would have them eagerly coming back. What I never imagined was that marketing directors who asked themselves the same question would settle on a circular solution—more giveaways.

A few weeks later, strictly coincidence, I had scheduled a meeting with Alan F. Balch, a man I did not know in person or by reputation, except that he was Santa Anita's vice president of marketing and was held by associates to be carving out new directions and achieving new levels of success. Very good! I had reason to be optimistic.

The paperback original of *The Handicapper's Condition Book* had just been released and was selling beyond expectations. Would Balch consider a version of the book's selection and elimination guidelines, a booklet, as a giveaway item? I presented a prototype.

Balch entertained the idea, took the prototype, and advised me Santa Anita would be getting back to me. Fair enough. During the meeting I had alluded to the tremendous success of Hollywood's tote bag giveaway. In a voice slightly raised and a tone slightly agitated, Balch had reacted by noting Santa Anita could not follow suit because Santa Anita's policy was not to pay more than a dollar apiece for a premium (giveaway) item, and tote bags had to cost more than that.

Though I said nothing, my instinct told me Santa Anita would not only be handing out tote bags as soon as possible, but two, one at Oak Tree and a second during the Santa Anita winter. That instinct proved correct.

A few weeks later I received by letter a well-reasoned response to my promotional idea for utilizing the information booklet. Santa Anita liked the product but had decided to pass for now, mainly because the track would likely be forced to hold a substantial oversupply from an original order of forty thousand, and the resale value of information products was considered poor. The track would put the booklet on file and might reconsider later. The letter was signed by a staff representative, not the vice president.

Before long the giveaway era had kicked in full-speed ahead. Tote bags had paved the way and were followed quickly by T-shirts, wristwatches, beer mugs, beach blankets, umbrellas, caps, calculators, jackets, jewelry, and on and on. On each of the appointed days, attendance rose significantly, but this was the age of no competition. The marketing effort was driven by attendance figures, not wagering dollars.

The giveaways have been successful, profitable, and fine, and there is no point in criticizing them, except as they are intended to substitute for the real reasons people flock to racetracks. They go there to play, and to bet.

The absence of marketing efforts intended to enhance those participative purposes has never been agreeable. Moreover, the long-term consequences of the prevailing marketing strategy, that is, to get the people to the racetrack, have never been seriously examined. A marketing strategy designed to lure people to the racetrack, again and again, for tote bags, T-shirts, and the rest, without a corresponding strategy for converting the interested customers into loyal fans, can only end at diminishing returns. After successive seasons of giveaways, the casual customers will have lost too much money, and most of them, sooner or later, will have decided to stay away. That unhappy consequence has been occurring for a time.

The same lamentable omission haunts the latest innovative promotions intended to extend a special invitation to the races to young adults, the twentysomething and thirtysomething crowd—Hollywood Park's "$1 Fridays," night racing, and Del Mar's "4:30 Fridays," twilight racing.

The young adults do come, attendance improves, and although per capita wagering shrinks, the handle increases. Everyone agrees the results exceed the comparable numbers on conventional Fridays.

No one regrets that the tracks still lack a mechanism by which the twentysomething and thirtysomething fans who become intrigued with playing the game might be converted to motivated handicappers and loyal customers. Once the young adults exit the tracks, how many of them can be expected to return at another time that isn't Friday night?

How many marketing directors the next week, upon reviewing the improved numbers and taking their bows, will be moved to ponder the inherent contradiction: "Hey, young people are coming, as we hoped, but we might be missing a golden opportunity here."

The sad truth is that the dire consequences of a tunnel-vision marketing strategy could have been, and should have been, avoided, or at least tempered, and, best of all, at low to moderate cost. A two-pronged strategy of linking the giveaways with programs of customer education might have bulwarked a marketing effort not only successful at getting people to the races but also successful at getting them to come back.

Eighteen months after my initial meeting with Balch I had a second encounter with the marketing veep, a brush that made it clear the vital linkage between giveaway promotions and customer education was not about to occur.

With *The Handicapper's Condition Book* now a top seller, and favorably endorsed by the leading figures in handicapping, I decided the moment was ripe for the first national conference on Thoroughbred handicapping. The national conference would legitimize the handicapping field, not only with racing's regular customers but, much more importantly, with the racetracks themselves. A large-scale collaboration might follow.

When Tom Ainslie, Andrew Beyer, William Quirin, and Steve Davidowitz enthusiastically agreed to participate, the plan was under way. A critical element was the formal participation of Santa Anita Park, and I knew the connecting force I wanted to convince.

I scheduled an appointment with one of the most distinguished figures in Thoroughbred racing: Santa Anita's senior vice president of racing, F. E. (Jimmie) Kilroe, the architect of racing in southern California for three decades, also a board member of the Los Angeles Turf Club, which runs Santa Anita Park, and a member of the Jockey Club. I had admired Kilroe for a decade as the most senior, mature, and impressive figure in southern California, a cultivated man, a fair and compassionate man, an outstanding man in every regard. I knew something else about Kilroe: He loved horse racing and he liked the handicapping.

In Kilroe's anteroom prior to the meeting I sat with numerous horsemen, all of whom were demanding stalls for dubious horses at the upcoming Santa Anita meeting. When I reached the inner sanctum, I began, "I'm not looking for stalls."

Kilroe responded, "You're one of a kind. Have a seat." So the meeting started on a lighthearted exchange.

I introduced myself as a writer on handicapping, explained the purposes and rationale for the national conference, and requested three favors: the formal participation of Santa Anita Park, such that the track's name might be attached to the venture, extending the conference legitimacy and credibility with the racing establishment; an investment by Santa Anita of $15,000, intended to seal the formal relationship, and which the conference would repay with interest; and Mr. Kilroe himself to deliver an after-dinner talk at a banquet at the Westin Bonaventure, in downtown Los Angeles.

Kilroe, an inscrutable man, rather shy, and to the point, listened intently, and sat quietly, stoically, for at least thirty seconds. His first words stunned me.

"I've read that book of yours, and I want you to know I think it is a first-class job."

In 1982 not one track executive in one hundred had read a decent book on handicapping. I was confident I had come to the right person. Another ten seconds of silence, and Kilroe said, "I think this conference is a good idea. Probably an idea whose time has come. I think Santa Anita should get involved.

"I'll tell you what. I'm having lunch with Alan Balch, our marketing guy, on Thursday. I'll run it by him. If he agrees, we'll go ahead."

On Friday, unable to control myself, I called Alan Balch at his office.

The Thursday lunch had proceeded, but at my asking Balch told me rather abruptly that although the topic had been broached, Mr. Kilroe did not push it strongly. I was stunned and frankly in disbelief.

The conversation drifted downhill from there.

Essentially Balch stated that Santa Anita could not be involved in "something like that." It was a condescending remark in a condescending tone, but I struggled to assure Balch the personalities would be legitimate, the leading writers and professionals in the field highly credible, the conference highly professional. I became somewhat assertive on the matter, but Balch could not be budged.

In the same condescending manner and tone, he said, and I quote, "Santa Anita has its own program of handicapping events, and we let the rest of that world go by."

Even then I requested a ten-minute meeting at which I might persuade him to change his mind. Balch rejected my request. He said he was too busy getting ready for the season.

It was a tragic moment. It meant that leading members of the handicapping community were nowhere close to being able to work collaboratively with the marketing efforts of leading racetracks. As Balch's star was in its ascendancy, it meant, too, the linkage I had imagined between the giveaway promotions and customer education had slipped away to the outer horizon.

An unexpected postscript to this debacle occurred a couple of weeks later and is worth reporting.

Accidentally I bumped into Jimmie Kilroe at the deli counter of a nearby supermarket. He smiled his hello.

I recounted the conversation with Balch, and finished by saying that although I knew Santa Anita was formally out of the picture, on a personal level I would still like him to deliver the after-dinner banquet talk.

Kilroe squirmed and wrinkled his brow, and it was clear I had put him in an uncomfortable position.

Another interlude of silence. And then, "I still think this conference is a good idea. I might be able to help. Come see me in a week or so."

When I went back to Kilroe's office, he mentioned his role on Santa Anita's board of directors and begged off giving the speech himself, but said he had talked to his racing secretary, Lou Eilken, about it. Would Eilken be acceptable?

I accepted enthusiastically. Lou Eilken gave an amazingly detailed, carefully prepared, well-delivered talk on the evolution of handicapping at the first national conference on Thoroughbred handicapping, and we have remained good friends ever since.

Alan Balch came out of Harvard in the 1970s with an MBA, and after a dalliance with show horses as a ringmaster, no less, he arrived at Santa Anita Park. He soon became the man in charge of marketing, and much else besides, and was on his march to the heights when I first brushed up against him. His credentials were of the unimpeachable kind: he was making piles of money for the company. As Santa Anita accumulated money, Balch accumulated power. The joint ventures continued and intensified for a long time.

If anyone wants to comprehend racing's marketing efforts, even today, they can benefit from a reprise of Balch's reign at Santa Anita.

Balch and the prevailing marketing strategy combined forces in the campaign for greater attendance, and the successes in southern California could be truly remarkable. Balch possessed undeniable talent. He inaugurated direct-mail marketing, and on a grand scale, with Santa Anita's mailing list containing in excess of 200,000 names. Everyone received a quarterly newsletter and other selected mailings. He refined the giveaway promotions, attaching them to specially selected days when stagnant attendance could use a boost. On one opening day at Oak Tree, a Wednesday, with the giveaway a transistor radio, I believe, the attendance exceeded 66,000 people. A Wednesday!

He understood the value of publicity vis-à-vis advertising. He was quoted as saying one dollar of publicity is worth thirty dollars of advertising. Deeply and continuously involved in community affairs, awarding the track's facilities to local events, Santa Anita enjoyed favorable publicity, and a wonderfully positive image.

When names like Bill Shoemaker, Laffit Pincay, Jr., Charlie Whittingham, and Laz Barrera were prominent, Balch invoked their feats impressively. Shoemaker once graced a poster, "The Shoe Wants You," for an entire year, when the poster market was the rage.

Ironically on this front—publicity—Balch committed one of his worst blunders ever, an egregious error that can only be characterized as sophomoric and silly. Unimpressed with the coverage of Santa Anita racing by the *Los Angeles Times,* Balch orchestrated a letter-writing campaign to sports editor Bill Dwyre. He sent letters to turf-club members and box holders, urging them to complain to the newspaper.

When missives of protest began piling up on Dwyre's desk, the editor quickly realized he had been bushwhacked. The letter-writing campaign was revealed and ridiculed. The effects were adverse, and embarrassing to the track. Why did Balch do it?

He organized a dynamic group-sales program, and Santa Anita's group sales were soon second to none. Several hundred groups of diverse demographics visited the track for consecutive years. Seating was good, and races were named for the largest groups, with the group leaders escorted to the winner's circle before and after the running.

Balch also knew how to exploit the magnificent environs of Santa Anita Park. With the San Gabriel Mountains all around, their scenic peaks and valleys in view of the frontside, the trees and lush greenery abundant, the large beautiful accessible walking ring behind the grandstand, and the most gorgeous infield in racing, Santa Anita was promoted heavily and appropriately as The Great Race Place. The races were accompanied by traditional flourishes most other tracks could only envy, with a trackside bugler in red coat and tails and the Budweiser Clydesdales pulling the starting gate. A sense of place was cultivated, the idea that Santa Anita was a special lovely park where individuals and families liked to go. And Santa Anita was a special place. People liked merely being there. I did too.

Balch even landed for Santa Anita the equestrian events of the 1984 Los Angeles Olympics, conducting horse shows on the racetrack during the off-season in the years prior to the world games. It was a glorious prize. As soon as the Olympics ended, so did the horse shows.

My pal Jon Bostrom occasionally reminds me of his experience on the Sunday of the 1985 Santa Anita Handicap, when he took his girlfriend, Kathy, to the races and 84,000 people went along.

"I live only two long blocks from the place," recalls Bostrom, "but when I picked up Kathy and drove to the track, I was forced to park at least a mile away.

"We were going to the infield and I had to carry beach chairs and beverage containers the whole mile. We were packed in like sardines. The betting lines were ridiculous.

"I'll never forget that day. That was only ten years ago. There's no chance of having that kind of crowd today!"

Later that year, in October 1985, the start of Oak Tree, it all began to unravel for Balch, Santa Anita, and southern California racing, events that would be reflective of the chronic recession in the industry nationwide.

As had other states, the state of California had legalized the lottery. In reaction, Balch, with great fanfare and expectations, instituted a new, exotic wager, the Pick 9. It was a $2 bet, widely advertised, and the underlying idea was that anybody able to pick all nine winners on a card would walk away from the races with a million dollars, perhaps several million dollars.

Since nobody could be expected to pick nine winners on any day at the races, a carryover provision was announced, and as soon as the Pick 9 pool had reached five million dollars, a mandated payoff the next day would go to the person or persons picking the most winners. Imagine the attendance and publicity on that exciting day, or so went the conventional thinking.

As talented as Alan Balch could be at racetrack marketing, he suffered a tragic flaw. Balch knew nothing about playing the races. The Pick 9 was a nonsense bet from the outset, having zero chance of competing effectively with the lottery. Its assumptions about pari-mutuel wagering, the racing game, and attendance were foolhardy. The most sensible racetrack response to the state's lottery would have been to ignore it.

In a discussion I had with a regional director of American Totalizator a few days after Santa Anita's Pick 9 had been launched, to extremely disappointing results, the director advised me of the assumptions that had been agreed upon in a planning session. It was assumed the five-million-dollar mark would be reached every eleven racing days. That assumed substantial pools to begin, the daily betting accelerated greatly by the carryovers, which did occur in Pick 6 wagering, the obvious but inappropriate model.

I forget the amount of money bet on the Pick 9 on its inaugural, but in the beginning I vaguely remember totals like $11,000. In contrast, the typical Pick 6 pool topped $120,000. Regardless, the Pick 9 attracted pitifully small pools. Instead of eleven racing days, the revised time line to five million dollars would be many weeks, assuming no one in the meantime actually picked nine, thereby forcing the betting to begin anew. This was not acceptable. The Pick 9 looked dead on arrival.

It was not. Instead of doing the right thing, and burying the body, Santa Anita attempted to restore the Pick 9 to good health. The format was revised.

Instead of $2, the Pick 9 now cost $1. Instead of five million dollars, the payback threshold was now three million.

In a wild display of chutzpah, Balch even attempted to manipulate the bettors into trying the Pick 9 by moving the daily double to the second and third races. Maybe the Pick 9 fans simply needed more time and fewer distractions!

Conservative, majestic Santa Anita, the track so dedicated to preserving the sport's hallowed traditions, the guardian of all that has been good and proper in the game, shoves the most hallowed betting tradition of all to the chorus, in favor of the most exotic wager in history.

As a racetracker known as Clocker Bob said to me in discussing the change, "That's power!"

It was the first great disturbing contradiction to come out of Alan Balch. Matters would never be the same again.

Although the wager continued in a bastardized form for years, the Pick 9 game was over. The $1 million payout occurred just once, won by an inveterate punter who took down $1.9 million during the Santa Anita winter meeting, and then lost the money within a year. Santa Anita had proved the racetrack could not compete with the lottery by implementing million-to-one exotic wagering games, a regrettable thought with the convergence of riverboats, Indian reservations, and casino games not long away.

About this time, in an attempt to distribute the product throughout the state, California failed by a photo finish to pass an off-track betting bill (OTB). Instead an intertrack wagering network was established such that any track or fairgrounds having a racing license might simulcast the races from operating tracks. The legislation meant regular handicappers, not to mention racegoers, could now play the races at an intertrack site closer to home. On-track attendance would begin to decline.

Similar (though better) betting bills were passed in other states, with predictable results. Instead of developing new markets, which the traditional marketing efforts had not been capable of doing, racetrack attendance would be redistributed, essentially away from the racetracks and toward the various off-track betting facilities.

In this context it's imperative to review again the prevailing marketing strategy. It's attendance-based, or attendance-driven. With giveaways, entertainment activities, and regular advertising promoting the featured races, the idea is to motivate people to come for a day at the races. Not to be overlooked or discounted, racetracks have traditionally obtained approximately 40 percent of their revenues from admission, parking, and concessions, hardly an incidental sum, though the percentage amount has plummeted in recent times, probably by half.

If the idea is to stimulate attendance on a given day, instead of bolstering racing's attendance base, by growing new markets, the marketing efforts do remarkably well. Attendance jumps. The promotions make money. The marketing directors are pleasantly satisfied.

With fewer and fewer racegoers traveling to the tracks, however, the prevailing marketing strategy has surrendered the center of its force. Nowadays giveaways work well only when combined with an especially attractive program of racing, notably a festival of stakes races that might be supporting one of the track's signature races. The top horses will be on display, the races exciting and competitive, and the giveaways provide an extra-added attraction for casual racegoers.

What happens to casual racegoers when they get to the races is still a pesky, nasty problem. Most of them lose more money than they would like to lose, which dulls the incentive to return. The prevailing marketing strategy has always suffered from this inherent weakness and from other structural weaknesses that have effectively prevented racing from competing intelligently once the competition from other forms of gaming began. To wit:

- The short-term emphasis subverts the long-term effect.

  How many tote bags can a naive horse player tolerate before he's lost too much money to persevere?
- Interested players, and potentially interested players, thousands of people, are lost to a strategy of benign neglect.

  Racing's customers cannot learn how to play the game, or even purchase a decent book on the topic, at a racetrack.
- However much attendance might be stimulated on a given afternoon, the attendance base remains the same, or stagnates, or declines.

  When crowds of 40,000 to 60,000 to 80,000 people were congregating at major racetracks in the 1970s and throughout the mid 1980s, if 3 percent had been converted to loyal race fans and regular players, racing's attendance base would have grown by 50 percent. Circumstances today would not be so disheartening.

The progressive marketing strategy, an innovative one designed to grow the attendance base, requires a definite shift in emphasis and resources, away from the passive purposes and toward the participative motives of a day at the races, or away from the spectacle of the sport and toward the gaming. People come to the races to play, to win, possibly to score, absolutely to succeed.

It's a game, not just a spectacle. Importantly the shift in emphasis does not mean that the spectacle of the sport, or the giveaway, must be abandoned. Both directions can be pursued simultaneously, and a natural nexus between the two can be forged. The marketing effort will have been broadened tremendously, not just rearranged.

The gaming package consists of education and training programs on how to play the races, and how to play well, as well as information services in support of the education and training.

Racing's casual customers qualify as the worst-educated sports fans in the country, the large majority ill-equipped to play a complicated game even satisfactorily. No indictment of the prevailing marketing strategy of the past twenty-five years could be more severe. The linkage I once thought natural between the giveaways and customer education might be resurrected successfully. Various training and education programs could be implemented as a matter of routine for occasional racegoers, for casual customers, for beginners, for intermediate handicappers, and for advanced handicappers. A fully integrated sequence of instruction and training for newcomers and novices who want to move from dilettante to journeyman to expert is entirely feasible.

Costs would not be prohibitive, and in any case would represent a capital investment, an investment in human resources. The payoff would be long-term, and would constitute a kind of loyalty to the sport and game that until now has been practically nonexistent.

If the education and training programs were successful, racing's attendance base would begin to grow. New markets the tracks have never been able to capture, of young adults, of women, of baby boomers, of members of the professional-corporate-technical elites, might be surprisingly responsive. Can anyone doubt that a certain percentage within each of these groups would like to learn how to play the races effectively? After all, as I have come to know and admire, there's a horse player in every family.

Regarding customer education generally, before meaningful change can occur, (a) a pervasive cultural value of the racetrack must be assiduously attacked; and (b) a key operational vacuum must be filled.

The cultural value in desperate need of repair is the idea that you can't beat the races. Hundreds do, and the marketing effort will be well advised to identify local handicappers who play well and promote these talented players as role models that newcomers, novices, and interested others might identify with. That kind of identification has been sorely missing at racetracks. Racing's customers do not identify with horses, or jockeys, or trainers, but they would identify with excellent players.

A perfectly legitimate, and timely, way to promote the gaming aspects of the racetrack is to compare and contrast the pari-mutuel wagering games with casino games. Playing the races is first of all, and most importantly, a positive-expectation game, which means that customers who develop the requisite knowledge and skill can beat the game.

The facts are sobering. A handicapper who gets 30 percent winners at average odds of 5–2 has a small edge (5 percent) on the game. If that player can improve to 33 percent winners at the same 5–2 on average, the winning edge jumps to 15 percent. As Dick Mitchell has observed, the player who improves his proficiency by 10 percent has tripled his profits. That can be marketed. At 35 percent winners, odds of 5–2, the edge is 22 percent, which is not chump change. The 40 percent handicapper at 5–2 average odds commands a 40 percent advantage, which can translate to meaningful profits season upon season. Those are attainable results. They also constitute positive goals for aspiring handicappers. The marketing effort need only make up its collective mind to tell it like it is.

Casino games, the competition so widely remarked and detested, are negative-expectation games. The house retains the edge, and no amount of knowledge and skill on the part of the player can reverse the odds. The more the customer plays, the more likely he or she is to lose. If marketing directors at racetracks want to know how to compete effectively with the spread of casino games, this is one self-affirming way. Persuade enough members of the target groups that playing the races for fun and profit makes sense, just as playing casino games does not.

The flowchart on page 182 contains an interesting comparison and contrast between pari-mutuel wagering games and casino games on several criteria. Examine the dichotomy.

COMPARISON AND CONTRAST

Pari-Mutuel Wagering	Casino Games
Positive-expectation games	Negative-expectation games
Percentages and probabilities	Random order
Knowledge and skill	Luck and chance
Information-based	Mindless
↓	↓
Gaming	Gambling
Thinking	Guessing
Player versus player	Player versus house
Subjective odds	Mechanical odds
Minimum boldness strategies are optimal	Maximum boldness strategies are optimal
Attractive overlays	Underlays only
Skillful players can win	Skillful players can't win
Fair	Unfair

More broadly, the essential racetrack experience might be promoted in crucial dynamic ways that until now have never been adequately explored:

- It's gaming, not gambling.
- It's recreation, not entertainment.
- You can beat the races, and skillful players do.

Gambling is guessing. Outcomes depend upon random order. Handicappers instead will be playing a game characterized by well-known, attainable results and having well-defined percentages and probabilities.

In addition, people do not go to the races to be entertained. They go there to do something—in essence to play the races. It's not a mere semantic distinction. Entertainment plays a support role. The entertainment value of watching the featured races and stakes horses, as well as ancillary entertainment activities provided by the track, can enhance the basic participation motive, and does. But the basic spur is still the recreation, not the entertainment.

As much or more than anything else, racing's customers need to realize that they can beat the races. If you can't beat the races, it makes no sense to try. People might as well roll the dice, spin the wheel, or turn the card, mindless games of random chance that is society's prevailing view of the outcomes at the track. That false impression can be changed, and must be, by the marketing effort.

Regarding the racetrack vacuum that needs to be filled, in a basic, almost primitive way, marketing qualifies as a fascinating, inexact, elusive discipline for which virtually everyone who is anyone recognizes himself or herself to be sufficiently qualified to succeed. Had a successful career in accounting, the law, real estate development, the stock market, selling medical supplies, playing basketball, building bridges? Fine, you're obviously bright, well educated, and successful. Let's see how well you can help us as a director of marketing. An excessive number of marketing managers have no special training or preparation for the role. None of them imagines for a moment he or she cannot do a fabulous job.

Juxtaposed with the lack of proper preparation for the job is the fallacy, almost universally indulged, that marketing can be equated with promotion and sales. Before the promotion and sales, as Thoroughbred racing is presently finding out to its chagrin, it's crucial to determine with a high probability of being correct what it is that should be promoted and sold.

In the marketing texts, though not necessarily in the marketing suites, it's the needs and wants of the market.

Do horseplayers want tote bags? No.

Do handicappers want a National Pick 7? No.

Would racegoers like to know how to play the races more successfully? Yes.

A positive trend in contemporary racing has been the addition of professional handicappers to the administrative circles of racetracks. The players may not have a clue as to effective marketing, but they do know what handicappers and bettors need and want. Randy Moss for a few seasons has been the director of operations at Oaklawn Park. In a maneuver that might accelerate the movement, in November 1994, Steve Crist was named director of communications and development for the NYRA. It's crucial that Crist succeed, although the obstacles will be formidable. No doubt other impressive handicappers have been finding their way onto the administrative ladders at racetracks. It's a healthy development that begs success.

Another new development that holds considerable promise for the more effective marketing of the racing game regards the newer, younger, sharper directors of simulcasting and managers of off-track betting sites. These positions have proliferated of late. The new directors and managers off-track strike me as much better attuned to the needs and wants of the players.

As a rule, management types at the nation's racetracks have long suffered a different reputation, fairly well deserved, of being generally inhospitable to, even contemptuous of, the bettors. A greater effort to identify the game's biggest bettors, and best players, and treat them favorably, is highly recommended. Word-of-mouth, the finest marketing technique of all, would improve immediately and immensely. These are not unimportant matters, and the evidence is accumulating that racing's best customers are likely to meet with much greater friendliness and hospitality off-track than on-track.

Last November (1994), two days after Thanksgiving, I visited the Upper Darby Turf Club, as they are called, one of the off-site betting parlors operated by Philadelphia Park, for a marathon day-night handicapping session. I had played in the Upper Darby Club perhaps five times.

On my arrival a boisterous argument had ensued between the admissions clerk and a severely agitated customer. The admission lines had backed up on two sides of the entrance. I stood six deep in the line.

Manager Gary Prestage was called to the scene. He calmed the customer adeptly and then recognized me in the line. Gary came over, shook my hand, stayed with me until I had moved to the desk, and then noted to the admissions clerk, "This is James Quinn, a good customer, and he's 'comped' today on admission, Racing Forms, and track programs." This pleased me.

Gary then escorted me personally to a dining table in the swanky clubhouse side of the parlor, motioned the waitress to the table, and told her to put my food and drink, lunch and dinner, on his account. We chatted briefly, and Gary departed. Within five minutes he had returned and handed me a VIP Gold Card. I examined the card, turned it over, and noticed a line notated with the phrase "Expiration Date."

In the blank space Gary Prestage had written two words: "No Expiration."

A lifetime pass!

Later that day I learned, not surprisingly, that Gary Prestage is one thoughtful manager in the habit of taking excellent care of his steady customers.

The Upper Darby Turf Club is filled to capacity, day and night.

How often in the past quarter century has that kind of wonderful service been delivered to the good customers at the nation's racetracks?

THE CART, THE HORSE,
AND CUSTOMER EDUCATION

More and more, in an industry that has practiced benign neglect of its core customers for decades, in organizational gatherings, in informal conversations, even in planning meetings, customer education has emerged as something of a buzzword. The buzz intimates that education qualifies as a direction the industry should pursue, but the substance of the talk suggests just as surely that racing officials do not comprehend what customer education means or how to do it well.

As much as the small talk can be found to consist of repetitive themes, at least two of the central threads do not bode well for the near future of the enterprise: (a) customer education means elementary education, certainly nothing advanced; and (b) to the degree fan education should be organized at all, the industry would prefer to do it on the cheap. There is, too, the messy problem of qualified staff, of which the administrative circles of racetracks are practically and peculiarly empty.

My rebuttal is direct and unequivocal.

Customer education represents nothing less than a secure future for the racing game. More than the televising of stakes races, expanded simulcasting, national exotic wagering games, or even interactive TV, customer education holds the promise of rapid and continual growth in the mature market, those cadres of regular racegoers optimistically known as handicappers.

To track executives who imagine that fan education can be reduced to the rescue of those poor, beleaguered fans who cannot interpret the data items of the *Daily Racing Form,* or do not know what a gelding is, aided and abetted perhaps by a deluge of statistical percentages describing the performances of trainers, jockeys, sires, and post positions, let them imagine as well what hope they would place in their children's education if it were suspended following elementary school.

186

The desirable kind of customer education will be a fully integrated program of events intended to deal effectively with the customer's wild array of know-how and skill. Just as children graduate from elementary school to high school, from high school to college, and from college to professional school, racetrack customers might evolve from beginners to intermediate players to experts to professionals.

Just as society and the workplace demand that its citizens be graduated at a minimum from high school, the tracks might prefer that its denizens progress to an intermediate level of success. If unexpected numbers of the players prefer to advance to expertise, a higher education, so to speak, that level of instruction should be offered as well.

In any event an emphasis on elementary education will be terribly misguided. Once instruction starts, most recipients wish to advance as quickly and as far as possible.

Of resources, customer education cannot be organized on the cheap, but costs to the industry should be low to moderate. On any cost-benefit analysis, notably in a large-scale development effort, costs will be revealed to be small and the benefits great. This is because the tracks can act as brokers in the deal, the education delivered by outside consultants and the expenses in the main assumed by the customers obtaining the services. The broader the educational scope, even less the costs to the local tracks, and even greater the benefits, which will include long-term loyalty in place of the traditional short-term trial, dismay, and desertion.

Whether it's skiing, golf, driver's education, scuba diving, computer programming, travel, tournament chess, or any number of activities dependent for success on an unfamiliar learning curve, the progressive model of instruction and practice works.

A second tenable model might be university extension, whereby instructors from the workplace provide a reality-based form of challenging instruction in the academic setting. The racetracks should not hesitate to adapt either model to their customers' education and training needs, which are multivarious and complicated.

It's crucial to grasp the increasingly fundamental role of customer education in contemporary racing. A particularly relevant, vibrant source of testimony will be the purveyors of electronic information services, including BRIS, Equibase, Track Master, and the dozens of their local counterparts. As 1995 began, BRIS was contemplating a national series of educational seminars for their own customers. Track Master was prideful of its growth rate, but equally mournful of the 30 to 35 percent of its subscribers who were dropping out during the first ninety days.

The reason in both cases can be linked to the customer's lack of education. An indecent percentage of subscribers to electronic information services will suspend their subscriptions within three months to a year. Of the survivors many will quit during the second year. The reason is the customers do not know how to use the information products effectively. Their game does not significantly improve. So they stop paying for the information.

The situation has become eerily similar to what has transpired between potential customers and the racetracks in the tracks' clumsy pursuit of a larger customer base. Not knowing how to play the races, the interested but undereducated customer eventually loses too much money and quits. Not knowing how to use the electronic data they download, eventually the high-tech customer recognizes that his game has not much improved and he quits.

Currently headed in the same direction is the Jockey Club's database Equibase. Intending to sell information products instead of data, a perfectly plausible plan and direction, Equibase will learn soon enough that its subscribers cannot use the information products effectively. Those disaffected customers will disconnect from Equibase. The more things change, the more they remain the same.

As early as 1985 I believed a meaningful remedy for racing's marketing problems would be information products and services. After all, this is the age of information. Computers could deliver innovative information products that handicappers might use immediately, successfully, and cheaply. Instead of users having to process the data items found in the *Daily Racing Form* with time-consuming, energy-depleting rating methods, handicappers would obtain the already processed data, or information, from the mouths of databases and personal computers.

Time and energy demands would be seriously and wonderfully diminished. The handicapping market would grow. Many more players would be successful. An extensive period of growth, success, and customer satisfaction would be under way.

By 1987 I had changed my mind. With partner Bill Quirin I had helped design a database that would be national in scope and would deliver daily to racetracks, other distributors, and consumers one dozen standard information reports, and any desired customized individualized reports, which would reflect the state of the art of handicapping information, including exact eligibility conditions, speed figures, speed and pace figures, jockey and trainer stats, new results charts, even a new and comprehensive version of the past performances, which would replace the customary data items with information, and much more. The database design was fabulous, or so I truly believed. Leading handicappers were hired and trained to collect the data. The database and the handicappers would have tremendous credibility in the handicapper's marketplace. This was futureworld.

Within a year it became crystal clear that futureworld was premature and still far away. The state-of-the-art database, the information reports, the highly credible handicappers on-line, none of that mattered very much. The educated market, handicappers and racegoers who might actually utilize the information products to play better, and maybe to win, was too small. The educational and training needs of the vast undereducated and uneducated audience of racegoers were too great. The mistake was basic, even primitive. We had put the cart before the horse. The great overarching need of Thoroughbred racing was not for information products and services, it was for customer education.

Customer education drives the information services. As customer education takes hold and moves, so will the corresponding information products. Eventually a complementary interactive effect carries the cause.

As to the importance of the education, the industry and local racetracks were not convinced, not interested.

The overarching problem surfaced again a few years later with the energetic publication of *The Racing Times,* a newspaper superior in several respects to the *Daily Racing Form* (see *"The Racing Times* and the *Daily Racing Form"*), and which also published professional speed figures the Form did not possess for the first time in the sport's troubled history. Expecting a 40 percent share of the handicapping market, *The Racing Times* settled instead for an 18 percent share. The demise of *The Racing Times* in one year may have resulted from multiple causes, but the explanation in the main resides in the haunting epitaph of editor

Steve Crist: "These people [racegoers] do not even know what a speed figure is." Once again, the cart was positioned in front of the horse.

As the electronic information providers of the 1990s will admit to their deep consternation, the cart is still running ahead of the horse. If the leading information suppliers hope to turn current events in their favor, they might begin by allocating decent portions of their operating budgets to customer education, not necessarily of their personal products but of the fine art of handicapping and effective pari-mutuel wagering. As might the local racetracks, they can view the education budget as a capital investment in human resources, which it is.

By the mid 1990s another prominent source began to press itself on the vital need for fan education. The new and growing rage is full-card simulcasting. Unfamiliar racetracks, unfamiliar horses, unfamiliar jockeys and trainers, all of the above and much more have been penetrating all racing markets via satellite technology. Regular handicappers relish the movement.

Well-targeted information services will descend upon the simulcast markets soon enough, but none of that will grow the handicapping market, or increase the customer base. To the extent that racetracks, their satellite signals, and information providers will be left to slug it out for slices of the existing mature market, a nongrowth, slow-growth sector, many of them will be forced to abandon the simulcasting business, and several non-competitive racetracks may be forced to close.

Which brings the matter of customer education full circle to where it rests, with the racetracks. The present state of affairs is not reassuring. Resources for customer education are poor to nonexistent. There are no budgets, no departments, no staff. Their creation and development would be costly, a strategic developmental cost most racetracks would prefer to omit.

Outside consultants who are handicappers may provide the cost-effective alternative, but a certain tension between the track officials and handicappers must be acknowledged. The two groups do not warm to one another cozily, though in the educational arena they are natural allies. Besides, the tracks generally do not know who their best players are. At the same time, the majority of handicappers will not qualify as planners and teachers. Matters of curriculum development and instruction cannot be discounted.

The issue of recruitment of qualified staff takes precedence, and deservedly so. Track customers who take part in education and training programs will prove a difficult audience for handicapping instructors to impress. These people will be betting their money. Above all, they want results. Content is key. The program must be demonstrably successful. Poor teaching substitutes will be revealed for the hollow ring they strike with the students, and quickly. A bad rap will set the education program back to square one.

In place of authentic customer education, it's instructive to review the few related services the tracks have been willing to indulge. One has been the notorious tout sheets, the colorful cards hawked outside the entrances. These supply the obligatory one-two-three predictions, and remain patently devoid of educational value. To the extent that the tracks perceive the tout sheets as supply lines to transient racegoers who otherwise do not distinguish the jockey from the horse, why not? To the degree the tout sheets are accepted as useful, educational, or beneficial to repeat customers, they are ridiculous. Racetracks not contemptuous of their customers' intelligence must be held to higher standards.

Day-of-the-races seminars that have become routinized on busy weekends can be somewhat educational, to the degree that the handicappers can support their selections with substantive, fundamentally sound explanations the customers might depend upon on their future excursions to the races.

Information products and professional speed figures sold on-track can be beneficial to regular customers, especially in the current rush to full-card simulcasting. Casual handicappers will largely be unable to use the products successfully. Again the prerequisite need for education, training, and guided practice. *The Sheets* and *Thoro-Graph*, for example, offer their trackside customers excellent tapes and seminars, the publishers having learned that unless the education is provided and the learning curve is shortened, the customers will be gone.

In recent years the racetracks and the *Daily Racing Form* have collaborated in a Partners Program, an aspect of which provides the tracks with an abbreviated program of fan education. The programs vary tremendously in substance, quality, duration, and effectiveness, but in general represent a thrust forward.

At Santa Anita, in 1995, three half-hour television shows on an independent station that also provides the nightly race replays were devoted to customer education, the first covering class evaluation, the second form analysis, and the third speed and pace. I watched two of the programs, and they were first-cabin, in no small measure due to the first-cabin handicappers in charge of the presentation, Brad Free and Jeff Siegel. The scripts were particularly well done. Anyone who observed the shows intently derived a real measure of learning.

Even as the patchwork of products and services has increased and improved at several tracks, none of it has amounted to an organized, well-distributed program of customer education that matters for the majority. The instinct to do the job as cheaply as possible retards real progress. Greater attention in planning has been past due. Initial 1994–95 efforts at a few of the majors, including NYRA and southern California tracks, while short-lived, have contributed some valuable lessons:

- Racetracks best contract for customer-education consultation and program development with outside agents, notably excellent handicappers who are not track employees.

  In the absence of budgets, departments, and qualified staff, which do not appear to be just around the corner, tracks will be well served by professional handicappers as planners and instructors.

  Few track employees can qualify as authentic handicappers. Besides, the participants (racing's customers) will not easily identify with track handicappers, at least at the beginning.
- Programs should be track-based.

  It's important that the educational services be strongly affiliated and identified with the local tracks, whose support systems will be vital to success. Marketing, publicity, and operations provide low-cost, ready-access assistance to the handicappers as instructors. The working relationship will be complementary. The handicappers can provide the curriculum, instructional materials, and training, and the tracks can provide the requisite support. The local tracks might subsidize the programs, paying the handicappers-instructors, or the participants themselves might pay relatively small fees, perhaps in exchange for small perks, such as free admission and free track programs on training days.

Whenever possible, classes and training sessions should be held on-track. If decent comfortable facilities are not available, the tracks might rearrange the furniture.

- A continuous, fully integrated program is highly desirable.

By fully integrated I mean a variety and sequence of programs, materials, and services that can satisfy the various educational needs of racing's customers, whether the participants are beginners, intermediate level, or experts. Where a fully integrated program is available and continuous, beginners can graduate to an intermediate level rather quickly, intermediate handicappers can rise to an expert level not so quickly, and advanced players might be ushered to a professional level of play—for meaningful profits.

- Handicappers who serve as instructors must satisfy the dual expectations of the customers.

One, they must be excellent handicappers, and accomplished players. Two, they must be adequate teachers. It can help enormously if the handicappers are also consistent winners, and will be perceived in that way, at least during the periods of application, when actual races are run and the handicapping instructors play alongside the pupils. To the extent that the instructors should happen to lose persistently, the instruction will not be especially reinforcing.

- Instruction as to effective handicapping and pari-mutuel wagering must extend to application, or actually playing the races.

The point is obvious, but crucial. Customer education targeted at playing the races does not occur in a vacuum. It occurs in a context of actual play, presumably successful play.

- At any instructional level, beginner to expert, customer education programs must improve the participants' knowledge, skill, and results. The programs should be held accountable to that severe standard.

The last is not least. It is indeed first. The mistake the industry and local tracks must not indulge is giving the customers a set of experiences and tools under the guise of education and training that can have no positive impact. In other words if the education does not improve the customer's play, the game has been lost once again. It's convenient at all times to remember that the customers will be risking their money.

If racetracks attend too elaborately or cautiously to the training needs of customers who cannot read the *Daily Racing Form,* or do not know what a speed figure represents, those tracks will be wasting their time. The low-level customer who has become interested in handicapping wants most of all to advance. Those players will master terms, definitions, and basic facts and figures quickly enough, but then they want to learn how to play more successfully. Improved play must be the bottom line in all situations, and a rudimentary stab at the relevant education and training will not get it done.

A track firmly positioned on the front lines of customer education has been Del Mar, near San Diego, in southern California. In 1994 the seaside course subsidized an eight-week intermediate-level program of instruction and training that was engaged by almost two hundred participants. I joined professional handicappers Tom Brohamer and Frank Romano in organizing and conducting the program, which was free to the participants. An encapsulated version of the same program had originated during Oak Tree at Santa Anita, in the fall of 1993, subsidized by Oak Tree executive Sherwood Chillingworth.

The curriculum was intended to reflect the handicapping process itself, from identifying contenders and representative races, to rating the contenders on speed and pace, to conducting a pace analysis, to recognizing meaningful performance patterns, to the entire range of the handicapping regimen, and including pari-mutuel betting strategies. It was analogous to Handicapping 101 perhaps, but at a college-entry level. Barry Meadow delivered a spirited presentation on betting strategy and money management. Joe Takach spent a day on recognizing equine body language. The participants were even required to read a few books between classes.

In a final report the participants relished the experience virtually without exception, and 64 percent reported the classes had improved their game substantially. Despite considerable confusion when the topics were introduced (mediated by backup sessions), when asked afterward whether the making of speed and pace figures was expecting too much of participants in an intermediate course, 90 percent reported making the figures was not overbearing after all. The self-reported evidence on the matter was conclusive.

In 1995 Del Mar repeated the instructional program and extended the education concept to include a makeshift Newcomers Area on-track and a weekly one-day course called "Simple Techniques," designed especially for beginners and novices. The linkage from newcomers to beginners to intermediate handicappers had been formed, and the program had evolved into a modest success. It's highly recommended as good copy to racetracks everywhere.

The Del Mar executive responsible for launching the education programs and for moving them full speed ahead is Craig Fravel. Interestingly, Fravel is relatively new to the racetrack, young, innovative, and refreshingly decisive, and formerly a securities lawyer for Del Mar. At first blush, Fravel admits, he did not know the difference between a claiming race and an allowance race. Maybe Fravel can identify more readily with newcomers and bewildered racegoers.

In an informal conversation following the 1994 experience at Del Mar, Fravel was observing how impressed he had been by the level of fan participation as well as the positive feedback he was getting, except, he wondered, wasn't diving into the making of pace and speed figures a little too advanced for casual handicappers and racegoers? He suggested that many racegoers do not even like speed figures; that they are not numerically oriented.

Agreed. But it's analogous to saying you want the kids to get a liberal education, well grounded in reading, writing, and arithmetic, but maybe we should leave out the arithmetic. Many children just do not like the numbers. They are not predisposed toward math.

Sorry, but racetracks should understand that the education cannot omit the speed and pace figures. By almost universal agreement speed happens to be the most important attribute of the racehorse, and handicappers simply need to know how fast the horses have run in the past. Speed figures tell the tale. Track executives concerned that their customers obtain a well-rounded, useful education in handicapping should remember that.

So should local tracks and high-tech information providers currently putting the cart before the horse.

So should those ever-cautious track officials who want to provide their customers with fan education but have it firmly in mind that it's prudent to begin and end at the elementary level.

WHO IS MART KOIVASTIK?

I haven't a clue as to how well Mart Koivastik performs at the windows, but on paper he's as good as it gets.

In January 1993, not long after the *Daily Racing Form* had purchased the database of the defunct *Racing Times* and had set sails on an innovative campaign of new editorial and statistical features, I had just sat down with four other hard knockers on a Saturday in a box at Santa Anita. It was five minutes prior to the second race, a six-furlong maiden sprint for 3YOs.

"Look at the comments for the No. 2 horse in the 'A Closer Look' column," I urged the group, whose members were not easily moved to making sizable wagers on somebody else's advice.

"Seeking The Gold is one of the very best sires with first-starters. His debuting maidens win an astonishing forty-four percent, and return a positive ROI."

The No. 2 maiden was a first-starting son of Seeking The Gold. He was posted on the tote at 11–1. The quartet of handicappers literally dashed from the seats and hustled to the windows. All got down on the No. 2. I had already climbed aboard.

The No. 2 maiden stalked the pace along the inside into the far turn, moved up briskly into the stretch, took the lead, and won. He paid $24.60, I believe. Lots of smiling, laughing, hand shaking, and generous celebrating ensued. A rare instance of opportunistic good fortune at the races had been shared by all.

The credit goes to Mart Koivastik. He's a *Daily Racing Form* handicapper who writes "A Closer Look" for two races a day in southern California and elsewhere, plus the same column for national featured stakes, plus occasional weekly articles on the fine art of handicapping. Without exception his material is top of the line. It's highly recommended for handicappers of every stripe, from the most casual racegoers, to weekend hobbyists, to everyday punters like me.

Koivastik has earned a spot on my list of handicappers who have helped me to improve my game. That's a deliberately short and select list, maybe of a dozen contributors. I hesitate to estimate the profits that have come my way via Koivastik's work, but it's in the thousands. I collected a swift $2460 when the son of Seeking The Gold scored in the second half of the daily double at Santa Anita in January 1993. Koivastik was supplying meaningful sire stats at least a year in advance of his colleagues and associates.

My interest in Koivastik had been pricked originally as I began to take notice of the performance statistics he selected, reported, and interpreted. The data struck me again and again as meticulously, accurate and appropriate. Moreover Koivastik had the enviable knack of selecting the statistics precisely appropriate to the handicapping context.

Mindlikaseive

Day's 2nd call (behind En Cascade); fabulous year for Ellis; in addition to overall excellence, barn also does well with dirt-to-turf move (24% wins last 2 years, according to Trainer Analysis Reports, published by Frank Tate of San Diego); Mari's Book has above-average record with first-time-turf horses: 12% wins, according to Bloodstock Research; chance.

Red Hills

Sire has tremendous record with first-time starters and some of them pay quite well; half to $51,476 earner Heavenly Dance; Mandella is tied for 7th in terms of most 2yo debut winners on major SoCal circuit since start of '92;

Silverbulletlover

Huge year for Baffert, including SA training title, but prefer barn with main-track horses – especially if they're going from dirt to turf; has tactical speed; Gulch with first-time-turf horses: 7% wins; has early foot and fact he ran well in debut suggests he can fire fresh; mixed signals.

Andtheliviniseasy

Although sire's stats with first-out 2yo are weak (5% wins), this guy has shown talent in a.m.; in recent years, no barn in SoCal has done a better job with juveniles; half-bro to 4 runners with career earnings exceeding $90,000, led by Tide ($234,459) and Let's Go Flying ($147,060); threat.

If today's race was on the grass, he unfailingly reported the sire's performance with turf horses. If horses were making their first or second starts on the turf, Koivastik relayed the sire's record with first or second grass starters. As pedigree data count emphatically when horses initially try the grass, those statistics were keenly relevant.

If 2YOs were the menu, handicappers could depend upon getting the pertinent data about trainers and sires, whether the juveniles were experienced, first-starters, or second-starters; whatever the situation dictated, the appropriate statistics would be presented.

Koivastik is unsurpassed with the juveniles. In effect he completes the handicapper's homework. His weekly column, "Baby Talk," brings handicappers up to snuff on the 2YO divisions at the local track.

If claiming races were on tap, the trainer statistics would be on the mark regardless, whether the situation involved claims, layoffs, rises and drops, speed figures, running styles, or whatever.

Soon enough I had determined that Koivastik was so adept with statistics, I would be likely to benefit more from his data and interpretations than from my own. I never fail to attend to his statistics and comments. It's convenient, too, that Koivastik is variously plugged into databases and computers. In addition, he surveys the data on trainer performance and trainer patterns distributed by local information services. A public handicapper who combines expertise with statistical data and a work ethic becomes a truly valuable resource.

Simulcast handicappers might appreciate the following little-known facts about popular southern California trainers Mike Mitchell and Bobby Frankel:

Total Tempo

Mitchell has good stats with layoff horses, including those who have been away more than 6 months; this guy runs okay fresh – 2nd for higher tag than today's in his first start of '94; looks as good as any from the standpoint of top Beyer figures showing in PPs; super connections; off-pace types can do okay at this distance: 17 of 33 winners through Mon. action were more than a length off the pace after a half-mile; can't argue with those taking favorable view.

In Case

With a generic trainer, the length of layoff or surface change would be major questions; however, barn excels with layoff runners and turf-to-dirt maneuver; Frankel first-time U.S. winners in SoCal this year (regardless of surface) include Lynton, Opera Score, Top Shape and Campanology; good post; intriguing.

Koivastik's statistics will sometimes stun me, as when he reports that journeyman trainer so-and-so has been 9 for 27 with an ROI of 1.89 when dropping in class in the first start following a claim in the past four years. How does he discover that?

Review the "Closer Look" comments by Koivastik below, taken from recent races at Hollywood Park during spring of 1995. The comments reveal how adaptive the handicapper can be to peculiar situations, and also reflect a range of handicapping talent that cannot be denied.

Hasten to Add

Was within a length of Romarin in the ET Classic after 6 furlongs despite some adversity, then faded; trainer took this event in '92 with 6-5 choice Sky Classic on a yielding course; hasn't competed beyond 9 furlongs since coming to this country, but won at 14 furlongs under 129 pounds and missed by a nose going 2 miles last year in Europe; Timeform experts gave him a 101 rating for '94, compared to 113 for Lassigny; more from Timeform on this runner: "big colt, impresses in appearance ... thoroughly game and genuine"; tricky call if he goes off at usual lowish odds; among several logical contenders in a competitive event.

Our Blue Michael

Hard to embrace on the win end, but trifecta shooters will note his trait of running 3rd at juicy prices; within last 10 starts, he's been 3rd at 6-1, 26-1 and 24-1; minor award may be best-case scenario.

Beautiful Crown

Didn't break especially well, then rushed up to set :44 1/5 half-mile split from the rail; that takes a lot of energy; he put up an incredible turn time of about :21 2/5; earned some strong speed figures in Arcadia earlier in the year; Kent, who has been aboard for each of the wins, returns to the controls; big chance to make amends.

Gold Land

Switch to dirt was a profitable move; gelded between the Feb. and April races and Drysdale has mentioned that change as a factor in the turnaround, too; no question he likes this track and distance; skeptics will note he had better posts for the previous 7-furlong tries, plus he was facing easier competition; however, Drysdale is tremendous in terms of placing his horses (27% wins on major SoCal circuit this year); Eddie D's in the Bay Area, riding Special Price for Drysdale in the GG Handicap; improving for a good barn, which makes him dangerous.

Hasten to Add was an import competing in the Early Times turf series that accompanies the Triple Crown. His record was not easy to decipher, until Koivastik gave it a meaningful context, including a Timeform comparative rating with another starter in the race (Lassigny). Is that good service?

Not one public handicapper in a dozen would even know to report on turn-time, let alone do the calculation and report the sizzling fractional-time in the context of a pace analysis. Pace fanciers realize that a turn-time of 21 ⅖ is superlative, and Koivastik does not fail to get Beautiful Crown's message across.

Casual handicappers, and not a few regulars, can learn everything they need to know about Gold Land and his prominent trainer in a twinkle.

I especially like the comments on Our Blue Michael, a long shot. Thinking like the talented, alert handicapper he obviously is, Koivastik takes a moment to remind trifecta bettors that the long shot has shown he can get a piece at a price.

In recent seasons Koivastik has even kept southern California handicappers informed about the track profiles at the regularly run distances. Track profiles alert handicappers to running styles that might be advantaged at particular distances and to biases that might be dominant. The profiles describe the beaten-lengths of recent winners at the first and second calls, respectively, and can be a helpful tool. Not only do track profiles guide a pace analysis but they also guide casual handicappers who cannot routinely attend the races.

Starting in each case with the first horse in the field, facing are recent comments from Koivastik regarding the track profiles at Hollywood Park, spring of 1995, at three distinct distances:

7 ½ Furlongs	1 ¹/₁₆ Miles	All Distances Grass

A CLOSER LOOK
5th Hollywood

A CLOSER LOOK
9th Hollywood

A CLOSER LOOK
4th Hollywood

T. H. Fappiano

Fast-track stats at this distance since start of '94: 12% wins from rail, 65% of winners more than a length off the pace after a half-mile; though Jory can strike at a price, none of his winners this meet have paid as much as $10; hasn't hit the board since being claimed.

Top Rung

How track played at this distance for first 21 days of meet (through Thu.): 36% of winners were on the lead after 6 furlongs, 77% were either on the lead or within 3 lengths of it at that stage; regressed in the A Gleam and will get first-time Lasix; has a Grade 2 win showing on the resume, though it came sprinting; hasn't hit triple digits on Beyer scale yet; has fewest starts in this field and perhaps more room to develop; maybe.

Sharp Words

Turf course has played fair in terms of running styles this meet; off-pace runner passed several horses here last month; has best last-race Beyer; ran okay at 10 furlongs in April at SA (led after 9 furlongs, was passed by hard-hitting Grooming); usually has earned a check this year, but most recent wins were vs. much cheaper at Hawthorne; chance.

The track profile at the odd distance of 7 ½ furlongs, programmed in southern California only at Hollywood Park, should be especially interesting to handicappers. The rail wins its fair share at 7 ½ furlongs, and most of the races will be won from behind the pace. It's nice to know.

Because Hollywood Park has experienced a negative speed bias along the rail at certain distances in recent years, Koivastik dutifully reports the performances of the inside and outside post positions at all distances at regular intervals. As Hollywood Park proceeded during spring of 1995, Koivastik at one point reported that at six furlongs the rail post had been 1 for 56. At the same distance at that time, the outside post position had accounted for 29 percent of the winners. Obviously handicappers would prefer contenders exiting from the outside, and not from the rail.

Yet in the absence of a rail bias or outside bias, Koivastik will not automatically report the performances of post positions at the various distances. Situational factors dictate the reporting of common statistics, heightening the meaning of the data in virtually all instances.

Maybe most impressive of all is the interplay between the considerable data Koivastik reports and the handicapper's interpretive and analytical skills. His opinions, when stated, invariably emerge from a highly objective base. It's in analyzing the country's featured races where Koivastik allows the objective-interpretive-analytical interplay to roam widely, and his comments can be quite persuasive. On Preakness Day 1995 examine Koivastik's comments on the upset winner of the Kentucky Derby two weeks before:

Thunder Gulch

Less-than-ideal post, but little dude somehow got a smooth trip from 16-hole to get the roses; his Beyer ranks 2nd (to Go for Gin's 112) among the last 5 Ky. Derby winners; impressed most by the way he earned the figure, staying close to fast pace that others couldn't cope with; 4 horses ahead of him after 6 furlongs in Derby finished 16-9-19-12; put another way, the horses who finished 2nd through 7th were in positions 10-12-9-19-11-18 after 6 furlongs; incredible year for Stevens, who has also won Santa Anita Handicap and SA Derby with non-favorites; though last 11 winners of this event raced in Ky. Derby, the only horses who won both races are Alysheba ('87) and Sunday Silence ('89); none of the others has won a Grade 1 race this year – he's captured 2; the right day to bet him was 2 weeks ago; whether he's a good investment at much lower odds is a tricky call; harder to overlook him this time.

—Mart Koivastik

In the 1995 Kentucky Derby, Thunder Gulch had stayed relatively close to a rapid pace before drawing away by two lengths in a powerful performance. Koivastik not only captured the essence of the colt's Derby victory but also documented the vigorous effort by describing how the other four stalkers had faded and how six horses in the bottom half of the field after six furlongs had managed to finish second through seventh. Very impressive!

As powerful as Thunder Gulch had looked in winning the Kentucky Derby, Koivastik cautioned that the moment to bet on the colt was then, not now, as a probable underlay in the Preakness. That's an impressively pragmatic piece of handicapping too.

As far as I'm concerned, the Form's "A Closer Look" column and Mart Koivastik offer a perfect mating of instant handicapping and excellent handicapper. His output day-to-day qualifies as the prototype his colleagues and other public selectors might strive to emulate.

In the eastern and central editions of the *Daily Racing Form,* "A Closer Look" often does not appear, in favor of a companion column, "At a Glance." "At a Glance" provides handicappers with an array of leading statistics under a number of criteria for the horses in today's field, without the corresponding interpretive and analytical comments. "At a Glance," in my judgment, is largely a waste of time and space. Its data supply little nourishment for handicappers, whether casual or regular. "At a Glance" might be eliminated in favor of "A Closer Look," with Mart Koivastik providing the prototypical commentaries and perhaps conducting a couple of in-house training sessions. Nothing personal, I hasten to add, just the optimal use of resources.

When I inquired about him, my friend and former Form official Scott Finley advised me that Koivastik was based in Phoenix, Arizona, one of the paper's two home offices, and that he was definitely a student of the game. No kidding!

Apparently the handicapper enjoys sitting at his computer in Phoenix, smoking over the past performances of southern California, New York, Florida, or Kentucky, and calling into play the handicapping data that might clarify events as much as possible. No doubt I speak for numerous handicappers in saying I keenly appreciate the approach.

Like my pal Dick Mitchell, maybe Mart Koivastik is a card-carrying member of that rarefied club of mature adults who gaze upon the personal computer as the world's most amusing adult toy. I hope he will continue to enjoy the handicapping game, and that he will continue to report his findings in marvelous detail.

It's none of my business, but I recommend too, that Koivastik be rewarded with a substantial pay raise. He deserves it.

BENNETT LIEBMAN'S REBUTTAL

I wish I had said that.

Have you ever taken part in a professional conference, a symposium, a meeting, or maybe an informal gathering of peers and associates, when suddenly a significant combustible issue arises, delineated perhaps by someone with authority and position, with the gentlemanly arguments having a certain face validity, but which at a deeper visceral level come across as hypocritical and false?

Wouldn't you have liked to have stood up and once and for all set the record straight, preferably at the expense of any false prophets in the room?

In December 1994 I got that opportunity, but I blew it. I did not countenance the harsh criticism of Thoroughbred racing I was hearing from a respectable source, but it never occurred to me what I might say in rebuttal. The absolutely correct response did occur, fortunately, to one Bennett Liebman, a member of the New York State Advisory and Wagering Board, and I have been envious of Liebman's rebuttal ever since.

The scene was Tucson, Arizona, at a resort hotel serving as headquarters for the annual five-day conference of the Thoroughbred Racing Association (TRA). A symposium on racing and the media was under way, and as I arrived partway into the presentations, sports editor Bill Dwyre of the *Los Angeles Times* was speaking rather critically about racing's credibility problem.

Also on the dais were NBC's Leslie Visser; *Sports Illustrated* editor Sally Bailey; author and handicapper William Murray, a friend who articulated the case for the bettors' point of view quite effectively; Drew Couto, lawyer for California's newly organized TOC, a horseman's group; and a representative of the Associated Press I did not recognize and cannot recall.

My tardy arrival had coincided with the tail end of Dwyre's attack on racing's credibility. The editor noted that if horse racing did not consider itself to be receiving fair and representative coverage in his newspaper (which it does not), the fault lay with the tracks themselves and with certain reprehensible practices the sport of kings has never seen fit to eradicate.

He mentioned the gambling, of course, and problems with the drug testing, and why doesn't horse racing publicize some of its more respectable owners, such as Bob and Beverly Lewis, of Newport Beach. A particular pet peeve of Dwyre's were those insidious 900-numbers that purported to sell winners to an unsuspecting public. I missed the major portion of Dwyre's criticism, but I had heard enough to become uncomfortably annoyed at the editor and his cheap remarks.

Dwyre's message was that horse racing could not reasonably expect better treatment by the media until it cleaned up its act.

The other panelists presented their views. The editor from *Sports Illustrated* was preoccupied with explaining why the magazine had not even covered the 1994 Breeders' Cup races—because Holy Bull did not go. She noted that horse racing has one of the weakest followings in sports, fewer readers than auto racing, sailing, cycling, and similar esoteric activities. The remedy was to produce more heroes.

Bill Murray bemoaned the depiction of racegoers in the popular media as sad and misleading. He took an aggressive stand on behalf of the poor misrepresented souls who enjoyed playing the races for fun and profit, occasionally referred to as handicappers. On occasion Murray invoked that enigmatic term.

The remainder of the session was concerned primarily with ways by which horse racing might generate better and more frequent publicity. The consensus held that racing's publicity directors must be more assertive, picking up the phones and calling in interesting timely stories, sending out the releases, and following up relentlessly, instead of waiting passively for the media to respond.

When the panelists had finished, the moderator opened the session to questions and comments from the audience. First to move to the microphone was Bennett Liebman.

Liebman addressed Bill Dwyre specifically and personally. How could the sports editor of the *Los Angeles Times* come to this conference, began Liebman, sit on this panel, and dare to single out Thoroughbred racing as having a lack of credibility? Liebman asked what Dwyre thought of the credibility of Donald Sterling, owner of the Los

Angeles Clippers. He wanted Dwyre to comment on the credibility of Bruce McNall, owner of the Los Angeles Kings. What did Dwyre think of Don King's credibility, and of boxing's credibility on the whole? And what did Dwyre think of the owner of the Los Angeles Rams, the remarkable Georgia Frontiere, and that organization's credibility?

As Liebman confronted Dwyre in a measured, rational, but forceful tone, it was a special dramatic moment for horse racing, a well-aimed arrow piercing its target's heart. Liebman finally stopped. Along with everyone else in the hall, I awaited editor Dwyre's carefully measured response.

It was halting, defensive, and frankly pitiful.

Dwyre conceded in a meek and grudging way that racing was indeed not alone, that other sports also suffered credibility gaps. Beyond that the serious journalist was not so forthcoming.

Dwyre did not allude to the steroids ingested routinely by football players and track and field athletes.

He did not mention the silly autographs baseball players sell to kids for outrageous fees.

He did not mention the drug abuses of the several major spectator sports, including the Olympics Games, or the associated drug-testing problems in those arenas.

He did not mention the massive illegal gambling on the Super Bowl or the widespread ceaseless gambling on football, baseball, and basketball games in every office and family room as a matter of course.

He did not mention the nonstop gambling on the golf courses in every professional country club in the nation.

He did not mention the recruitment practices of leading colleges and universities, the bogus graduation rates, or the financial entanglements among alumni, the athletic departments, and the athletes, or the indecent conduct of the striking owners and players toward the national pastime.

Dwyre mentioned none of that and much more as he conceded that racing was not alone in the credibility bind. He retired rather humbly from the rest of the discussion.

Dwyre might have conceded as well his own hypocrisy, in his role as sports editor of the *Los Angeles Times*, in treating horse racing as a sport with a credibility problem while not treating football, baseball, basketball, ice hockey, boxing, and the rest as sports having similar, indeed greater, credibility problems, not to mention those luminous sports impressarios who lie and cheat their way to the summit or the sports bettors galore who make the handles at racetracks look like chump change. All of that betting expressly illegal.

Thus my heartiest respects to Bennett Liebman. At the perfect time, in the perfect place, he had the savvy, nerve, and common sense to unmask a hypocritical editor who should have known better and re-instated horse racing on a leveled playing field with those other darling sports. I dearly wish I could have said what Liebman said.

Coincidentally, seven months later in an editorial in the *Daily Racing Form,* Bennett Liebman was saluted warmly for his decision supporting the race-day use of Lasix in New York.

According to the account, Liebman had steadfastly opposed the use of Lasix for years, but had changed his mind after a wrenching soul-searching that was resolved ultimately on a best judgment as to what was best right now for the game. Still, Liebman could not endorse the use of Lasix with enthusiasm, but he had become even more concerned with the small fields, declining attendance, and horse shortages that were crippling New York racing.

In an eloquent, carefully modulated decision, Liebman had determined that on balance, Lasix would benefit New York racing more than the diuretic could possibly harm it. The *Form's* editorial proposed that the sport might be revitalized successfully if more officials like Liebman could be drafted.

Bennett Liebman's rebuttal in Tucson should serve a more noble purpose than its admonition of the *Los Angeles Times's* myopic sports editor. Fearful of the gambling connection, horse racing historically has indulged the slings and arrows of social critics who do not know what they are talking about. In consequence, notwithstanding the several crunching problems contemporary racing faces, the sport's bleak image in the society at large has endured as pervasively negative. That image is long overdue for a makeover. The tolerance of knee-jerk criticism must end. The sport deserves its makeover, and the new look must be presented by leaders in the game who purport to care about horse racing.

In truth the horse-racing game is deceptively clean, and certainly so in the relative sense—in comparison, that is, to other sports and other games. The doping of horses and the fixing of races has never been more than an incidental nuisance, and belongs mainly in the romantic traditions of Damon Runyon and Nathan Detroit. When a dedicated racetrack racketeer was asked at trial in the 1970s why he attempted to fix races in New York by bribing the jockeys instead of drugging the horses, he responded, "The horses won't cooperate."

For the same compelling reason, horses are not drugged and races are not fixed, except in highly unusual circumstances. Even then nobody gets rich. The horses do not cooperate.

On the broadest of good-bad scales, horse racing is relatively clean, well policed, and a fair shake for all participants, from owners to breeders to jockeys, and even to bettors. Season after season the best horses and best players will be more likely to prevail.

When charges of corruption, contamination, and credibility raise their ugly heads, racing people have no excuse for backing away. Instead horse racing warrants an honest, aggressive defense. Let everyone remember Bennett Liebman's rebuttal.

To fair-minded people, it hits home, hard and true.

CHARLIE

O nce, just one time in a quarter century, I heard one of his fellows criticize Charlie Whittingham.

The assailant was that irascible Irishman Tommy Doyle. Tommy was standing at the rail near Clockers Corner at Santa Anita, early 1980s, watching a couple of his nicely bred 3YOs in training. Years before he had won the 1975 Belmont Stakes with his pride and joy, Avatar, the crown on Doyle's outstanding career as a Thoroughbred trainer.

Tommy was saying how easily horses fly on airplanes, that they experience none of the tension and anxiety that humans feel, when the conversation quickly veered toward the development of young horses. Gazing at his latest hopefuls, I asked Tommy whether his greatest thrill was shaping the talent and careers of 3YOs.

The horseman's eyes brightened, his posture straightened, his very being seemed to spring to life as he nodded yes, affirmative, absolutely, developing the young ones was the cat's meow for a horse trainer. A cynical man, intelligent, engagingly critical, articulate, carrying something of a chip on his shoulders, probably hinged to the contrariness of the racing game, all the well-laid plans that can be constantly spoiled, Tommy lit up at the topic and began to reminisce on the development of Avatar and the other good ones he had guided to completion.

And then he suddenly said, "You know, Charlie has never developed a young horse in his life. He's just never had to do it. I don't think he could do it. It's not his strength. He gets them fully developed. They're sent to him. They've already matured as racehorses.

"Tell me, what's the last colt Charlie developed as a two-year-old or young three-year-old into a top horse? Name one young horse Charlie has developed into a champion."

I might have named Porterhouse, 2YO champion of 1953, or Turkish Trousers, 3YO filly champion of 1971, but at the moment I did not recall either horse.

Besides, this was not a version of Trivial Pursuit. With a muted resentment winding its way throughout his broadside, in his customary cynical, harmless style, Tommy Doyle was merely trying to insinuate that in one important facet of the craft he could do as well or better than Charlie Whittingham, everyone's king of the backstretch.

The kernel of truth in Doyle's critique was that for the past twelve years Whittingham had been sent mature, extremely talented, well-developed horses by the likes of Nelson Bunker Hunt, Aaron Jones, Howard B. Keck, Claiborne Farm, Mary Jones Bradley, Quinn Martin, Serge Fradkoff, Robert Sangster, and numerous others. His mere presence meant to the clients the difference between a degree of success and the Grade 1 titles, the championships, the abundantly rich purses, and the multimillion-dollar breeding syndications. He got the great Ack Ack at four, three seasons into the colt's career, from the fabulous raconteur Captain Harry Guggenheim.

True as well, Whittingham in his prime concentrated mainly on the Grade 1 races and other stakes for older horses, 4up, going nine to ten furlongs on the dirt and especially at any route distance on the turf. His 3YOs were relegated to a minority status, and Whittingham rarely bothered to run a 2YO. For that matter he rarely started a sprinter.

To put the prime years in perspective, Whittingham had never surrendered even a passing thought to the Kentucky Derby. When confronted on the matter, the trainer reiterated his position that reflected an attitude, that he did not believe in pushing young horses too fast.

More than once Whittingham had advised the racing establishment that racing 3YOs at a mile and a quarter on the first Saturday of May was ridiculous. As the Kentucky Derby was horse racing's premier event, indeed the sport's truest identity, in a strange and unfortunate way, and notwithstanding the roll call of champions, near-champions, division leaders, and stakes winners from 1968 to 1985, Charlie Whittingham could never be raised on high and carried through the market square as the centerpiece of his own private domain. In this fundamental sense Whittingham was strictly out of it. Charlie didn't give a damn.

So Tommy Doyle cannot be faulted entirely for forgetting about Porterhouse, Turkish Trousers, and other youngsters that Charlie indeed had launched.

And that is why I have concluded, when at age seventy-four Charlie decided to go for it, and promptly won the Kentucky Derby twice within four years, that this man, the Bald Eagle, Sir Charles, was the greatest trainer of them all.

The achievement is almost unimaginable. After three decades of looking the other way, of playing another game, of working almost exclusively with older horses, all at once, as if on a whim, Charlie directs his attention to the younger horses, and practically overnight he takes down the sport's greatest prize, with Ferdinand, in 1986, and then, as if to drive home the lesson, he does it again, in 1989, with Sunday Silence.

No one sent him a grown-up Ferdinand. No one sent him a grown-up Sunday Silence. For good measure, in 1994, at age eighty-one, Charlie finished second in the Derby with Strodes Creek. Maybe Charlie will win the roses again when he grows a little older.

When Ferdinand won, Charlie practically brushed the moment aside. Naturally members of the media wanted to know why he had traveled to Churchill Downs with a 3YO after all the intervening years, and all the brusque refusals.

"I got tired of hearing people tell me I was no good because I had never won the Kentucky Derby," explained Charlie, tongue firmly in cheek.

As Whittingham constructed the story, people he met would ask him what he did for a living. When Charlie revealed he trained racehorses, the first thing people asked was whether he had ever won the Kentucky Derby. When Charlie admitted no, he hadn't, the people expressed disappointment and the conversation subsided.

When Sunday Silence won, that was quite different. That one meant something, a shining moment actually, to Charlie. The opponent was Easy Goer, an odds-on favorite, leading son of Alydar, bred by the Jockey Club's Ogden Mills Phipps, the quintessential blueblood, and trained by Shug McGaughey, the finest young horseman in the land. Easy Goer was New York, and Sunday Silence was southern California, the polar opposites, and Charlie delighted in the geographical conflict as well.

When Sunday Silence crossed the finish line first, and the network cameras panned to Charlie, there he was all aglow, smiling wide, shaking hands even, a demeanor not at all characteristic of Charlie Whittingham, unfailingly stoic and unassuming in victory.

In counterpoint the pained frustration on the face of Shug McGaughey rendered it clear that the New York contingent had fully expected to win. Everything that had transpired to that point had assured them they would be running the better horse.

But Easy Goer and Shug McGaughey had run headlong into Charlie Whittingham's greatest asset: the ability to focus on the main objective so totally, so relentlessly, with such competence, that nothing stands in the way. The ability to win the big one—that was always Charlie's trump. He did that better than anyone else.

Once Charlie had decided that Sunday Silence could win the Kentucky Derby, that he wanted to beat Easy Goer on that memorable day, the die had been cast. The result was not preordained by any means, but Easy Goer had better deliver his number-one race in the Kentucky Derby.

Another illustration of Whittingham's greatest asset is well worth recounting. It happened in the fall of 1978, and to this day the race remains my favorite. This was Charlie's finest hour, a coup de grace, a singular achievement.

Charlie trained a turf star named Exceller, a deep closer owned by Nelson Bunker Hunt, the eccentric multimillionaire, who had paid a paltry $25,000 for the horse, and the best racer "Bunky" would ever own.

Early in 1978 Exceller had won a Grade 3 dirt stakes when the race was moved off the turf due to January rains. From January to July, Exceller had collected five Grade 1s, four on grass, and the Hollywood Gold Cup on the main track.

Seattle Slew, at four, was back in action for an abbreviated campaign on the East Coast. Charlie thought Exceller deserved a shot at Horse of the Year. He knew Seattle Slew would be handed the award, unless Exceller could beat the Triple Crown hero in his own backyard.

Charlie rarely traveled, but now he shipped Exceller to New York and announced in no uncertain terms the objective would be the Jockey Club Gold Cup, at a mile and one-half the country's ultimate handicap challenge.

In preparation Charlie entered Exceller in Belmont's Grade 1

Woodward Stakes, at a mile and one-quarter. Seattle Slew went favored in the Woodward. Prior to the Woodward, Charlie emphasized he expected Exceller, who had not started since late July, to be short and to lose. In the running Exceller raced forwardly, not his normal style, chasing Seattle Slew, the lone front-runner, all the way. The two finished one-two.

Three weeks later, in the definitive Jockey Club Gold Cup, Exceller dropped far back, as usual. The track was sloppy. Besides Seattle Slew, the small brilliant field included Affirmed, and those two brilliant champions ran together on a pace of 45 ⅕, 1:09 ⅖, to the mile in 1:35 ⅖. Exceller was practically distanced. In the grandstand far above, Bunker Hunt had lost hope.

Between the half-mile pole and the upper stretch, Exceller dispensed a tremendous rally, gaining no less than twenty-two lengths. In the meantime, Seattle Slew had drawn clear. Affirmed proved no factor.

Exceller caught Seattle Slew at the eighth pole. The pair fought furiously through the long Belmont stretch, Seattle Slew under Cordero, Exceller under Shoemaker.

At the wire it was Exceller by a nose. Bunker Hunt would call it the greatest race he had ever seen. In the aftermath Cordero suggested he might have won in another jump. Shoemaker, who rarely indulged these exchanges, strongly disagreed. He insisted he had horse left, and could have held Seattle Slew safe for another sixteenth.

It was Charlie's greatest triumph, or one of them. The Woodward prep aside, Exceller had annexed six consecutive Grade 1s, on dirt and on grass, from January to November, defeating the best horses on both surfaces, including Seattle Slew in the year's definitive test.

The voters slipped the prizes to Seattle Slew—the Eclipse Award for Older Handicap Male and for Horse of the Year. Exceller did not even get an Eclipse as grass champion. Charlie's reaction was typically subdued. He wondered what those people (the voters) could be thinking about, but he let it drop at that.

A crusty, rough, acerbic man, a drinker, a fighter, an ex-Marine, Charlie was fastidious with his horses. Every horse was trained to the minute. Each was aimed at specific objectives. Charlie's workouts were classic, perfectly spaced, every five days, every horse, most expensive to least expensive, for three decades. He got to the barn early each morning, like clockwork, and the daily routine began.

He stayed in California. Until 1970, when the onslaught of stakes winners began, his best horse had been Pretense, bred by Llangollen Farm, Charlie's major client during the first half of his career. In 1967, Pretense won six major stakes, including the Gulfstream Park Handicap. It's the only stakes Charlie has won in Florida. He has never won a stakes in Maryland, New Jersey, or Arkansas, but it's only been half a century.

The occasional exception was New York. Charlie would go to the Big Apple, but only when the Horse of the Year title was on the line, as with Exceller. Otherwise Charlie stayed put, attending meticulously to the hundred-plus horses in his care.

His relations with owners were strictly business, and Charlie was the boss. By and large the clients were pleased to have a presence in the barn. The flare-ups on record involved jockey assignments. Charlie used Bill Shoemaker first call, Don Pierce second call, and Fernando Toro third call. Shoemaker's special dimensions apart, the three were waiting riders, with excellent timing, and unusually talented with latecomers on the grass, Charlie's specialty.

Charlie affected a disdain for jockeys. In bars, over drinks, he would allude to them scornfully as size-three hats. Shoemaker, he allowed, was a size four. He did not often retain Laffit Pincay, Jr., the greatest rider of his day and of Charlie's prime. A rugged individualist, possessing tremendous strength, and all-out on his mounts in all circumstances, Pincay was ostensibly too hard on the horses. He would bring them back a little the worse for wear. Charlie did not like that.

When Shoemaker retired, in 1989, for several weeks Whittingham used a green apprentice, Fernando Valenzuela, a lightweight, literally, which Whittingham liked. The young Valenzuela could not win enough, however, and Charlie eventually switched first call to Chris McCarron.

During primetime the trainer enjoyed a special relationship with jockey Shoemaker, and the match worked wonderfully well for both men. Charlie relied upon Shoemaker's light, magical hands to teach developing horses to do what Charlie wanted them to do: to rate kindly, to relax behind the early pace, to respond when asked, to finish strongly. As the horses matured and learned, the jockey was willing to lose. When the horses were at last prepared to strike, Shoemaker won the stakes races their blue-blooded pedigrees and fastidious training programs had entitled them to win.

Once, as long ago as 1972, after a Hollywood grass stakes that had been bungled, Shoemaker dismounted, and I watched Charlie approach him in a temper, waving his arms. Apparently Charlie said something the jockey did not endorse and the two of them stood there toe-to-toe near the winner's circle arguing vehemently and gesticulating wildly. I never saw that scene again.

One of the final scenes between the trainer and the jockey was played out in romantic, dramatic fashion at Churchill Downs with Ferdinand in 1986. Ferdinand was difficult to train (an underachiever) and he was difficult to ride (he pulled himself up when in front), as both men had consistently complained. Shoemaker had not won the Kentucky Derby since 1965. Whittingham had never even entered the race. Shoemaker was fifty-six, Whittingham seventy-four.

When Ferdinand won, following an incredibly smart, talented ride by Shoemaker, the trainer and jockey were hailed as racing's Sunshine Boys. They liked the tony reference. The tag line fit, was pleasingly apt. On the winner's stand, the garland of roses draped around his neck, Shoemaker even sobbed. The 1986 Kentucky Derby served as a culmination of sorts for the sport's bellwether practitioners, its leading jockey, and the leading trainer.

Quick, how many champions has Charlie Whittingham trained? The number is a solid rounded ten. The first was Porterhouse, in 1953, the latest was Flawlessly, in 1992, forty years in between.

Which was best of show?

When Sunday Silence won the 1989 Kentucky Derby, followed two weeks later by the Preakness, followed six months later by the Breeders' Cup Classic, accumulating five Grade 1s in the process, and was voted Horse of the Year as a 3YO, the consensus formed that this must be Charlie's best-ever.

Charlie agreed, but like witnesses on the stand, it might have refreshed his memory to review the actual record.

As good as Sunday Silence was, he was only second banana, not nearly as talented as Charlie's greatest horse.

Charlie's greatest was Ack Ack. A 5YO of 1971, the midpoint of Charlie's grand career, Ack Ack was a terrifying force from six furlongs to ten furlongs. He won on the dirt, and he won on the grass (undefeated). In eight 1971 starts, Ack Ack won seven major stakes, and he took them wire-to-wire at every turn. He carried 130 pounds three times, 129 twice, and in the mile and one-quarter Hollywood Gold Cup Ack Ack completed the course under two minutes (1:59 ⅘) while carrying 134 pounds. As only a handicapper and Ack Ack devotee would recall, believe it or not, in a short field, with Ack Ack at 1–3 odds, the Gold Cup exacta paid $235.

In that amazing season, while never leaving California, Ack Ack was voted unanimously (a) Horse of the Year; (b) Older Handicap Horse; and (c) Champion Sprinter. How many horses have completed that triple? Very, very few!

Ack Ack

HORSE OF THE YEAR

BEST HANDICAP AND SPRINTER HORSE

(Bred by H. F. Guggenheim. Owned by Forked Lightning Ranch. Trained by C. Whittingham.)

Racing Record, 1971

Date	Track	Race	Dist.	Wt.	Fin.	Time	Odds	Value
Jan 2	Santa Anita Park	Palos Verdes Handicap	3-4	129	2	1:08¾ gd	4-5	$ 6,000
Jan 16	Santa Anita Park	San Carlos Handicap	7-8	126	1	1:21 gd	6-5	34,150
Feb 6	Santa Anita Park	San Pasqual Handicap	1 1-16	129	1	1:41⅖ ft	4-5	33,300
Feb 27	Santa Anita Park	San Antonio Stakes	1 1-8	124	1	1:47 ft	1-1	54,450
Mar 13	Santa Anita Park	Santa Anita Handicap	1 1-4	130	1	2:03 sl	4-5	100,000
Jun 17	Hollywood Park	Hollywood Express Handicap	5 1-2 f	130	1	1:02⅗ ft	2-5	19,500
Jly 5	Hollywood Park	American Handicap	1 1-8 (T)	130	1	1:47⅕ fm	3-5	45,900
Jly 17	Hollywood Park	Hollywood Gold Cup Invitational Handicap	1 1-4	134	1	1:59⅘ ft	1-3	100,000

Recapitulation

Year	Age	Sts.	1st.	2d.	3d.	Unp.	Won
1968	2	3	1	2	0	0	$ 6,075
1969	3	11	7	3	0	1	177,491
1970	4	5	4	0	0	1	59,775
1971	5	8	7	1	0	0	393,300
Total (4)		27	19	6	0	2	$636,641

Photo by Tony Leonard.

On the final day of Del Mar, 1970, Whittingham stunned a rookie handicapper by entering Ack Ack in an unimportant sprint at 5 ½ furlongs. I could not understand the maneuver.

What could possibly be the purpose? This was the best horse in America. What's up?

Ack Ack promptly recorded a record 1:02 ⅕ seconds, a speed standard that stands today, twenty-six years later. The horse was sensational.

Later I came to realize Ack Ack probably had been kicking down the stall door. The Del Mar dash released a gusher of pent-up energy.

Ack Ack was so supreme, so thoroughly dominating, that even Charlie dubbed him great. In his later years Charlie frequently, and rather carelessly, praised his horses, overrating several, but during primetime he rarely bestowed his praise. A truly talented horse was nice, or maybe good, but he was never great.

Charlie's reticence bothered small-time client Burt Bacharach, who toiled in a setting where you were great if you were merely good. Bacharach that season campaigned a stakes winner with Charlie named Advance Guard. To Bacharach's chagrin, Charlie would allow only that Advance Guard was nice.

Charlie anointed Ack Ack a great horse.

At age fifty-eight Charlie was named Outstanding Trainer of 1971, his first national honor. That year the Eclipse awards were inaugurated, too, and Charlie would be accorded the honor twice again, in 1982 and 1989.

Following 2450 wins and 650 stakes winners, it's difficult and perhaps pretentious to isolate the best horses Charlie has ever trained and to elaborate a top-ten list, but it's also fun to do, and I have definite opinions about both.

CHARLIE WITTINGHAM'S BEST-EVER TEAM:

Best Older Handicap Horse	Ack Ack
Best 3YO	Sunday Silence
Best 3YO Filly	Turkish Trousers
Best Older Filly and Mare	Tallahto
Best Turf Horse	Cougar II/Fiddle Isle/Perrault (tie)
Best Turf Female	Dahlia
Best Sprinter	Ack Ack
Best 2YO	Porterhouse

CHARLIE WHITTINGHAM'S TOP TEN HORSES:

1. Ack Ack
2. Sunday Silence
3. Perrault
4. Fiddle Isle
5. Cougar II
6. Tallahto
7. Pretense
8. Quack
9. Turkish Trousers
10. Exceller

Honorable Mention: Ferdinand, Porterhouse, Flawlessly, Dahlia and Kilijaro.

Charlie dominated his colleagues and foes in southern California so thoroughly for so long that any meaningful comparisons seem unwarranted, but the one nemesis he feared and never did thwart was John Henry. The gutsy, infinitely determined gelding not only frustrated Charlie's turf cavalry in the early 1980s but also whipped Perrault by a disputed nose in the 1984 Santa Anita Handicap, a million-dollar prize, and a milestone Charlie has captured nine times. Charlie admired old John Henry, one racehorse he would have loved to handle.

At Santa Anita, in 1995, at age eighty-two, Charlie started 115 horses and won with 9 of them, an 0.08 percentage. He went 0 for 17 in the subsequent weeks at Hollywood Park. The inevitable slide that had begun a few years before now gathered momentum. No one ships Charlie a good horse anymore. Unsentimental handicappers discount his contenders.

Only aging cornered Charlie. A curious change in his personality occurred regarding his uncharacteristic boasts about his horses. The same stoic, sullen horseman who had refused to call a stakes winner anything better than nice was suddenly showering praise, even before the horses had accomplished the minimum.

In 1987 Charlie was quoted by the *Daily Racing Form* as believing a journeyman performer named Swank would be his best grass horse ever. Huh?

He suggested in 1987, too, that the unexceptional Temperate Sil might win the Kentucky Derby. A year later he suggested that a truly ordinary one-run closer named Lively One might win America's race. Apparently Charlie had been smitten with the roses after all.

And in 1990 Charlie created a media furor that would last for two seasons when he dubbed the untested 2YO Excavate his Derby horse. Overbet to even-money or thereabouts repeatedly on Charlie's empty boast, Excavate never won a stakes. As the 1991 Kentucky Derby approached, Excavate was still eligible for nonwinners once other than maiden or claiming. Excavate was just a horse.

None of those horses, or others Charlie had coronated prematurely, would break into the Top 100 on a list of all-time Whittingham bests.

But Charlie's okay, doing just fine. He's working at the racetrack, at the job he loves, as a horseman. The $110 million his horses have plundered will remain a matter of record. A shrewd investor in his own horses (in 1971 he acquired one-third of Ack Ack by suspending his sales fee and forgiving the training expenses), Charlie has probably pocketed more money from the racetrack than anyone in history. Yet the money has never meant as much to him as the work.

Charlie had compiled so much, or had come to care about money so little, that in the 1980s one of his administrative employees embezzled a tidy one million dollars from him without his knowledge. When the matter came to light, Charlie expressed his regrets. The woman got ten years.

He's known as a racing legend, of course, and a book has been written (*Whittingham,* by Jay Hovdey, published by The Blood Horse, 1993), the tributes so well deserved now coming due.

Santa Anita has hung a portrait of Charlie in its clubhouse, a full-length reflection of his racetrack persona. The portrait has a majestic aura to it, Charlie standing tall, in his familiar suit with the familiar pate, as if striding above the memories his time evokes.

The portrait is wonderful, so, too, the biography, the dinners, and all the other tributes, but a full-sized, stone-carved monument to Charlie would be best, near the paddock at Santa Anita. Like the monuments at Yankee Stadium, Charlie endures astride his sport in a magnificent way. Southern California racing is deeply and eternally in his debt. He is the eternal racetrack figure. Strong. Solitary. A hero. A good man.

Best of all, Charlie goes about his business these final days with the deep respect and affection of his fellows. Charlie is liked by all. As ever, he is much admired for who he is and what he has done. It will always be so.

He's been good to the horses, every one of them. With a single exception, a Bacharach-owned claimer in front wraps, I cannot remember a Whittingham horse breaking down on the track. They returned to the barn whole. If they suffered the slightest ailment, they did not train, they did not race. The infinite patience, so much remarked.

But when the horses were healthy and ready to roll, Charlie struck with an iron fist, and the results cannot be denied.

LAZARO'S LEGACY

The racing game being the devil's cauldron of disillusionment and despair that it so commonly is, for owners, breeders, horsemen, and handicappers alike, it's always invigorating to spend some time with the winners. One of the most indomitable spirits in the annals of the sport was Lazaro Barrera, gone since 1991, but never to be forgotten.

In front of a hundred horse players at a day-of-the-races seminar in the early 1980s, Lee Rousso quizzed me as to which trainer of southern California I considered the bettor's best friend. It was a shrewdly phrased question, and I answered instantly—Laz Barrera. The versatile trainer had practiced in southern California only five years, but he had long since taken command.

Laz was equally adept with claiming horses, allowance horses, and stakes horses. He won going short, and he won going long. He won on dirt, he won on grass. He won with fillies as well as colts. He won with 2YOs, with 3YOs, and with horses 4up. He won after claims, with first-starters, up in class and down in class, after short layoffs and after long layoffs, with front-runners and with closers. He won with shippers and with imports. He won in New York, and he won in southern California. He won in Cuba, in Mexico, and in the United States, entering the Hall of Fame in each of the three countries. As a local report on trainers summarized, when analyzing Barrera, "He has no discernible weaknesses."

Perhaps it will stand as the horseman's greatest testament that during the two seasons of 1978 and 1979, when the great Affirmed was three and four, and so overwhelmingly on his mind and schedule, Barrera produced an additional eighteen stakes winners. Not a single horse in the stable, one of the nation's largest, suffered because Affirmed was there. It was a remarkable feat.

Beyond the habitual winning for which he will be immortalized, Barrera's legacy extends in three-part harmony to others, two of his contributions of benefit to his fellow trainers, and the third a special unexpected gift to California racing.

One, Barrera made the difficult, complicated transition from the claiming game to the nonclaiming game as quickly, surely, and successfully as any horseman in history.

Barrera had struggled with claiming horses for almost two decades when the offer came from Harbor View Farm. He was not Lou Wolfson's first choice, and not the second choice. As events proceeded, Wolfson considered that Laz had upset the 1975 Belmont Stakes wire-to-wire with Bold Forbes, stretching the colt to twelve furlongs impressively against all odds, and when he received a push from Angel Penna, private trainer for the Phipps family, he extended Barrera his chance.

Laz grabbed the opportunity and rode it into the stratosphere. Good fortune smiled, which helps. In 1977, the job still brand-new, Affirmed arrived as a Harbor View 2YO. The next several seasons would go down in recorded history.

Harbor View shot to the top of the money-won standings, and the operation stayed there for four years. From 1978 through 1981 Barrera won four consecutive Eclipse awards as the nation's outstanding trainer. It's a standing record, and may persevere.

Whatever the overlaps, handling claiming horses and non-claiming horses requires as well a uniquely differentiated set of skills. Instead of turning them upside down and around on a conditioning regimen, and dropping or rising a level or two, as in the claiming game, trainers must guide better horses through carefully delineated stages of development. They must master the eligibility conditions, placing developing youngsters where they belong, advancing neither too quickly nor too slowly, else the horse or the future might be lost.

As nonclaiming horses mature, trainers must identify their distance, footing, and pace preferences. They must select riders that fit the horses, regardless of owners' preferences, which can cause annoying conflicts. In the stakes, trainers must judge exactly what degree of competition their horses can withstand, how far they can go, how much rest they need between races, and what it takes to bring the horses to a perfect pitch at just the right moment.

If nicely bred nonclaiming 3YOs are brilliant, as many are, trainers face the delicate problem of refining that speed, rating it, controlling it, such that the horses do not exhaust themselves in a pitiful premature burst or get chewed to pieces on a hotly contested pace.

None of the necessary precision occurs because the trainer wishes it.

Among contemporary horsemen, Bobby Frankel has engineered the change from the claiming to the nonclaiming game as impressively as anyone. A genius with grass runners and older handicap horses, Frankel's achievements in the stakes ushered him into the Hall of Fame in 1995, alongside Charlie, Laz, Woody, and other training greats.

In 1980, fed up with the claiming routine and anticipating loftier achievements in the important races, Frankel bragged privately that he was just as good as Laz and that he could beat Barrera if he got the opportunity.

Barrera had already produced a Triple Crown winner, a second classic winner, and four champions. Frankel had accomplished none of the above. By 1995, Barrera having produced six champions and Bobby having had his opportunities, Frankel had produced exactly one champion, Bertrando. Bobby is still searching for his first classic winner, not to mention the Triple Crown, but it's only been fifteen years. As fabulously talented as Frankel is with grass horses and older handicap types, he has consistently pulled up short with the younger ones, the nonclaiming threes and twos.

It's not a piece of cake, and the comparison is intended only to magnify the claiming-to-nonclaiming transition accomplished by Barrera.

Two, as much or more than any other horseman in the modern sport, Barrera's work with Harbor View Farm reinforced and solidified the perception, long appreciated by handicappers, that training beats breeding.

For years before Barrera arrived, the sons and daughters of the foundation sires Raise A Native and Exclusive Native were there, and so were the fabulous dams, yet Harbor View was unable to crack the top thirty in money-won, let alone capture the classics or win the game's biggest events.

Barrera came on the scene, and the Triple Crown, the four money-won titles, and the nonstop stakes victories quickly followed. No one who reviews the record objectively will imagine for a moment that Affirmed would have won the Triple Crown from Alydar or have succeeded as a two-time Horse of the Year except for the presence of Laz Barrera. The farm was recognized with multiple Eclipse trophies as leading owner and leading breeder. From the platform Lou Wolfson thanked Laz Barrera profusely.

The contemporary analogy belongs to Shug McGaughey, who replaced Penna and promptly led the Phipps armada on a stakes pillage the operation could not have anticipated. The Damascus line, other leading sires, and the fabulous dams had been present for decades.

By 1982, with Affirmed at stud and Wolfson wanting to watch his homebreds, the partnership between the two horsemen had begun to dissolve. Wolfson did not like air travel. He did not fly to California much, unless Affirmed was performing in a glamorous event.

The new trainer would be Stanley Hough, an impressive comer. The Harbor View horses would now be sent to Florida in winter and New York in spring, summer, and fall.

Life was never the same again. The stakes wins abruptly stopped, revenues fell, and Harbor View Farm quickly dropped off the money-won leader lists. The sons and daughters of Raise A Native and Exclusive Native were still present. So were the blue hens. So, too, now were the offspring of Affirmed. Training beats breeding.

Three, and Barrera's proudest legacy, Laz put California racing on the map.

By sheer coincidence Barrera had planned to move the Harbor View operations to southern California in the fall of Affirmed's 2YO season. By then, Affirmed's juvenile skirmishes with the mighty Alydar had reached national proportions, the pair of juveniles obviously superior, but the jury hung on which was better. The moving plans well laid, Lou Wolfson did not stand in Barrera's path, hardly an unimportant point. If the Affirmed-Alydar 2YO matches had preceded the shipping plans, Affirmed's change of address would probably not have occurred, at least not until the 1978 Kentucky Derby, the Preakness, and the Belmont Stakes had been wrapped.

No sooner had Laz Barrera set down in California than a torrent of criticism pursued him. What does Barrera think he's doing? How can Laz possibly believe he can train Affirmed to win the classics from a California base? Everybody knows the tracks there are glib as glass, and the competition weak as water.

Some of the most vitriolic criticism was hurled by John Veitch, trainer of Alydar, and for storied Calumet Farm, to whom Alydar represented nothing less than the messiah, an economic savior. Uncharacteristically Laz said nothing. He stayed quiet as 1978 opened and the harsh criticism climbed to mountainous peaks. It became a feeding frenzy, the eastern media and establishment horsemen piling it on and gathering like vultures around the carcass of a staked-out Affirmed.

Barrera had been such a fool to take Affirmed to southern California!

To complicate Laz's life immensely, it rained relentlessly in southern California during the winter of 1978. Barrera could not train Affirmed properly. As weeks passed into months, not only did Affirmed not start, the 3YO also did not work out. Gallops and gallops galore, only gallops.

By March 1, the Derby two months away, the critical chorus was laughing at Laz. In Florida, Alydar had looked sensational, blowing away his opposition. Veitch, and others, pumped up the rhetoric. Going to California to prepare Affirmed for the Kentucky Derby was the dumbest thing Laz Barrera, or anyone else, had ever done. Still, Barrera remained silent.

Slightly past the middle of March, Affirmed finally started. He trounced an overnight field at 1–9.

Barrera broke his silence. Not to worry, said Laz, Affirmed would be ready by May 1, and he would win the Kentucky Derby. The critics scoffed and scowled and howled. Veitch was moved to say he considered Alydar, who had just recently annihilated the Florida Derby opposition, a sure thing.

Next, in early April, Affirmed won the Santa Anita Derby.

Now Barrera attacked his critics. He assured the world Affirmed would prove he was the greatest racehorse ever. He would beat Alydar again, just as he had in three of four of their 2YO showdowns. Furthermore Barrera lauded California racing, assuring everyone the California surfaces were excellent and the California 3YOs were as good or better than the eastern colts.

The grudge match was set.

Two weeks later Affirmed won the Hollywood Derby, looking splendid all the way.

Barrera lashed out at Veitch and his cronies with everything he had. He promised Affirmed would win, not only the Kentucky Derby, but also the Triple Crown. He declared flatly that California racing was better than New York racing, and he insisted the California 3YOs that Affirmed was beating were more talented than the eastern 3YOs Alydar had been beating.

Nobody had ever stood up for California racing like that. And nobody, not a single horseman of southern California, rallied to Barrera's side. He was crying out alone. He was marvelous.

When Affirmed humiliated Alydar in the Kentucky Derby, and proceeded to win the Triple Crown in consummate, breathtaking style, standing in the winner's circle beside Laz Barrera was California racing. The mighty Alydar, scion of Calumet Farm, had been defeated, and again, and again. Nobody in horse racing would ever again say the California tracks could not deliver a classic horse.

Wayne Lukas took it from there. In the 1980s the new entrepreneurial money poured into California racing, select yearlings were brought from the tony auctions at Keeneland and Saratoga to California farms, and southern California horses would begin to dominate in the classics as they never had before, and as no one had dared to imagine they could.

When Laz Barrera was inducted into the Hall of Fame at Saratoga in summer 1980, one of the introductory speeches was delivered by Santa Anita's senior vice president of racing F. E. (Jimmie) Kilroe, by a clear margin the most important figure in the history of California racing. Kilroe called Barrera a son of southern California. The trainer had been active in the region less than five years. Kilroe knew. What had transpired was nothing less than a changing of the natural order, and everyone should now and then remember how it came to pass.

In the mid 1980s, the Harbor View horses gone, the relentless competition winding down, Barrera relaxed. He had fashioned a sort of sunset companionable relationship with the delightful Dolly Green, heiress to the land under Beverly Hills, an elderly but surprisingly spry philanthropist who was now in fragile health. Dolly loved horses, which she had ridden as a child in Los Angeles at the turn of the century, as well as the racehorses her father had campaigned at Santa Anita and Hollywood Park in the 1940s and 1950s.

Dolly predicated her late entry into Thoroughbred racing on having Laz Barrera as her trainer. She liked to reminisce about the time she first saw him, standing astride a red sports car on the backstretch

at Santa Anita, looking "like a handsome, debonair Latin charmer."
Marge Everett arranged the meeting.

In building the stable, Laz and Dolly arrived together at the prestigious yearling sales. Whatever youngsters they wanted, they got.
Money was no obstacle. Dolly gave Laz a 10 percent payment on all
purchases, twice the standard commission, not because Barrera had
requested it but because she wanted it that way.

Dolly never missed one of her horse's races, and at dusk she would
venture to the barn and feed carrots door-to-door to the entire Barrera
entourage.

On race days the sight of Laz and Dolly strolling arm-in-arm to the
paddock and walking ring soon became a familiar racetrack scene, as
if out of a movie. If Dolly's horse had won, the two of them again
walked arm-in-arm slowly to the winner's circle. They were the picture
of success. For Dolly it was all a romantic fantasy she loved to live and
relive. For Laz it was a season to relax, and to enjoy.

In 1986 Laz took Dolly and one of her impressive 3YOs to America's race, the Kentucky Derby. The racing media took Laz too seriously
that week when he kept insisting that Dolly's colt had a heckuva
chance to win.

On Derby Day, President Carter, no less, requested a formal introduction to Dolly, and the grand dame of Beverly Hills obliged, although she was feeling tired from the parties and ceremonies of the
occasion.

On network television, when Dolly's horse did not get a serious
call and finished unceremoniously in the bottom half of the field,
Howard Cosell, in his distinctive voice and manner, remarked, "Well,
Laz Barrera can have no excuse for that horse."

What neither Howard, nor Laz, nor President Carter had realized
was that during the running of the Kentucky Derby Dolly was alone
in the Churchill Downs directors' room, where she had fallen sound
asleep.

Despite quadruple bypass surgery, once repeated, Laz just could
not adhere to his severely restrictive diet as the weeks and months
passed. At the track he favored soft drinks that contained the sugar he
was not permitted to take. He indulged other dietary violations, without a doubt.

On a weekday of racing at Santa Anita the end came swiftly, surprisingly, and sadly, from a bout of pneumonia his heart could not tolerate.

He was no longer there, in his box near the finish line at Santa Anita and Hollywood Park. That's the simple image of Laz that endures, the country's leading horseman sitting upright in the front row of the box. He possessed an imperial presence in that box, and he never left it. Others came to visit him, friends, associates, colleagues, and fans. He dressed well, in suit and tie. He wore cologne, which the ladies liked. As Dolly often remarked, Laz was a ladies' man. He was also a man's man.

An enormously proud man who wore the pride of profession on his sleeve, Laz had developed a deep admiration for Charlie Whittingham, and the two fabulous trainers were obviously respectful peers.

He held strong political views, a circumstance that does not mix well with most of the solitary, independent mavericks of the racetrack. He was a rabid anti-Communist, a scathing opponent of Fidel Castro, telling me that Americans do not understand how easily they might lose their vaunted freedoms.

Laz also felt a deep commitment to family, as well as to the extended family, the clan gathering regularly at the races during the holidays and at crunch time. It's curious that not many years after his passing, his sons, Larry and Albert, drifted away from the racetrack, even though their father had represented an overbearing presence; a new beginning was probably a good idea.

Laz arrived early, before the first race normally, and stayed unswervingly until the ninth race had been run. He was a dyed-in-the-wool racetracker, his very name so identifiable to everyone in the sport. He was Laz to friends and acquaintances, Lazero to intimates.

From Cuba, to Mexico, to New York, to California, wherever he went, Lazero left unforgettable marks, a legacy that lives.

HOLY BULL

H oly Bull just did not do enough. The nation's most brilliant race-horse of 1994 had ascended the Thoroughbred throne, where he belonged, but with reservations among some of the subjects as to how impressively he would rule.

That Holy Bull was dubbed 1994's Horse of the Year by nearly unanimous acclaim was partially a formality, not altogether a mandate emerging from the colt's sensational 3YO performances, but in part a concession, as early as mid September, recognizing that no substantive alternative could be found.

That Holy Bull had beaten older handicap horses twice in prestigious New York stakes collapses as a certifiable credential the moment it's admitted that the older handicap horses of 1994 must be regarded as the most untalented crop in years. In the season's championship event, the Breeders' Cup Classic, 3YOs finished one-two-three-four.

That Holy Bull had provoked comparisons to Secretariat, as well as to Seattle Slew, Affirmed, and Spectacular Bid, class demons of the 1970s, can be assigned not only to people's capacity to forget but also to a troubled industry's almost obsessive desire to fill its popularity void.

The comparisons do not apply.

Secretariat won the Triple Crown in unparalleled style and time and he erased five course records as a 3YO, in the process devastating perhaps the finest 3YO crop of the decade and a ferocious division of older handicap stars.

In the first running of the Marlboro Cup at Belmont Park in the fall, Secretariat set the standing world record at nine furlongs (1:45 ⅖). His thirty-one-length tour de force in the Belmont Stakes was probably the greatest race ever run. In just two starts on grass, Secretariat demonstrated he might also have been unparalleled on the turf. He was voted America's Athlete of the Year. The glorious red colt was one of a kind. Facile comparisons are ill advised.

Seattle Slew and Affirmed also carried the Triple Crown with distinction, the latter defeating Calumet Farm's outstanding Alydar in a storied succession of spectacular finishes. In the Kentucky Derby, Seattle Slew broke slowly, burst between horses in the rush to the clubhouse turn, and continued to lead all the way in a convincing performance. Both colts became undeniable champions at four.

Spectacular Bid sparkled in the Kentucky Derby and the Preakness, established the world record at a mile-and-one-quarter (1:57 ⅖) at Santa Anita as a still-developing 4YO, and walloped older horses so savagely that he was granted a walkover in New York's Woodward Stakes (Gr. 1).

By those regal comparisons, Holy Bull remained an heir apparent.

Of the five Grade 1 stakes Holy Bull annexed in 1994, only one, the Travers, at Saratoga, limited to 3YOs, had the shine of a classic. Holy Bull set no track records, equaled one. In passing the Breeders' Cup Classic, Holy Bull postponed his taking the test of champions. He was retired before he had defeated the cream of the 4up handicap division at America's classic distance of a mile and one-quarter. One-turn middle-distance events at Belmont Park cannot substitute for that.

None of this is meant to intimate that Holy Bull was not the genuine article, an outstanding racehorse. He was America's best. Only that the crucible of greatness lay ahead. Moreover, a worthy opponent, maybe two, would be waiting.

If he wished to be remembered as king, Holy Bull had to win two Grade 1 events on his carefully sculpted 1995 agenda. Next he was scheduled to run in the million-dollar Santa Anita Handicap, the distance a mile and one-quarter, and the most rugged definitive handicap of winter racing.

The southern California handicap division is usually crowded with the country's top horses, although the winter of 1995 will be empty of scintillating memories. A few of the leaders may not have made the race, including the ranking 4up champ, The Wicked North, but others would have. Pace can be an elusive rabbit to predict, but Holy Bull should have been forced to run relentlessly hard against talented Grade 1 winners for the entire ten furlongs.

One horseman who understood the confrontation at Santa Anita as the critical juncture it represented was Holy Bull's owner-trainer Jimmie Croll. In the fashion of Charlie Whittingham, Mack Miller, Ron

McAnally, and Allen Jerkins—traditional conservative horsemen who have seen it all and suffer no illusions—Croll had appreciated Holy Bull's special dimensions from the outset, but he had remained reluctant at every stage to advance his case prematurely.

Croll and his ever-cautious brethren typically come across as anti-heroes, unwilling to extend high compliments to horses until every obstacle has been circumscribed. They know well the precarious character of racetrack speculation.

"If Holy Bull wins at Santa Anita," Croll had suggested, shortly after his gray streak had returned triumphantly at Gulfstream Park in January by torching a seven-furlong sprint stakes, "I think he will be undefeated for the rest of the year."

The remark not only expressed the trainer's confidence but also placed Holy Bull's circumstances in the proper context, implying the colt must accomplish future goals before he deserved to be coronated.

Croll also confessed publicly what so many others had hardly paused to ponder, that Holy Bull's main problem at Santa Anita and later may have been distance. Up to nine furlongs, Holy Bull and his kind (brilliant, precocious, speed demons that prefer to run on or near the front) are virtually unstoppable. They can simply run away and hide.

Performances at middle distances, however, do not translate reliably to classic distances. Abundant, irrefutable data confirm the point.

The explanation attaches primarily to pedigree. Racing aptitudes transmitted to progeny by sires, maternal sires, and grandsires interact on a continuum from high speed to high endurance. Notably among stakes winners at ten furlongs, the crucial attribute is a certain statistical blend of speed and stamina. Holy Bull did not possess the desirable blend. Too much speed, not enough stamina.

This does not mean Holy Bull would not have defeated older Grade 1 cracks at a mile and one-quarter. Only that he should be fully extended to do it. To be sure, Holy Bull's best race, the Travers, occurred at ten furlongs. Following the rapid pace he pressed, and completely extended, that day Holy Bull withstood by a neck the late charge of the 3YO Concern.

Concern promptly won the Breeders' Cup Classic, flattering Holy Bull's Travers and setting the stage for a 1995 rematch. Concern had qualified absolutely as the 1995 challenger previously remarked. The same horse Holy Bull had repelled by a short margin at Saratoga dispensed a tremendous four-furlong run from far behind to win decisively at ten furlongs on Breeders' Cup Day.

If Holy Bull had participated in the 1994 championship race, the Saratoga result might have been reversed. At some moment in 1995, maybe at Santa Anita, Holy Bull would have been required to withstand Concern's terrific charge again.

Not only that, entering 1995, Concern personified the rampantly improving 4YO that may no longer be denied, reminiscent of California's Best Pal at a similar career stage. That's because deep closers that rely more upon stamina than upon speed tend to mature impressively during the final months of the 3YO season and the first months of the 4YO season.

Speed horses tend to develop earlier. The maturation continues at four, but at a reduced momentum. Holy Bull would have needed greater reserves of speed and stamina than he possessed in 1994. In other words, at a mile and one-quarter Concern might well have been the better 4YO.

As events proceeded, Concern did not mature as expected, and despite a few undeniably powerful finishes the colt dispensed an inconsistent four-year-old campaign. The vacuum was filled by a model of consistency. No matter how fast Holy Bull had run in 1995, he might not have run faster than Cigar, even at middle distances.

It's not easy to imagine any horse conquering Cigar in the 1995 Oaklawn Park Handicap, the most heavily loaded middle-distance handicap of the year in which Cigar at 8–5 was dazzling. Cigar's Beyer Speed Figure on that day would be 121. Holy Bull's highest Beyer ever, a 122, was recorded in the Metropolitan Mile, a one-turner.

With Cigar popping onto the scene, even if Holy Bull had prevailed at Santa Anita, he might not have experienced the uninterrupted passage during spring and summer that Jimmie Croll had predicted. Then would come the Breeders' Cup Classic at Belmont Park, Holy Bull's home base. That meant a final vicious and relentless mile and one-quarter. Cigar would be present. So would every other Grade 1 stakes winner hoping to make a lasting impression.

To be celebrated as royalty, Holy Bull first had to win that one too.

FULL-CARD SIMULCASTING

I t's the most seductive siren call ever for racetrack regulars, a positive development, to be sure, the handicapper's great leap forward. The practical advantages of full-card simulcasting are captured full force by this 1990s incident at the Mirage Hotel, in Las Vegas.

A matronly handicapper rose following a symposium with six of the nation's leading figure analysts and addressed the panel in dry, serious tones. "You gentlemen are professional handicappers. That means you play for profit, for a living.

"Tell me, how many races a day do you play? How often do you bet? I'd like each of you to respond to that."

Scott McManus, of Chicago, spoke first: "Usually two or three key bets a day. No more than that."

Jeff Siegel, of Los Angeles, followed: "Me too. I make only a couple of serious bets a day."

Tom Brohamer, also of Los Angeles, spoke next:

"Yeah. I might play just one race some days. I pick my spots, like most serious players."

Andy Beyer was next.

"Well, I played forty-six races today, and I'll be getting up at five A.M. with the roosters to get ready for many more bets tomorrow."

Beyer brought the house down. In the somber, melodramatic context in which the quip was lobbed, it was genuinely funny.

The punch line was also pertinent. Beyer has always reveled in poking a sarcastic swipe at the characterization of the serious, semipro handicapper, sitting at the races patiently, waiting for the one, two, or maybe three good things on which he or she is willing to risk a dedicated amount.

The same dedicated handicappers, while awaiting the key horses, can typically be found with a pocketful of exotic tickets on doubles, exactas, trifectas, Pick 3s, overlays, and long shots. The horses and combinations are referred to as action bets, a euphemism for wagers that as often as not represent the antidote to tedium.

The tedium has now been replaced instead by full-card simulcasting. The semipros who could find only one, two, or three bets a day in 1990, by 1995 could locate the same number of key horses at four, five, or six racetracks.

The implications of the innovation are fantastic. Putting first things first, full-card simulcasting affords excellent handicappers an opportunity to make a living, at least a handsome partial living, by playing the races.

At one track, two keys a day, handicappers can anticipate four-hundred win-bets a season, tops. If $200 wagers are placed on each, the investment will be $80,000. A 25 percent edge translates to a profit on key horses to win of $20,000; nice, but not much of a living. If the edge is a sensational 40 percent (40 percent winners at average odds of 5–2), the profit on win keys jumps to $32,000.

When inquiring minds want to know why excellent handicappers do not simply make a living trading on their knowledge and skill, the answer should be plain. It just hasn't been practical.

But now it is.

If two key horses can be found at each of five tracks a day, the action has intensified, and so has the investment. At $200 per, the simulcast handicapper invests as much as $2,000 a day. If he plays for two-hundred racing days a year, the annual investment soars to $400,000. The profit potential soars as well. Handicappers having a 20 percent edge now earn six figures, or $100,000, which is a comfortable existence indeed.

The sensational handicapper having the 40 percent edge now collects $160,000. That handicapper is living in luxury and he hasn't bet an exacta, trifecta, Pick 3, or Pick 6 to get there. Life is good, life is fine.

None of this jibes with the conventional adjustment to full-card simulcasting. Handicappers typically concentrate on two favorite tracks, with occasional bets at other tracks. The practitioner's lament abhors the lack of time and energy for attacking the several programs concurrently. This amounts to misplaced sorrow. Of the options simulcast handicappers might consider, an amateurish attempt to cover all races at all simulcast tracks is the worst.

A balanced approach might supplement the conventional handicapping at the home track, with pet plays and selected races at simulcast sites. For serious handicappers, the semipros hell-bent on profits
and success, a positive adjustment focuses on strengths and avoids
weaknesses. A variation of the strategy combines an emphasis on well-
documented strengths at multiple tracks and a reliance on pattern
plays that have tossed profits anywhere they appear.

In the fall of 1993, while in Washington, D.C., I visited handicapping colleague Mark Cramer, who lives in Gaithersburg, Maryland, and
fancies an OTB parlor in a nearby restaurant called the Cracked Claw.
I pulled into the parking lot at two-thirty P.M. on a Tuesday afternoon,
hardly the heaviest pari-mutuel betting day of the week. The lot was
so crowded I could not find a spot.

The Cracked Claw was large. Two spacious rooms lined with comfortable tables were filled with simulcast bettors, most of them prospect-
ing the local card at Laurel, with side bets at Arlington Park, Hollywood
Park, Fair Grounds, Philadelphia Park, and the Meadowlands.

Cramer was the fascinating exception, which is nothing unusual
for handicapping's iconoclast. Mark was playing only the grass races
at Arlington Park, Hollywood Park, Fair Grounds, and later the Meadowlands, assuming, to be sure, he could find a first or second grass
starter having a successful turf sire. It's a spot play that has rewarded
Cramer with provocative overlays. His other scattered bets covered
other angle plays, perhaps backing the horses of underrated trainers,
or horses satisfying handicapping criteria and price supports Cramer
had previously identified as profitable.

"That's what I do now," said Cramer. "I look for the plays I like,
the ones that have been winners for me. I come here regularly, make
my favorite plays at several tracks, and leave. It's a brand-new ballgame, and I like it this way. I don't bother with races I hate, or full
cards anywhere, or low-priced horses I have no edge in betting."

Cramer's lament was the absence of New York from the simulcast
menu, as he likes the grass racing there. That prohibition ended in
1995, increasing Cramer's opportunities, and probably his profits.

I thought wistfully of Al Fisher, a recreational handicapper and
good friend who has lived in Las Vegas for a decade. He covers northern
California, maybe southern California, but always the horses entered
in the East by a pair of intriguing trainers. His trainer angles have been

successful year after year. Sorry, but I guaranteed Fisher I would not reveal the specific trainers and patterns.

A personal adjustment for me might concentrate only on non-claiming races, the stakes and turf races especially. Substantial profits await handicappers who understand the stakes and can follow the national divisions from track to track, fastening especially on shippers that might hold a class edge and will be underbet. I relish that tactic, and full-card simulcasting supports the endeavor.

A radically dissimilar adjustment might be entertained by Tom Brohamer. Brohamer would focus on the mid-level to high-priced claiming races. His pace methods can be deadly accurate with the middling claimers, regardless of racetrack. Brohamer would pass turf races, the stakes, and the maiden-claiming plugs.

Beyond amplifying the size of the annuity from key horses four-fold, full-card simulcasting allows handicappers to apply their strengths selectively and eliminate their weaknesses wholeheartedly. Multiple cards also permit a significant number of spot plays that qualify as pet angles. For regular handicappers, those new permits can be viewed as the advances of a lifetime.

In a recent marathon session at the Upper Darby Turf Club, my favorite OTB spot, just west of Philadelphia, I played seven tracks from noon to midnight, possibly surpassing Beyer's forty-six races in Las Vegas, an achievement of sorts. To make the point, I found a couple of excellent bets at every track. An investment in two dozen horses to win would have been feasible, and profitable on that day.

Unfortunately for Brohamer, me, and handicappers of southern California, and of New York to a lesser degree, the adjustment to full-card simulcasting remains a motion-in-waiting. By 1995 the country's metropolitan tracks on each coast had fallen clumsily behind the times. New York's out-of-state simulcasting program improved significantly in 1995, with better times ahead, while California was clinging to the status quo, apparently wanting the distinction of being the last to change.

In reaction, the migration has begun of handicappers from New York and southern California to Las Vegas, and to other climates offering full-card simulcasting from numerous tracks. The simulcast program in southern California today, July 1, 1995, included a stakes race from Arlington Park; the full card from Pleasanton, a minor oval in northern California; the full card from Woodbine, in Canada; the Cal Expo harness races, a full card; and the Los Alamitos quarter horses, a full card. This is presented to southern California handicappers as a contemporary, full-service simulcast extravaganza. It's one of those intervals when a handicapper muses longingly on leaving the state.

A paradox of full-card simulcasting has touched the business of racing. The manifest anxiety creeping over racetrack officials, and horsemen too, that full-card simulcasting would be a terrible blow, has steadily given sway to a grateful calm as handles soar and the bettors have refused to be knocked out of the ring. As handicappers appreciate, but track officials and horsemen do not, what slays the bettors mercilessly is not too many races but too many underlays. In a curious, unanticipated way, full-card simulcasting has acted as a countervailing force against contemporary racing's parade of underlays, especially at tracks where nonclaiming fields have been persistently small and the low-level claiming races just as persistently dreadful. It's been full-card simulcasting to the rescue.

The latest track to count the blessings of full-card, out-of-state simulcasting (June 1995) has been Sportsman's Park, in Chicago. On the first afternoon, a weekday, simulcasting boosted Sportsman's handle by half a million. The increases ranged from $500,000 to $800,000 for weeks. Chicago racing officials were singing in the rain. Track revenues were improving, and so would horsemen's purses. The terrible blow that full-card simulcasting was thought to inflict instead has the unique but not unprecedented potential of saving racing officials from themselves.

An adaptation to full-card simulcasting not recommended to handicappers is the high-tech solution. In coping with multiple cards, the instinct to download the past-performance data into personal computers and process it by applications software, while tempting, must be resisted. The applications software misses too much. So do computer-generated power ratings provided for every horse at every track. Computers can be helpful, but handicappers should observe sensible limits. Handicapping software that purports to serve simulcast handicappers by being all things at all tracks is just an illusion. No method of handicapping succeeds in every circumstance, and neither does a computer program.

The remedy that applies is to emphasize personal strengths and to identify spot plays that come sharply into focus as always, by comprehensive handicapping, a methodology that applies everything handicappers know to every race they play.

It's no surprise that most handicappers favor full-card simulcasting. In the East and Midwest, at the finer OTB parlors, the rooms are jammed and bustling. The practical adaptations that will accommodate the future of handicapping are well under way. It's a fascinating time, an exciting time. Real change. New possibilities.

An intelligent mix of live racing and full-card simulcasting beckons the future, not only of racetracks that hope to stay in the game but of excellent handicappers that envision the chance to win more money than they have ever won.

HOME BETTING

B etting at home on the races has been imagined increasingly by racetrack officials, notably executives bending under the weight of the industry's recession, as (a) inevitable; (b) the cutting edge; (c) the logical extension of off-track wagering; (d) a waterfall of revenue; (e) a technological innovation the bettors will find irresistible; (f) horse racing's high-tech savior; and (g) the greatest single development in the history of the sport.

If those propositions were viewed as alternatives in a multiple-choice item, handicappers might be invited to circle the likeliest eventuality.

My choice is *c*. The other alternatives can be ascribed to wish fulfillments that may be illusions rather than happenings. It depends. The racing industry's approach to off-track betting has been so far unmistakably plain. Under a rubric of marketing, intended to penetrate new markets, off-track betting has been managed instead as a means of distributing the wagering opportunities, and thereby redistributing the existing attendance base.

Instead of betting at the racetrack, handicappers can now bet at intertrack sites, OTB parlors, restaurants and bars licensed to take the signals, and to a limited extent in the home. The logical extension of the migration is home betting for everyone. All studies have revealed that the off-track legislation has resulted in the redistribution of the existing market, not the development of new markets, and no persuasive logic or evidence can be presented to indicate that the same will not be true of the people betting at home.

In the rosy scenarios so conveniently elaborated, the problems associated with home betting are never admitted, of course—a negative spin on the future and the last critique a declining industry needs to face. A few of the stickier problems can be accommodated here.

Up front I have always affected a kind of bemused, ironic posture on home betting. The last outpost of off-track wagering to me represents the last place many racegoers and handicappers will be predisposed to bet on the horses.

Two developments, however, have forced me to alter my stance. One has been the recent and continuing experiments in New York. The second, far more instrumental, is hinged to the potential of interactive TV, although the thought recurs that there the potential may far outstrip the reality.

Not to be overlooked, home betting has been available in Pennsylvania for years, and tiny Penn National in the central region of the state has marketed the telephone betting it entails aggressively. At Penn National, handicappers from Pittsburgh to Harrisburg might open an account at the track, phone in bets, and watch the local races on cable. People might also bet at freestanding facilities called Autovend machines, obtain a voucher, and watch on cable.

Numerous accounts were opened. In short time, many of the accounts lie dormant, one of the underestimated perils of home betting. Skeptics might cite the minor-league racing, but that's begging the question, and Penn National is good minor-league racing.

Similar home-betting opportunities have been in place at Philadelphia Park. As long ago as 1982 I recall a visit to the family home in a Philadelphia suburb and lunch at a local bar and grill. On the pub's television, a cable channel, were the races from Philly Park. What I cannot forget is how awful the cable telecast had been; interminable screens presenting the odds, no live shots of the horses, no commentary, no prerace or postrace analyses, no information about scratches, track conditions, or jockey changes. The telecast first caught sight of the horses approaching the gate, entering the gate, and leaving the gate.

When I visit my brother today on the main line outside of Philadelphia, the same cable channel showing the races continues all day, now complementing the local races with full-card simulcasting from Maryland and occasional simulcasts from Florida, Kentucky, Illinois, and even California. If my brother possessed the good sense to open a telephone-betting account at Philadelphia Park, I could jump to the phone and bet any race I liked.

What has changed is the quality of the cable telecast. It's definitely improved, and Philly Park analyst Jenny Ohrenstein shines. On my last visit, in a turf race, she advised the TV audience that trainer so-

and-so had started fifteen runners on the grass, with six of them winning, four finishing second, and two others finishing third. Obviously that barn must be taken seriously on the turf. I cannot obtain those specifics from TV analysts in southern California.

Nonetheless a second peril of home betting regards the poor-to-awful programming of cable telecasts. Something has to be done, or the home-betting boom will be quickly doomed.

As at Penn National, and at Philadelphia Park, though out-of-state simulcasting has altered the situation, many phone accounts lie dormant. It's one step for handicappers to open home-betting accounts apparently, and quite another step to activate them regularly.

So I was amazed—at first—when ninety days after home betting was legalized in New York in 1995, the New York City Off-Track Betting Corporation (NYCOTB) reported that no less than 11,138 telephone accounts had been opened. The revenue from telephone betting totaled $34,432,106 for the three months from March 1 to June 1, up from $7,308,489 in 1994, a 377 percent increase. The telephone betting proved so rampant that its revenue dragged NYCOTB from $7 million in the red to $4.5 million in the black.

Was home betting in New York a popular innovation whose time had come?

Not so fast. New York's home-betting legislation had erased the 5 percent surcharge at the OTB parlors throughout the city. New York City bettors switched allegiance immediately, from betting at OTB parlors to telephone betting. The impetus had to be the surcharge as much as the telephone.

Another aspect of the home-betting legislation contributed significantly to the outpouring of phone betting at NYCOTB. New York really would be conducting a dual experiment. At the NYRA, phone accounts were opened with a minimum of $450. At NYCOTB, no minimum balance was required. So, what happened? NYCOTB opened twenty times as many phone accounts as did the NYRA.

The legislation extended home betting, with at-home cable television of live races, for one year, its continuation dependent upon a contractual relationship between the NYRA and NYCOTB. NYRA's Steve Crist was so chagrined at the $450 advantage extended to NYCOTB that he soon began threatening to suspend the city's use of

NYRA's satellite signal. NYCOTB's president, Allie Sherman, responded by insisting the city would simply take another signal.

The posturing on both sides was simply a negotiating stance. NYRA would not dare pull the plug on the Apple's bettors. NYCOTB would not dare to deny the Aqueduct-Belmont-Saratoga programs to the city's suitors. Home betting on out-of-state races would not be remotely as popular, at least not to begin with. The continuation contract will probably specify the same minimum balance for everyone, or no minimum balance.

The New York home-betting legislation also approved a cable telecast of the live races, at first for a March 1st–May 15th window, later extended for one year. A "Race Day at Aqueduct" show was hastily put together by the NYRA. Stay-at-home bettors got the odds, some comments about the races, and the races themselves, the now-traditional and just-as-boring cable format. Sherman, whose background in cable programming at Time-Warner and pay-per-view sports landed him the NYCOTB presidency, became the cable show's worst critic.

"NYRA put that show together quickly," Sherman told *The Thoroughbred Times*, "so that they could present the message and information they wanted to get out, namely odds, some comments on the races, and the races themselves.

"I would think they would want to flesh it out and do more. You have to do more than the event. Like other sports, you have to provide an educational and entertaining thrust. Don't just talk about the races, talk about the personalities.

"What makes any sport interesting is that people can develop an expertise in it. We have to give the public a vision of the sport."

Sherman, former coach of football's New York Giants, understands well that the popularity of football soared once the viewing audience learned what pulling guards did, what the nickel defense meant, and how wide receivers tended to run post patterns against zone coverages but preferred to go down and out against the man-to-man. Tendencies, defenses, patterns, plays, coverages, and much more of the game's strategy brought the viewers into the action.

In the same way, par times, speed figures, pace analysis, class evaluation, biases, trips, body language, trainer patterns, jockey tactics, and the rest can bring the viewers into the race. A peril of home betting that must be avoided, but probably will not, is the traditional lifeless, boring cable telecast. Information, analysis, and critical thinking will make a difference.

Another impediment to home betting rarely remarked is the nuisance it becomes to loved ones and the family. People uninterested in horse races abhor watching them on television. If football and golf have become anathema to television widows, horse racing will be worse, even intolerable. The bettors' rejoinders that they're risking money on the outcomes will not save the situation. Cable telecasts of live races may not be accepted in living rooms, family rooms, or kitchens.

Bettors who want to watch the races on television at home must be prepared to do so in isolation. The vision of handicappers alone in the den or home office watching a procession of local races and simulcast events that they might have bet by telephone does not square with family life or with familiar activities in the house.

In consequence, home betting may become a catchall phrase that in practice will mean betting at restaurants, in bars, and in other public places taking the track's signal. Although handicapping effectively qualifies as an individual, independent, even lonesome pursuit, playing the races contains a social aspect that should not be underestimated. Sharing opinions and experiences at the races facilitates a familiar, comforting, almost therapeutic release, in no small part because so many of the shared experiences will be negative.

In sum, the problems associated with home betting will be several:

- Phone accounts, once open, can lie dormant.
- Cable telecasts of races to the home tend to be poor-to-awful.
- Betting on the races at home will be a nuisance to loved ones and to the family.
- Family life interferes with the solitude and information-processing requirements of effective handicapping.
- Playing the races contains a social aspect that should not be denied.

Under two conditions home betting may generate the stimulative effect track officials like to envision, and in a best-case scenario, may be potent enough to develop new markets.

The first is to extend the advantage of opening NYCOTB phone accounts to home bettors everywhere—no minimum balances. And a logical extension of no minimum may be less of a radical remedy than it seems at first blush, home betting on credit.

Credit limits would be specified, dependent upon credit histories. Payments, including installment payments, would be required weekly. No payment would mean no play, and monthly interest charges would begin after thirty days.

Anyone who considers home betting on credit ludicrous might first consider the existing models. Shopping on credit, traveling on credit, eating on credit, and borrowing on credit—all of the conventional financing and terms apply. Credit cards drive the modern economy. Anyone who believes shoppers, travelers, and diners are more credit-worthy than horse players cannot support the assumption with evidence.

If shoppers, travelers, and diners do not repay the credit debt within thirty days, the banks have not the slightest reservation at leveling usurious interest rates, as much as 19 ½ percent annually. Is that a fair bargain for credit users? The interest charges may be insidious, but the model exists, and for the large majority of credit customers it works. The same would be true of racetrack customers.

Besides, another model of home betting on credit, less dubious than the banking practice of issuing credit at crushing interest rates, has existed for horse players and sports bettors for as long as the oldest profession: All horseplayers have access to the friendly neighborhood bookie. In the bookmaker's model, the bookie extends a week's credit to horse bettors, who will typically be phoning bets from the home or office. Legal or not, for anyone who wants to bet, home betting with bookmakers has been available for centuries. Neither the tracks, the horsemen, nor the state get a bite.

The bookmaking model has worked remarkably well, notwithstanding the inherent dangers to the bettors, which do not entail the widely remarked cracked bones. No installment payments are accepted and on those memorable occasions when the gigantic payoffs come home, the bettors still lose. Not because the bookmakers suddenly refuse to pay—their reputations are absolutely hinged to reliable payments, which can be trusted as automatic—but because they pay only to the limits.

Everyone remembers the special occasion at Del Mar when a long-shot double paid $365, but the bookie paid only 50–1, or $102. A $20 double that should have returned $3560 instead returned $1020, a tidy difference of $2630. Did that happen to me?

My introduction to home betting occurred toward the end of my sophomore season. My playing partner and I had surrendered a few thousand for the season at tricky Del Mar, the races in southern California suspended in mid-September for people living near San Diego.

A track acquaintance offered us a home-betting account. From mid-September until Thanksgiving we played the races at Bay Meadows, in northern California, by phone, practically daily. Betting small, we could not lose. I used $5 exactas and $10 win parlays almost exclusively. My playing partner was worse. He relied upon $2 and $5 round-robins, typically covering four or five races. A CPA, he delighted in calculating the payoffs. Day after day the results were positive. They must have admired us down at the office.

We skipped the races during Thanksgiving week, but were back on the phone, calling from home, by the first of December. The bookmaker had cut us off. We had been betting small and winning big. Our convenient home-betting account had been deactivated, which in combination with limits has been reason enough for excellent handicappers to abandon the bookmaker model of home betting. The better you play, the less likely you will continue to play.

Ultimately home betting will be successful or not, depending upon racing's comprehension of interactive TV. Home betting cannot be racing's economic savior, but interactive TV might.

Content, or product, will be everything. Process, the technology, and the system, will be next to nothing.

If racing makes the fatal mistake of viewing interactive TV as another means merely of distributing its wagering opportunities, the game will have been lost again. If it's a hyperbolic example of showing the odds, some comments on the races, and then the races themselves, the trilogy Allie Sherman loves to hate, the growth of home betting is guaranteed to be slow, minimal, and disappointing.

On the other hand, if racing develops its interactive TV channel as an information system—a convenient means for the individual to obtain and manage information about unfamiliar racetracks, unfamiliar horses, and unfamiliar trainers and jockeys, complete with a true relational database, an inquiry utility, standardized and customized information reports, as well as state-of-the-art applications software by which handicappers might process past-performance data as they please, not to mention entertaining talk, interviews, and activities— now the possibilities are exciting, and tremendous.

Bettors can integrate their handicapping with computer technology, information systems, home betting, and watching the races. They might access the system at any time for information they want, for a tutorial on speed handicapping, for replaying the races, for watching actual races, and much more.

All sorts of fantastic possibilities will be available to the handicapper's imagination and to racing's customers, who will be playing, not only the local cards but also full-card simulcasts from faraway places. Best of all, with proper planning it will be easy, effective, and cost-effective.

Home betting is not a mechanism for distributing pari-mutuel wagering opportunities to the home. It deserves a much broader context. Home betting will be situated best as part of a management information and education system for racing's good customers, present and new.

THE BANKROLL

Proper money management begins with the size of the bankroll. It must be $10,000 or more. Any smaller amount cannot be manipulated intelligently in the modern game, or worse, amounts to scared money. Casual handicappers may not care, but regular handicappers must. No matter the force of the individual's handicapping acumen, scared money loses.

The bankroll represents capital. The money is intended solely for racetrack speculation. It's not income, savings, or money that might be needed for emergencies or unexpected bills. The bankroll is strictly an investment in the handicapper's knowledge and skill. If lost in its entirety, life rolls on without skipping a beat.

Of the pratfalls handicappers take at the races, none should involve money management. Inept horsemen, jockey mistakes, the mishaps horses encounter in races, the putative misjudgments of the stewards, all the disheartening errors and interference, none of it falls under the jurisdiction of the handicapper, but the bankroll does.

Put the bankroll aside. It's fundamental to do that. A separate bank account for racetrack revenue is highly recommended. Besides separating the racetrack bank from income and bills, a private account serves the affirmative purpose of tracking exactly how much money has been won or lost. Handicappers keep score by counting the money.

Experience suggests the real reasons handicappers refuse to deal seriously with money management are psychological. Many moons ago I conducted a seminar on money management and betting strategy for upscale handicappers. The idea was to maximize the profit potential by eliminating errors associated with betting practices. A certain level of handicapping expertise was assumed.

The participants were required to record their bets, amounts, and results. No one kept accurate records. The reluctance persisted week after week. Stumped, I finally realized handicappers do not keep records because they do not want to face their losses.

Fair enough. Recreational betting consists of behaving exactly as one pleases. Seminars on money management and betting strategy qualify as the least appealing to handicappers. People may be curious to know what effective money management and betting strategy means, but they retain the inalienable right to do whatever they want with their money.

The profit motive alters the equation, or should. A separate account for track bets can substitute for comprehensive record keeping. At least handicappers will be aware of the increases and declines. The record becomes an incentive to persevere, or to improve.

Having learned the folly of delivering copious advice that will be ignored, I'm tempted to stop now and trust handicappers will have been sufficiently persuaded to equip themselves with the separate $10,000 bankroll. On the other hand, the complications inherent in the current juxtaposition of exotic wagering and full-card simulcasting have nudged me to make one final pitch.

For handicappers motivated to succeed and wanting to improve on the money management and betting-strategy fronts, here's a one-year streamlined experiment that might assist:

Divide the $10,000 bank in half, $5000 for straight wagering to win and $5000 for exotics.

In betting to win, bet 2 percent of the bank to begin. First bet will be $100. Win-bets are restricted to key horses, either at the local track or at any simulcast tracks. Regardless of win-loss patterns, never bet less than 2 percent.

The low fixed-percentage bet of a legitimate capital means that decent handicappers will never be out of the game. The most money that might be surrendered to a desperately hapless season will be $3000. If handicappers customarily have lost more than that sum on straight wagers, they have a genuine incentive for engaging the experiment.

On the plus side, if five key bets can be found during each of two hundred racing days, a thousand bets will have transpired, involving at least a $100,000 investment. The expected profit will be $15,000 to $22,000. Profits might be considerably greater, but in the spirit of streamlining, let's not get carried away.

In the exotics, pursue your fortune in the favored pools, just be careful to invoke the correct strategies when playing exactas and trifectas (see "Betting Strategies"). The underlying strategy to adhere to in exotic wagering is bet small, win big. In other words, regardless of bet size, demand good value, not fair value. All exotic wagers are low-probability bets, a principle of exotic wagering that should not be forgotten, notably if losses have been persistent and painful. A pair of 2–1 shots has a 10 percent chance of occurring in either direction, which means handicappers can expect to lose similar exactas in eighty of one-hundred attempts. Ouch!

No one can predict how much money excellent handicappers should win in a season of exotic wagering. No a priori edge exists, only the advantage that might attach to a specific situation. Handicappers who won $50,000 in the exotics last season may lose twice that much, or half that much, this season. The trifectas that became bonanzas last year may constitute a black hole this year. So might the daily doubles, exactas, and Pick 3s. Pick 6 bettors who snatched a cool quarter million last season may not prosper again for a decade.

Respecting the low probabilities, I have argued repeatedly that handicappers who live in the exotics will die in the exotics. It's just a matter of time. In my personal play a gradual shift to exotic wagering has picked up momentum lately. In 1994 I crushed them. In 1995 they crushed me. So, what's new?

For that reason the $5000 bank for exotics should be nonrenewable. If the bank is bankrupt, exotic betting for the fiscal year is best suspended. The strategy contains the reassuring aspect of capping the seasonal losses. In a good cycle handicappers might amass six figures. In a bad cycle only $5000 can be lost.

Once I encountered a magazine piece saluting a dentist who lived in Las Vegas and ate lunch once a week at the Sands. It seems the doctor knew something about craps, namely it's nice to be playing the pass line when the dice are rolling.

Each week at lunch the dentist brought $50 for wagering. After lunch he walked to a nearby craps table, played the pass line, and subsequently the come line, until he had covered the requisite numbers. If he lost the $50, he left. If the dice were rolling, he stayed in the game for fifteen passes. He took the odds, and basically played his hand quite well.

The Sands did not want his business. Frankly they wished he'd eat his lunch somewhere else. The casino could take $50 a week from the doctor, maybe fifty times a year. Once or twice a year, however, the dice indeed would be rolling. During the positive spins, the dentist would win $30,000 to $50,000, maybe as much as $100,000.

Bet small, lose small, win big. That's the way to play the exotic-wagering game at racetracks. One implication of the strategy is so important, handicappers are invited to write the message on their foreheads.

In exotic wagering, anytime handicappers are torn between two or more horses that might be included, always, always, always include the horses having the higher odds. So if handicappers decide to use one of two horses in a trifecta, one a 10–1 shot, the other an 8–5 favorite, abandon the favorite.

If handicappers ingest nothing else about exotic wagering from this brief recitation on the bankroll, they will benefit enormously from including the higher-odds horses more often than not. Needless to say, most handicappers approach the exotics by doing exactly the opposite.

The bankroll and its management are crucial. As outlined here, in the worst years, losing in the straight pools and in the exotics, losses will remain somewhat below $10,000.

In the best years, winning in the straight pools and in the exotics, profits can exceed $100,000.

In any typical year profits in the straight pools should comfortably exceed any losses in the exotic pools, at least for excellent handicappers.

It's only a one-year experiment. Forgive the patronizing tone, but handicappers are strongly urged to stop sabotaging their best efforts and give themselves a fighting chance to join the ranks of winners.

THE COMPETITION

How difficult can it be to compete effectively
with a mindless game like Keno?

—ANDREW BEYER, 1994

Craps can be fun. If you take the pass line and the shooter rolls a number, you get the number. If you take the come line next and the shooter rolls another number, you get that number too. You can bet the come line again, and again, and again. If any of your numbers is repeated before the shooter craps out, you win. If the shooter rolls seven, you lose the bets on your numbers. If the dice are passing, perhaps ten, eleven, or twelve times in succession, and you know how to play the game, that's exciting, and someone might win a small fortune.

Isn't that a provocative game? Millions must think so, for they play craps endlessly in casinos around the world.

It goes downhill from there. Casino games of chance have not grown famous for the mental activity they demand of the players. The roll of the dice, the turn of the card, the spin of the wheel, those are the highlights. Placing the bets requires a thought or two, but the exercise soon becomes automatic as the previous bets placed seconds ago have been swept clear of the table and board.

The one-armed bandits warrant a special place in casino discourse. Now the players are relieved as well of the thoughts required to place the bets, but apparently the repetitive yanking of the handle supplies the overcompensating entertainment.

It hurts to admit as much, but this is the competition the racing industry has dreaded. The fear has become so penetrating, so obtuse, track officials would prefer their customers be permitted to play casino games at the racetrack, and not a few of them would be willing to build their own casinos to get a piece of the action.

The future of Thoroughbred racing does not rest comfortably in those official hands.

Once, in Minneapolis, I testified on behalf of Ladbrokes and Canterbury Downs in a court hearing on the proposition that pari-mutuel wagering qualifies as a lottery. Lotteries are expressly forbidden by Minnesota's state constitution. In rehearsal the night before at a downtown law firm, the senior partner representing Ladbrokes and Canterbury asked me to describe the ideas and methods handicappers use.

Provided with a blackboard, I proceeded to outline the most prominent methods of speed handicapping, class handicapping, and pace analysis. The presentation lasted roughly twenty minutes. The law partner was provoked by the procedures.

He said enthusiastically to his partners, "This is fascinating stuff. The handicapping methods are highly rational, organized, detailed, and sequential. The contrast with betting the lottery could not be more stark.

"Tomorrow, in court, why don't we just ask Jim the same questions we've asked him here, bring in an easel, and let him present the handicapping methods until the judge tires of it and stops him?"

The judge let me demonstrate for the court for fifteen minutes. Ladbrokes and Canterbury eventually won the point. Pari-mutuel wagering was judged significantly dissimilar from betting the lottery.

Is it an acrobatic leap of logic to suggest to racetrack officials that not only are the methods of handicapping and the lottery essentially distinct, but also so are the players, the customers, and the market of each.

Casino gamblers should be strictly a tertiary market for Thoroughbred racing. Estimates of the market overlaps vary from 5 percent to 20 percent, the majority toward the lower estimate. Management consulting firms supplied the estimates when Caesar's World was planning to build casinos in Illinois. Las Vegas race and sport book managers have testified continually that customers move more frequently from the casino floor to the race book than vice versa.

So why would a rational racetrack executive react to the advances of casino gaming by throwing untold unreasonable resources in that direction? Since it began, racing's response to casino gaming has developed the shine of the knee-jerk reaction, lodged by officials who have engaged no competition in the past and have suddenly been frightened of the future.

The rational alternative is to grow new racing markets. An intelligent combination of customer education and information services could increase the core market of Thoroughbred racing by 20 percent within three years, maybe five years, wiping out the crunch of the desertion so widely remarked. Within seven to ten years the same affirmative programs would grow the track's attendance base by 50 percent, and maybe more.

So why is it, with the young adults, the women, the baby boomers, and the corporate-technical-professional elites up for grabs in the national drift toward gaming, that racing staggers, gropes, and falls farther behind its mindless competition year after year?

Maybe it's because too many track executives haven't got a clue? Too many of them do not understand their product sufficiently to market it successfully. They comprehend so little about playing the races that track officials cannot tell the difference between pari-mutuel games and the lottery.

As a point of departure, racetrack executives might consider the tremendous advantage they can exert with people who like to play games. These people prefer to win at games they play. Casino games are negative-expectation games. Pari-mutuel wagering games are positive-expectation games. You can't beat the casinos. You can beat the races. Is that a fantastic marketing edge?

Racetrack executives who can accept that distinction and are willing to run with it will find success with large cross-sections of customers. The tracks will afford themselves a possibility of making loyal fans of anyone who likes to pursue games they play well and have a legitimate chance of beating. By relegating the racing game to a status interchangeable with casino games, all of them bundled together and targeted indiscriminately toward people who are hell-bent to gamble, the racetracks have done themselves a magnificent disservice, for which they have been paying a magnificent price.

Another perception on the gaming revolution may be even more distressing. Racetrack officials who believe they have met the enemy have not met the truly dangerous competition at all. Lotteries and casino games will not be life-threatening to horse racing, but sports betting may. Betting on sports is also a positive-expectation game. Skillful players can win. Players can study the sport, collect the information they need, analyze specific situations, and bet on outcomes when they think they have the edge.

Sports bettors are eerily similar to racetrack bettors. The players form highly practiced opinions, and like to bet on them. If track officials want to know where the authentic competition for the racetrack dollar lurks, it's sports betting. Someday, maybe soon, maybe not so soon, sports betting in America will be legalized. Thoroughbred racing had best be properly prepared.

While the advantage remains intact, it's an excellent idea to set about growing the loyal racing market. Strategic planning, systems analysis, program development—all the basic management concepts apply.

All that is needed is leadership.

THE GHOST OF HK AND
KERMIT'S KERNEL

The 1995 season was my worst ever. I lost at the ninety-day Santa Anita winter meeting, my home base, not just in the exotics, but also in the straight pools. The Pick 3s that I had relied upon for eighteen months with boastful confidence betrayed me absolutely. Favorites disappointed unrelievedly with major money on the line and beat my overlays relentlessly otherwise. The pattern persisted for many months.

In the simulcast from northern California, no less than nine times I needed leading jockey Russell Baze (virtually a 30 percent rider), eight of them on favorites, for four-figure Pick 3s. I went zero for nine.

My decision making became equally inept. In structuring Pick 3s, if I bought the field minus the favorite in unpredictable and contentious situations, invariably the favorites or low-priced contenders prevailed. When I spread or passed, the long shots upset, keying astronomical payoffs. I cashed none of the astronomical payoffs. This pattern, too, persisted for months.

After six months the season had evolved into a miserable experience, the losing run by a wide margin more prolonged and irritating than I can ever remember. I had encountered my share of losing streaks in the past, but nothing resembling this. On particularly disastrous days I left the track babbling to myself.

In times like these I'm visited by the ghost of a would-be handicapper I'll call HK. HK had been a highly successful securities investor, by some unofficial estimates having accumulated 300,000 shares of McDonald's common stock. I first met HK at UCLA, and for the next several years we crossed paths at the university and in the west Los Angeles vicinity, where we both lived. HK usually inquired about my handicapping exploits, and I relayed the news enthusiastically.

In the midseventies, without warning, HK began to frequent the racetrack. He had dabbled in the game occasionally, flashing $2 win tickets on selected horses he had backed, but HK was suddenly something of a regular practitioner.

His interest grew. At Hollywood Park that season HK played daily. He devoured the leading handicapping books. He recorded copious trip notes. He collected each day's results charts. He kept meticulous records of his wagers. HK was a player's player. I had no doubt HK would be successful at the track, and regularly told him as much.

Just as suddenly HK no longer attended the races. He was conspicuously gone.

For months I did not see him again, though mutual friends had advised me HK remained active in the market and stayed busy pursuing his other interests.

Several additional months passed, and I did not see HK at the track or anywhere else.

Extremely curious, I finally phoned.

"Why did you quit playing the races? You obviously loved the handicapping. What happened?"

"There's just too much error in the racing game," HK replied. "The error factor got to me. The bad trips. Jockey mistakes. The irrational upsets. The form reversals. I got tired of all the mishaps. It's contrary to my temperament. I'd rather play the market any day."

The error factor, to be sure, is large and depressing, exactly as HK had described it. The misfortune does not play evenly. Good handicappers suffer significantly more from the error factor than do untalented handicappers, who depend more upon chance than form to win. The occasional good fortune handicappers experience does not compensate for the lost opportunities and financial setbacks attributable to error, either human or animal.

My temperament can tolerate the error factor. Many handicappers cannot. Like HK, they should probably cease and desist. The game is not compatible with their psyches. They belong in the stock market, or at the chessboard, or on the golf course, games of skill where the risks and errors can be controlled to considerable degree by the individual.

If talented handicappers can tolerate the error factor without losing control and perspective, they will have broken down one of two psychological barriers to consistent and generous success.

The other barrier is losing runs. These are entirely normal and to be expected. The best handicappers lose six to seven of every ten bets they make. Once in a while the losing can become chronic and debilitating, though even extended losing streaks should be considered normal. Computer simulations show that handicappers having a 35 percent win proficiency can expect to lose twenty-two to twenty-five bets in succession if they persist for one thousand wagers, which equates to two and a half seasons.

Losing runs of twelve to sixteen plays can occur more frequently. The same computer simulations that reveal the expected loss patterns also reveal a substantial profit if the 35 percent handicapper can withstand the storms. In competent hands the bottom line remains positive, and even generous.

An analogy to baseball hitters is apt. The best of them will be out seven out of ten at-bats. When the unsuccessful at-bats accumulate, the hitless streaks stretch to twenty, twenty-five, maybe thirty attempts. But the leading hitters bat .300 and somewhat higher in the end. They do not alter their stance, swing, or habits when fighting the doldrums. They do not cave in mentally either. In the worst-case scenarios the good hitters experience an occasional bad season. They finish well below average. But they bounce back gloriously the next season. Good handicappers can do the same.

Southern California handicapper Kermit Hollingsworth believes the ultimate test of the winning handicapper is the capacity to survive long losing runs.

"That's the real test," says Kermit. "Long losing runs defeat many good handicappers. They can't take it, and they give up. If they would realize instead that the losing will stop and that positive patterns will reappear, many of them would be capable of beating the game.

"But long losing runs cause handicappers to lose their bearings. They begin changing their game, making poor decisions, stabbing, chasing, all the bad habits losing players repeat all the time.

"This is a game of percentages and probabilities. The losing is part and parcel of the experience."

The best handicappers can do during abnormally long losing runs is to minimize the financial setback. The worst handicappers can do is to stop playing to their strengths and altering winning habits, assuming they have been playing a winning game for a time.

The error factor and abnormal losing runs are the two psychological barriers to success handicappers must strive to overcome. Do not be intimidated by the ghost of HK. Honor Kermit's kernel of good advice.

I look forward to a resounding comeback in 1996.

THE PIRATE

There has never been a jockey more dedicated
to his profession . . . than Laffit. Not me, not
Arcaro, and not anybody. I don't care who
he is.

—BILL SHOEMAKER,
Sports Illustrated, 1986

When the trigger snapped in Linda Pincay's hand, January 1985,
her husband, Laffit, was changing silks for the ninth race at
Santa Anita. He was the greatest jockey in the world, and had been for
the past fifteen years.

The vision of Laffit Pincay, Jr., tearing down a Los Angeles freeway
in jockey silks toward the end of his wife's life might be translated
easily to the death of his sensational career. By the jockey's admission
Linda Pincay had formed the backbone of their duet, taking scrupulous
care of Laffit's diet and his regimen, since his weight problem had
become debilitating a decade before.

A few weeks of insurmountable grief and ennui passed by. On his
inevitable return, when he won a stakes on Laz Barrera's Adored (Gr. 1),
Laffit collapsed in Laz's embrace in Santa Anita's winner's circle, and
the two horsemen sobbed.

In the weeks and months that followed, Laffit Pincay, Jr., began
riding like a man-child on emotional fire. He was suddenly every ounce
as talented, consumed, and daring as the young swashbuckling Laffit,
the Pirate who had stolen purses with verve and abandon, the twenty-
year-old who had emigrated from Panama to America in 1966 and soon
had migrated to southern California, where William Shoemaker had
been kingpin since 1950.

By the conclusion of 1985 the year could be remembered primarily
for Pincay's riding exploits, an astonishing display of resilience and
chutzpah, as furious a comeback as any champion has ever displayed
under adverse pressure. He had won 289 races, with a win percentage

of .20 and purses of $13.4 million, the most money taken by a rider ever.

In May he delivered that incredibly powerful ride under a weary Spend A Buck in the Jersey Derby, securing the biggest purse in history ($2.6 million). On August 25 his lifetime purses passed $102 million, eclipsing the venerable Shoemaker, and a bounty that had seemed untouchable only ten years earlier. In November he capped the performance by winning the Breeders' Cup Juvenile at Aqueduct on Tasso.

In December, for all Pincay had done, on merit alone, he was awarded the Jockey Eclipse. It was his fifth Eclipse in fifteen years. No other jockey had won three. The country's leading jockey may have been burying his sorrow in his work, but he had also rehabilitated himself for a remarkable unforeseen future.

When 1986 began, the numbers and achievements were no longer the mark of the man. By standards that count, three jockeys have dominated the national winner's circle in modern times, and alongside Eddie Arcaro and Bill Shoemaker, Laffit Pincay, Jr., of Panama, was one of them. The record had been a tapestry of excellence. He had done it, too, in high style, with aggressiveness and unparalleled strength, but with the leading rider's finer attributes of handling and timing too.

Pincay's trump had been a dashing physical strength that never faltered, not even for a single race. One of the lasting images for people who understand the game will be Pincay pumping on a tiring claiming horse, propelling the sullen creature to the finish line. As the railbirds liked to observe, Pincay carried the horses.

In the long run of a career, however, it would be Pincay's character that rendered him the all-time champion who will endure in the hearts and minds of racetrackers. He has possessed a quiet dignity, professional grace, even modesty. No nonsense, no cheap remarks, no egoistic bombast has passed from Pincay to the public arena. He has remained reserved, so unprepossessing about his achievements that the media chose to discount them and him, rendering Pincay one of the most underpublicized champion athletes in history.

As the years collapsed into decades, horsemen and jockey agents began to issue unsolicited compliments saluting Pincay's character. These are hardened men, not given to sentiment. The jockey kept his commitments, they avowed, true to his word, about riding engagements, not only in the afternoon when the money was fat but in the mornings, too, when immature, unseasoned horses needed to be exercised and trainers would be pleased to obtain the services of ranking jockeys. And he never took off his mount in the ninth race of a long afternoon just because he felt like it. In a quarter century nobody could recall a truly ugly incident involving Pincay.

Never to be underestimated are the bettors, the sharpest-tongued critics of them all, and Pincay's biggest boosters. The bettors admired Pincay's all-out efforts under all circumstances. He afforded racing's bettors everything he had on a mount, a singular distinction the racing crowd will not forget. Pincay has never been booed at racetracks, not even as his win percentage stooped from the perennial 20 percent to 13 percent in the mid 1990s. The jockey has been awarded the abiding respect of the bettors. No one at the races can claim a higher ground.

An initial indication of Pincay's special dimensions was revealed in 1978, when his bout with body weight knocked him down. Until then Pincay's world had been a spinning wheel of success, riches, glamour, and fun. In recent seasons he had traveled east following the summer sessions at Del Mar to compete for national honors and money-won titles in New York. Amassing primetime numbers, hard-driving agent Vince DeGregory had been scheduling Pincay in double-headers, riding at Belmont Park during the day and at the Meadowlands at night.

During the preceding years Pincay had been fighting the extra pounds the old-fashioned way. Every day he spent thirty minutes, or longer, in the sweat box. He ran laps. He abstained from the table, or ate sparse, nonnutritious food.

His system broke down. Pincay, at thirty-three, was exhausted. He was losing his vaunted strength. Doctors ordered the jockey to rest.

Pincay took off his mounts for an indefinite period that fall. He changed agents, replacing DeGregory with the older, more relaxed George O'Bryan. When Santa Anita began in winter, Pincay rode again.

Yet something essential had changed. Pincay had switched to a nutritious, high-protein diet. He had abandoned the sweat box. His wife, Linda, supervised the diet and also assumed a wider management role in her husband's career, taking responsibility for his behavior outside the track. As a result Pincay's riding weight stabilized at 117, a few pounds above scale for numerous mounts, which trainers readily accepted.

In one of the most amazing statistics of the jockey's career, Pincay's riding weight has stood steadfastly at 117 for nearly two decades. His weight does not vary, not even by a pound. In recent years Pincay himself has become a master of the high-protein diet, and he delights in passing himself off as an expert on nutrition and weight control.

When his weight management faltered in the latter 1970s, no one imagined that Pincay would ride beyond his fortieth birthday in 1986. Since turning thirty, acknowledging the deadline, almost longingly as the weight wrestling tortured him, the jockey himself had hinged his retirement to age forty.

When age forty arrived, Pincay rode on, as brilliantly as ever. Shoemaker persevered to age fifty-six as a leading man, and Pincay might duplicate that feat too. Shoemaker's continuity featured the same relentless daring and consistent winning, Pincay staying firmly in place at the top echelons of the sport. To racing people having knowledge of the debilitating effects of overweight on a jockey's career, Pincay's run has been unparalleled, even incomprehensible. Winning the battles with his weight will be positioned prominently as one of the jockey's all-time accomplishments.

On track, a curious aspect of Pincay's career has been a relative omission of glamorous times, identifiable horses, and special events. Everybody in racing remembers with relish the ten consecutive victories aboard the great Affirmed in 1979, when that Triple Crown champion was four and had been in the clutches of a four-race losing streak. Pincay replaced Steve Cauthen, and Affirmed would lose only one additional race.

Pincay, in his robust riding and aggressive handling, was a perfect glove for Affirmed, who could run away from most horses but defeated the few who contested him in the late stages with infinite tenacity throughout the stretch. When asked occasionally to name his best horse ever, Pincay responds immediately by recalling Affirmed.

He has won the Kentucky Derby just once, aboard Swale in 1984 for leading New York trainer Woody Stephens, who rated Pincay above all other jockeys. When the retirement finally begins, and people discover Laffit to be an ex-jockey, inquiring as to whether he has ever won the Kentucky Derby, at least Pincay, in his customarily modest and self-effacing style, can state flatly that he did.

The next Triple Crown season, 1985, would bring Pincay's greatest ride, so sensational in its exhibition that probably no other rider could have succeeded in the race, and a historic event to boot that will be recorded as an oddity in racing lore.

That year investment banker Bob Brennan reopened Garden State Park, in New Jersey, and promptly threatened the sport's very foundations by challenging the Triple Crown. Brennan offered a two-million-dollar bonus to any horse that could win in succession the Cherry Hill Mile (Garden State), the Garden State Stakes (Garden State), the Kentucky Derby, and the Jersey Derby (Garden State), the latter event to be run on Memorial Day, in between the Preakness and the Belmont Stakes.

No sooner had Brennan brandished the bonus than he received outrageous good fortune. The speedy Spend A Buck won the Cherry Hill Mile and the Garden State Stakes, and then he scampered wire-to-wire at Churchill Downs in the third fastest Kentucky Derby on record.

When Spend A Buck's managers chose to contest the Jersey Derby for the two-million-dollar bonus, abandoning the final two legs of the Triple Crown, the controversy swirled. Would racing's hallowed Triple Crown ever be the same again?

Angel Cordero, Jr., Pincay's alter ego on the East Coast, and a great rider, had been named aboard Spend A Buck. But Cordero faced a scheduling conflict for a top client in New York on Jersey Derby Day. Trainer Cam Gambolati selected Laffit Pincay, Jr., to ride Spend A Buck for the money.

It would be a thrilling, memorable occasion. On his customary lead, turning into the stretch, with horses looming up on the inside and horses looming up on the outside, with a quarter mile to run, Spend A Buck was laboring obviously to retain his slight advantage, and he looked haplessly beaten. At the eighth pole Spend A Buck's slight advantage had virtually disappeared, three horses noses apart and others bearing down relentlessly from not far behind.

Fully leveraged on Spend A Buck, in perfect rhythm with the colt's stride, Pincay summoned his incomparable strength and aggressiveness to keep his horse's dimming chances alive. The final furlong seemed to last forever. The race caller intimated Spend A Buck had taken his final gasps. The announcer could not imagine that Spend A Buck might prevail, and neither did the millions watching the race, including the gallant colt's owner and trainer.

Spend A Buck did prevail. He won the Jersey Derby by an unlikely head. The victory demanded a rare combination of power and finesse by the jockey. Spend A Buck and his greatly enriched connections had been fortunate to have hired the greatest finisher of all time. Anything less on that day would not have been good enough.

Pincay's other flirtation with celebrity would be unnecessarily and unfairly interrupted. For two years Pincay had accompanied the great gallant gelding John Henry, possibly the finest grass runner ever. He had ridden John Henry flawlessly during that span, but while Pincay was on suspension, Shoemaker guided the gelding in New York, against easy opposition, and won handily. Grateful owner Sam Rubin decided he wanted the more popular, more fashionable Shoemaker to ride his champion. Shoemaker stayed.

Jockeys are thoroughly hardened to these circumstances, which recur annually, but this wound went too deep, and qualified as a low blow. Agent O'Bryan cried foul. He was decidedly correct. John Henry performed on the national stage for another five seasons, earning $6.6 million. The loss of income and reputation to Pincay exceeded all reasonable limits.

The incident can be accepted as telling. Barerra excepted, Pincay never emerged as especially fashionable with leading stakes trainers on the West Coast. He rode hundreds of stakes horses, of course, but not so often the top bananas. Charlie Whittingham used Pincay surprisingly sparingly, on certain horses only, and not as first, second, or even third call as a matter of routine.

Ron McAnally, Neil Drysdale, Bob Wheeler, Gordon Campbell, Tommy Doyle, Willard Proctor—none of them reached automatically for Pincay. In his ruggedness Pincay could be unsparing of horses. He might bring them back more fatigued than the trainers preferred. He was not a sit-still rider à la Shoemaker, Baeza, and other leaders, whose style depended more on touch and finesse rather than force and strength.

Moreover, throughout the 1970s, Pincay's prime, southern California boasted few prominent breeders, the horsemen whose progeny grace the stakes events on a standardized rotation year after year. Pincay sculpted his record and reputation in the overnight races as much as in the stakes. In the claiming, allowance, and maiden races, however, he enjoyed a tremendously enviable edge. Everyone wanted him and competed for his services. Getting Pincay to ride an authentic contender in a nonstakes race was tantamount to winning.

Of jockey rivalries, Pincay has experienced just a few that have transcended the normal day-to-day competition. The keenest occurred with Shoemaker. By migrating immediately to southern California, Pincay assured himself he would struggle in Shoemaker's long-fabled shadow for the duration. As Pincay's star kept rising, soon shooting high, the two battled furiously for mounts, victories, and dominance. Both won.

As a pleasant and agreeable consequence of a fierce rivalry between champions, not unusual in sports, the two men evolved as best of friends. All jockeys, if not quickly, eventually would come to admire the Shoemaker mystique—the hands; the seat; the balance; the timing; the classic form; the long, loose hold out of the gate; the quick, staccato whip in the drive; the reserves of energy saved to the finish—and Pincay was no exception.

Shoemaker correspondingly would come to admire Pincay as the best of his times. Sometime in the 1970s, his own career now surpassing a quarter century, Shoemaker conceded the throne to Pincay. He could not deny the combination of ferocity and finesse he witnessed daily, and after seasons had elapsed into decades, Shoemaker praised Pincay's longevity of high achievement that ultimately separates the great from the good.

Asked once to name the jockey who had succeeded him as best of show, Shoemaker glanced at his interrogator incredulously, as if the answer was self-evident. "Laffit, of course," said Shoemaker. "He's been the greatest for years. Who else?"

By the 1980s the pair of jockeys had grown personally close. Their companionship and social activities away from the track increased. It was Shoemaker who substituted on Pincay's mount in the ninth race on that fateful day. And it would be Shoemaker who delivered the tender eulogy for Linda Pincay.

In the midseventies, after it had become clear that the baton had passed to Pincay, Sandy Hawley arrived from Canada to ride full-time in southern California. Hawley was five times leading jockey of North America, no less, and one of the best ever. He was talented enough to rival Pincay at the top.

On Hawley's first full season at the ninety-day winter meeting at

Santa Anita, he led Pincay by thirty winners with approximately a month to go. Pincay dispensed an unbelievable furious finish to retain his title as leading rider. Jockey titles at regularly scheduled race meetings are overblown to a fault, but this contest had captured the public's imagination. To be sure, Pincay had looked brilliant and unquenchable during the rampage of winners.

To be fair to Hawley, at the next meeting, Hollywood Park, during spring-summer, the Canadian challenger won five times on opening day and proceeded to whip Pincay for the season by no less than fifty-five winners. Pincay had never been distanced in that decisive way by any rival.

Hawley's comet burned out relatively quickly. Sandy did not persevere at the summit. He did not care enough. Pincay regained his position atop the jockey standings the next season, and stayed there. Even today Pincay has designated Hawley as the toughest rider he has ever attempted to pass in an all-out driving finish.

The sternest, longest, most controversial rivalry Pincay faced, however, indeed the challenge for supremacy from 1970 to 1984, came from the opposite coast, from New York, in the person of Angel Cordero, Jr., who had emigrated from Puerto Rico. The two jockeys dominated the standings on their respective flagship circuits, and the arguments flew feverishly among handicappers on both sides as to which jockey was best.

Like Pincay, Cordero would be defiantly, aggressively rugged, a strong finisher, and a fierce competitor, in overnight races as much as in the stakes. He possessed the finer skills to superlative degree, and eastern bettors judged him an intelligent rider, an expert at recognizing and exploiting track biases. Cordero, like Pincay, positioned his horses where they commanded an excellent chance to win.

Cordero was quite a stylist as well, dismounting from his numerous winners with a trademark liftoff, a combination bounce and jump. Cordero flashed the flair that Pincay eschewed. Cordero fanatics in New York could be indefatigable in knighting Angel as the world's greatest jockey. Cordero would make anybody's short list, to be sure.

A statistical comparison of the two superstars throughout the prime years, from 1970 until 1984, reflects their leading positions in the sport. During the fifteen years, amazingly, with one exception in each record, neither man failed to finish among the top five in money-won. Pincay led the ranks six times, Cordero four times.

In strikingly similar manner the pair divided the spoils in stakes races, from 1974 through 1984, with one exception each, never ranking lower than fifth in money-won. Pincay led the stakes winnings four times, Cordero twice.

An examination of the statistical comparison in the table on page 269 reveals the unmatched consistency of Laffit Pincay, Jr., in his prime. Pincay never failed to win with 20 percent of his mounts; only twice did he rank lower than third on win percentage. In contrast Cordero won with 20 percent of his mounts just three times.

Pincay won with 25 percent of his mounts four times. Cordero never approached that percentage of winners. The lifetime statistics indicate Pincay held approximately a 5 percent statistical advantage against his archrival.

More than any other jockey, Pincay anticipated, avoided, and evaded the trouble spots that are commonplace in horse racing. Sometimes it seemed Pincay never experienced mishaps. He never took up, never even checked or steadied. He never was caught in traffic, never was blocked. He came through narrow holes with a fast and furious burst. His instincts were rapier sharp. He wedged his way through tight traffic, even along the rail. His courage was boundless. If Cordero exploited track biases, Pincay was a trip handicapper's delight.

Out of the gate, a tactic I detested, if his horse broke on top and showed high speed, Pincay invariably persisted at full throttle. More than occasionally he failed to clear the early-pace contest with the tactic, ending in a speed duel. But when the horses began to tire from the early efforts, Pincay would summon his might and carry the weary animals farther than they otherwise wanted to travel, and frequently, to the finish line. Obviously the jockey had learned he could risk the tactic, and prevail regardless, at least much of the time.

If Pincay had a flaw, a shortcoming, it would be the one-rally run from the back with deep closers. Like so many aggressive riders, Pincay preferred to maneuver into striking position as early as possible. He surrendered a few close calls in that way, but he probably stole just as many by the same tactics, again propelling tiring horses all the way.

Stealing races had been a Pincay specialty since the early days. His persona, even in the formative years, of the Pirate, a swashbuckling

PINCAY VS. CORDERO, 1970-1984

Year	Pincay Money-won (millions)	W%	Rank	Cordero Money-won (millions)	W%	Rank
1970	$2.6	.20	1	$2.2	.16	4
1971	3.7	.23	1	2.3	.15	4
1972	3.2	.21	1	3.0	.17	2
1973	4.0	.24	1	3.1	.18	4
1974	4.2	.27	1	4.2	.18	2
1975	$3.4	.22	4	$3.2	.19	6
1976	4.3	.27	3	4.7	.18	1
1977	4.3	.22	3	5.2	.18	2
1978	4.1	.20	7	5.3	.18	3
1979	8.1	.25	1	5.6	.18	2
1980	$6.5	.20	3	$7.1	.20	2
1981	7.9	.26	2	7.1	.18	3
1982	9.0	.20	2	9.7	.22	1
1983	8.8	.21	3	10.1	.20	1
1984	10.9	.21	3	11.9	.18	2

Year	Stakes-money (millions)	W%	Rank	Stakes-money (millions)	W%	Rank
1974	$1.4	NA	1	$0.9	NA	3
1975	1.2	.20	5	0.8	.11	10
1976	1.5	.29	4	1.6	.23	3
1977	1.7	.18	3	2.0	.18	1
1978	1.2	.17	7	2.3	.18	2
1979	3.5	.26	1	2.2	.18	2
1980	$2.5	.16	2	$2.0	.14	5
1981	3.3	.23	3	2.7	.22	4
1982	4.8	.26	1	3.5	.20	2
1983	4.4	.23	1	4.0	.21	3
1984	6.2	.22	3	7.1	.19	1

Lifetime (Thru 1984)

	Yrs.	Mounts	1st	W%	Money-won
Pincay	19	26,770	5,976	.22	$92.6 M
Cordero	23	30,460	5,502	.18	$94.0 M

renegade of a rider who took closely matched races as he pleased, was richly deserved. He stole races on cheap front-runners. He captured them late with flying finishes. He overpowered them in the upper stretch. He wrestled them from other jockeys in long stretch drives ending in close margins. The Pirate persevered as a fitting stickpin.

In 1995, riding at 13 percent winners, Pincay might barely have been noticeable beyond his stellar reputation if it were not for the Quest. He rides few stakes stars now, no divisional leaders. His late career has been advanced in an important way instead by trainer Bill Spawr, on a deluge of claiming horses and occasional nonclaiming types. Spawr himself is a highly consistent winner, one of the finest claiming horsemen in southern California. Pincay accompanies the majority of Spawr's winners, and the supply should not run dry.

Spawr's supply line feeds Pincay's quest. The fifty-year-old jockey has taken aim on Shoemaker's all-time number of wins, 8866. An untenable goal for a full-bore jockey fighting weight in his prime, Pincay's character and perseverance have served his cause so well for so long that by now it has become plain to all that Pincay is the man who deserves to break the record. Even Shoemaker is rooting for him, keenly aware that Pincay conquered nasty weight problems he himself was never forced to confront.

Pincay needs another 400-odd winners, which puts him four seasons away from the prize. If he can avoid a serious injury (the jockey has broken his collarbone nine times), Pincay will undoubtedly pass Shoemaker.

The racing industry has never bothered to correlate Pincay's milestones with the usual promotions and celebrations. Pincay will not be indulged in the national tour of racetracks that celebrated Shoemaker's final ride.

When Pincay passed eight thousand winners at Del Mar a few seasons ago, a fabulous milestone previously achieved by a single jockey, Del Mar officials forgot about it. Only a few days later when the media reported the milestone did track executives even become aware of the opportunity lost. So it goes, and so it has gone for three decades for horse racing's most underpublicized champion and ideal citizen. The long-suffered neglect has become an embarrassing slight.

If the industry's inattention has failed to motivate Pincay's quest, something significantly more important and personal has filled the void. Pincay has constructed a new, fully functioning personal life. Newly married in 1990 to Jeneen, Laffit has gathered to him another child, a new home, and a new lease on life and work. The family will keep him active, growing, and striving. The unofficial spokesman for a nutritious high-protein diet advises all who inquire that he's happier than ever, feeling great, and will continue, intent on surpassing Shoemaker's "untouchable" number of winners.

When he does the deed, the lucky track where it happens will be brimming with long-standing admirers. No one will think the achievement or jockey undeserving. Shoemaker will testify he's pleased his proudest accomplishment has been exceeded by the greatest jockey and one of the finest athletes anyone has had the privilege to know.

The celebrations and tributes arranged by the industry may be late, but they will be gloriously fitting. And Laffit Pincay, Jr., will be filled with pride. Feeling prouder of himself and of his achievements than he has ever felt before. Amen.

1 mile

start & finish

HIGH-TECH
HIGH JINKS

3yo (May) gelding, gray

Dam: Groomstick
by Jig Time

Wet:
Turf:

13 10.06

Gr.3 Kelso Handicap Stakes

27Mar91 8Bel ft 3+ Stk500000 1m 22.14 44.26 :09.29 1:35.45 88 14/14 3 5⁴¼ 7¾⁴ 7⁵ 10¹ 15³ J Garcia 107 b 13.2

Gr.1 Metropolitan Handicap

26Apr91 8Hol ft 3 Stk71050 7f 21.50 44.10 1:08.70 1:21.30 88 5/3 3 3⁵ 3⁴¼ 1⁶ 1⁷¾ E Delahoussaye 122 8b 1.

Harry Henson Stakes

11Apr91 8SG ft 3 Stk53700 6f 21.90 45.30 57.50 1:10.30 87 2/5 3 4⁵¼ 2, 1⁷ 1⁴ C Nakatani 122 9b 0.4

Pluebleikof Stakes

28Mar91 8SA ft 3 Stk58000 6½f 21.30 44.10 1:09.70 1:16.10 88 2¾ 1 2¹ 2⁹°   , 1¹⁶ E Delahoussaye 111 9b 1.8

DATA ARE NOT INFORMATION

The splendid promise of the computer for handicappers of the information age can be communicated in a word—information.

Databases would become storage bins of data for every track, race, horse, trainer, and jockey on the highway. Database-management software would link the data items to one another in any conceivable way, processing, summarizing, sorting, and calculating the data in ways that produce ready-to-use information. Applications software (methods of handicapping) would do the same, processing inordinate amounts of data instantaneously and converting the data to ready-to-use information.

The data-processing tasks (chores) of comprehensive handicapping would become a relic of the past, the horse player's dinosaur.

The promise has gone unfulfilled. Handicappers are still dealing with data and data processing on a large, increasingly prohibitive scale, the desirable information either nonexistent, inaccessible, overly expensive, or ineffective.

In the age of full-card simulcasting, handicapping's transition from a data-based activity to an information-based activity is no longer desirable, but imperative. If handicappers will be attacking two tracks, and more, they need information, not data.

The past-performance tables of the *Daily Racing Form* represent the familiar data source that illustrates the problem. Before viewing the past performances, handicappers must appreciate the distinctions between data and information.

Data consists of elements of fact or items of calculation, or numerous facts and items in combination. Examples would include final times, fractional times, racing positions, and beaten lengths. Final times and fractional times are data. Data are useful as a basis for discussion, calculation, or summarization.

Information is processed data, or meaningful data. Information has meaning. It tells users something they did not previously know.

When related to a goal or problem, information represents a basis for making a decision or solving a problem. Data that have not been processed lack meaning. They form no basis for making decisions or solving problems. Executives in the organization want information, not data. Handicappers should want the same.

Speed figures represent information, or processed final times. Final times and speed figures may be numerical representations of how fast horses have run, but final times remain raw data, unrefined, unprocessed, and not adequately related to making effective handicapping decisions.

Final times become information, or speed figures, by calculations that involve other data items, including par times, projected times, daily track variants, and beaten lengths. Final times are converted to speed figures; data are converted to information.

Now consider the familiar past performances:

Argolid
Own: Pegram Mike
DOUGLAS R R (—)

Dk. b or br g. 4
Sire: Saros (GB) (Sassafras)
Dam: Procne (Acroterion)
Br: Ridder Thoroughbred Stable (Cal)
Tr: Baffert Bob (—)

L 113

Lifetime Record:	17	4	5	2	$213,487						
1995	4	1	1	1	$48,325	Turf	2	0	0	0	$3,666
1994	11	2	3	1	$142,362	Wet	0	0	0	0	
BM	1	0	1	0	$10,000	Dist	6	2	2	1	$61,350

24Aug95-3Dmr	fst	6½f		:224	:453	1:091	1:151	3↑ Alw 53000N3X	97	6	2	42½	31	1hd	12	Nakatani C S	LB 117	*1.00	95-09	Argolid1172 Flying Standby114nk Swank1172	Strong hand ride	6
31Jly95-3Dmr	fst	6½f		:22	:444	1:083	1:144	3↑ Alw 53000N3X	84	1	3	1hd	2hd	43½	58	Stevens G L	LB 117 f	*1.10	89-10	Moscow M D117no Goldigger's Dream1177 Trumpet Solo117½	Inside duel	6
13Jly95-8Hol	fst	7f		:222	:45	1:09	1:213	3↑ Alw 51000N3X	102	5	2	21	31	1hd	2hd	Stevens G L	LB 116 f	5.00	94-12	Score Quick114hd Argolid1161¾ Alphabet Soup1162¼	Led, outnodded	8
27May95-9Hol	fst	6f		:213	:444	:564	1:091	3↑ Alw 51000N3X	99	7	6	41½	31	3nk	31¾	Stevens G L	LB 116	6.10	92-11	In Case116½ Beautiful Crown1161¼ Argolid116nk	4 wide into lane	9
19Nov94-8BM	fst	6f		:221	:443	:563	1:084	3↑ Saratoga H54k	95	3	3	1hd	1hd	1½	21¾	Belvoir V T	LB 117	2.40	95-12	Ackachina's Day1141¾ Argolid1171 Canaan Land1151½	Held gamely	8
29Oct94-5SA	fst	6f		:211	:434	:56	1:091	3↑ [S]CalCupSprntH100k	63	8	5	51¾	74½	97	1113½	Nakatani C S	LB 115	4.30	78-09	Uncaged Fury116hd Ke Express115½ Wild Gold1161¾	Drifted in 5/8	12
13Oct94-8SA	fst	6f		:213	:442	:562	1:084	3↑ Alw 38000N2X	96	4	4	1hd	13½	16	12½	Nakatani C S	LB 113	*1.10	93-13	Argolid1132½ Goldigger's Dream1163½ Paster's Caper1174½	Ridden out	8
29Aug94-8Dmr	fm	1 1/16	(T)	:241	:481	1:13	1:432	3↑ Alw 48879N2X	92	1	1	11½	11	3nk	42	Delahoussaye E	LB 116	2.70	87-15	RoyalChariot1171¼ MementoMori117nk ViaCondotti114½	Rail, outfinished	7
17Aug94-8Dmr	fst	7f		:222	:45	1:092	1:22	[S]RealGoodDeal67k	88	1	4	1½	1½	11½	2nk	Nakatani C S	LB 119	*1.20	93-07	El Alerta116nk Argolid119½ Windwood Lad1153½	Drifted out lane	7
27Jly94-5Dmr	fm	1	(T)	:22	:454	1:103	1:361	[R]Oceanside69k	60	1	6	51½	3½	85¾	915½	Valenzuela P A	LB 116	2.80	74-10	Powis Castle1161¾ City Nights1141 Makinanhonestbuck1141¾		10

: 5 wide bid, took up sharply 3/16. Run in divisions.

WORKOUTS: Sep 10 Dmr 5f fst :583 H 2/37 Sep 4 Dmr 5f fst :594 H 5/58 Aug 21 Dmr 4f fst :462 H 2/50 Aug 16 Dmr 6f fst 1:122 H 4/29 Aug 9 Dmr 5f fst :592 B 8/63 Jly 22 SA 4f fst :471 B 3/36

Beginning toward the left, handicappers can appreciate that the fractional times and final times presented for the various races and distances represent data, not information, and that the times have no substantive meaning until processed by speed handicapping methods.

Instead of final times and fractional times, handicappers would be better served by speed and pace figures.

Next handicappers see data items that have been combined to provide information about relative class. Here the past performances have been greatly improved. Uncaged Fury is exiting not merely an allowance race but a classified allowance event having a $60,000 purse and limited to horses that had not won a specified amount of first money since a specified date during the current year. That has meaning—it's information.

If today's race is a sprint stakes at Bay Meadows having a $200,000-added purse, which it is, handicappers might use the class column of the four horses as a basis for making a decision as to whether each fits the race. If the class information is combined with other data items (finish position, beaten lengths, speed figures), that information can be meaningful.

Next handicappers are provided Beyer Speed Figures. At a studious glance they can compare the speed figures among horses coming together from various racetracks and races, contested at different distances, on different days. Extremely useful information.

Next appear the data items describing positions and beaten lengths at four points of call. Until processed, these data items have scarcely any meaning for handicappers. When processed by various methods of analysis, however, the data inform handicappers on several fronts—early speed, early pace, pace analysis, improving and declining form, good-acceptable-poor performances. When related to the final times and fractional times, the data also form the basis for a pace analysis, but handicappers must first process the data, and produce the analytical information. How convenient if the information were provided instead.

The remaining data items in the running lines must be processed as well before decisions can be made or problems solved. Handicappers are working with data, not information.

On the other hand, the past performances now supply handicappers with tabulations revealing how performance data have been summarized to obtain meaning. Handicappers get horses' lifetime records, plus records for this year and last, turf records, records on today's tracks, and records of performances on wet tracks. The information helps enormously. In its absence, can handicappers imagine the data-processing tasks? Not many seasons ago the summaries were not provided.

In the past five years the past performances have provided greater amounts of information (speed figures, exact eligibility conditions, statistical summaries). The tables also contain several data items having minimal utility value unless processed by methods of handicapping. Someday the past performances will consist of information alone, not data in need of processing. Full-card simulcasting will press the matter heavily. Full-card simulcasting practically demands it. The elimination of needless time-and-energy-consuming data-processing requirements qualifies as a lofty universal goal—an attainable universal goal. Handicappers can arrive at the races, or at their favorite OTB parlor, purchase ready-to-use low-cost information reports for the races and horses at any track on the menu, and in an abbreviated period of study make decisions and solve problems.

That's the way it should be today. That's the way it can be tomorrow. That's the way it must be if this industry hopes to grow, not merely to survive.

THE NEXT GENERATION

High-tech handicapping has typically consisted of data processing by applications programs intended to represent the basic methods. The first computer programs produced numerical ratings or rankings of horses that were not particularly convincing. Rushing to fill a vacuum, more ambitious applications purported to analyze the races utilizing more powerful software that encompassed as many as thirteen handicapping factors, or seventeen, or twenty-eight, or maybe forty-one.

The computer was heralded as the handicapper's panacea. Unfortunately handicappers were forced to input the data. The more factors to be analyzed, the heavier the data-entry burden. Ugh! Not much of a bargain, after all.

Other problems, such as the independence among the factors or the effectiveness of the program in picking winners that paid decently, might be shrugged off, but the onerous time and energy demands pressed by the machines guaranteed that high-tech handicapping would not be experienced by the majority as good, clean fun and the personal computer might be viewed as another item on a long-lost laundry list of secrets of beating the races.

Into the gloom stepped the download. The downloading frenzy quickly followed. Instead of entering data ad nauseum, high-tech handicappers could download the pertinent data items from a data source and the innovative computer programs would be up and running, speedily and efficiently.

Not only that, beyond the raw data, certain additional kinds of information might be downloaded—trainer stats, pedigree stats, perhaps the class ratings of other handicappers.

A brand-new world of high-tech handicapping had been discovered. Numerous data files, each of them logically designed to complement the applications of users, might be downloaded, and the data

processed against multiple applications programs. Algorithms soon began to convert the output from multiple handicapping applications to
higher-order ratings, the so-called power ratings.

Instead of speed figures, pace ratings, class evaluations, form de-
fects, and the rest, handicappers were equipped with power ratings,
all-in-one, and one-for-all. The power ratings could be translated into
betting lines. Presto! The handicapping process has been fully com-
puterized. Just in time for full-card simulcasting. As everybody knows,
contemporary handicappers are playing multiple tracks, handfuls of
tracks a day, such that the computer has become the necessary hand-
maiden of handicappers.

Except for the nasty problems:

- Data processing completes only the primitive stage of handicapping, not the refined later stages characterized best by thinking, evaluating, and decision making.
- Between the only two national data sources (the *Daily Racing
  Form* and Equibase) and the thousands of high-tech handicappers stand dozens of information providers whose data files and
  downloads may not be perfectly compatible with the player's
  applications after all.
- Applications software works best when the program represents
  a narrow slice of the handicapping regimen, as opposed to a
  holistic approach, which means, output in hand, a considerable
  amount of heavy-duty handicapping remains to be done.
- The more handicapping factors an applications program em-
  braces, the less effective it's likely to be because the fundamental factors of handicapping are not independent but
  interdependent, contributing to a tendency to assess the same
  phenomenon (speed, pace, class, form) again and again; this
  redundancy delivers noise, not positive results.
- The relations among various types of output (speed, pace, class,
  form, consistency, trainers, etc.) are analytical, not mathematical. Power ratings and their ilk cannot substitute for the users'
  ability to think.
- The fair-value betting lines delivered to handicappers by computer programs have invariably ignored at least half a dozen
  handicapping factors that will be relevant today, at this track,
  in this race; handicappers will still need to do a great deal of
  juggling with the betting lines.

The first generation of computer applications has not advanced the cause by more than a couple of data-processing steps. Downloading data that are processed by computer applications is not essentially different from buying the *Daily Racing Form* and processing the same data manually and mentally. Both activities consist of data processing. The computer will be faster, but will it be more accurate, and more effective? Sometimes yes, and frequently no.

Another delicate problem has haunted the first generation of high-tech handicapping, an overarching concern not easily managed. What about quality control? Unless applications software has been logically designed by successful handicappers, excellent handicappers, what's the point? The output will probably prove next to worthless.

If computer programs deliver speed figures, for example, or pace ratings, or various numbers dependent upon adjusted actual times, how have the daily track variants been calculated? To the degree track variants are tethered to computer algorithms, they will be inaccurate and misleading, at least much of the time. If track variants are omitted, or have been calculated by some innovative technique that does not really assess the day-to-day speed of the track surface, the figures and ratings will be inaccurate and ineffective, at least much of the time. What's the point?

If class ratings are produced, how have the ratings been developed? Who are the handicappers and what are their credentials? Have the class ratings proved demonstrably effective across representative samples? What kind of empirical evidence has been accumulated to support the ratings' effectiveness? Without persuasive replies to these questions, high-tech handicappers who rely on the class ratings may be spinning their wheels.

Not wanting to become a killjoy, I have no doubt high-tech handicappers can benefit enormously from a logically designed, high-quality applications program, in particular a program clarifying the speed and pace factors. One or two effective applications already exist. Downloading data is preferable to entering data. But the download of data has no future.

Instead of downloading data, the next generation of high-tech handicappers should be downloading information reports. The data processing will have been done. Handicappers can obtain the reports, study them, and make their handicapping and wagering decisions.

Frankly I'm surprised, and chagrined, that by now, in the middle nineties, information reports have not become standard fare for high-tech handicappers. In a more desirable computer world, databases should be pouring out information reports for all racetracks, for networks of racetracks on a circuit, for tracks within a geographical region, or even for the local track. Beyond the downloading to handicappers' computers, the databases would download the standard set of reports to racetracks and other venues, which would then print the reports as hard copy and distribute them to on-track, intertrack, and OTB customers at low prices.

My database would issue the following reports at consumer-friendly prices daily:

1.	Speed and pace figures	$2.00
2.	Trips and biases	1.50
3.	Class and form report	1.50
4.	Pace report	1.50
5.	Trainer patterns	1.00
6.	Track profiles	0.50
7.	Pedigree report	0.50
8.	Equipment and medication	0.50
9.	Horses to watch/Horses to beat	0.50
10.	Workouts	0.50
11.	The long report	3.00
12.	Customized reports	1.00

The long report (no. 11) would consolidate several of the particular reports into a new version of the past performances. Instead of data, the past performances would present processed data, or information.

Customized reports refer to any personalized, individualized reports that handicappers prefer. Any combination of data items in the database could be provided in a customized format. Suppose a handicapper wanted a short list of first-starting maidens on today's program having a sire that wins 15 percent with first-starters, a trainer that wins 15 percent with first-starters, and the past ten workouts of the horses that qualified on sire-trainer stats. That report could be developed, and delivered to the player's computer every racing day.

Matters of database design and quality control would remain irritating issues. Handicappers would be relying on information produced by other handicappers. Excellent handicappers might produce the output for each of the information reports provided by the database, but other handicappers would prefer alternative concepts, methods, and information.

Racing's customers would obviously not purchase all of the reports, or even several of them, but merely the information they prized and desired. Handicappers who eschew figure handicapping would not want speed and pace figures. Handicappers who collect personal-trip and bias notes would not buy the trips-and-biases report. Players who do not believe in class would not want the class-and-form report.

The database would nonetheless contain something for everybody. Important information would become accessible at a low cost, and with no sweat. As multiple tracks were engaged on a single afternoon, local handicappers might depend upon personal information resources for the local horses but avidly want a few key reports for the simulcast tracks. Figure analysts would want speed and pace figures for each of the simulcast tracks they play.

The information reports issuing daily from well-designed, high-quality databases would complement full-card simulcasting. They should contribute as well to improved play and the betting churn that racetracks will find so endearing as regular handicappers play multiple tracks instead of one. Informed, skillful, successful handicappers will contribute disproportionately to the churn as never before. They will represent the tracks' best customers absolutely.

The next generation of high-tech handicapping cannot arrive soon enough for my tastes. When the downloading of information reports replaces the downloading of data, that's when I want to be on-line.

MPH SOFTWARE AND COLTS NECK
DATA ONLINE

For five years when handicappers pinned me as to the computer programs I liked most, I responded with some enthusiasm that I didn't use any of them. Actually I did employ a truncated early-energy program that required four inputs to a handheld Sharp computer and helped me to predict whether (a) horses' running styles would fit the energy demands of today's distance at today's track; and (b) sprinters might stretch out from sprints to routes effectively. Both the computer and the software were gifts.

Not only do I detest data input, I had my own information system, manual and quite elaborate, that took me approximately thirty minutes a day to update. I had remained satisfied with the manual system, mainly because it had worked well. The change that has shoved me toward high-tech handicapping is not some super software program, but full-card simulcasting. As do most handicappers, I like full-card simulcasting, and will typically play races from two, three, or more tracks. The personal computer supports that cause admirably.

Nonetheless I still prefer information reports to applications software. Applications software suffers ineluctable disadvantages for handicappers. The computer programs ignore too many relevant factors, miss too much, and therefore leave too much to be desired. If the programs attempt to overcompensate, embracing a dozen factors or more, the data processing is confounded by noise and the output becomes obtuse.

The applications programs that have impressed me the most deal extensively and cleverly with speed and pace, crucial handicapping factors that lend themselves extremely well to data processing. Even so, with the output in hand I am constantly and keenly aware that the handicapping process is not done. Class, form, distance, trips, biases, pedigree, trainers, jockeys, post positions—all of that or some of that may be important today, the nuances, variations, and interrelationships not apparent to the computer and its software.

When I'm asked about applications software now, I recommend Tom Brohamer's MPH Software, not because Brohamer has been my friend and a handicapping partner for a decade but because the program is an outstanding representation of pace analysis, a subject both difficult and elusive for many handicappers, and not easily manipulated manually.

The software also satisfies the telltale criteria. It deals with a fundamental and manageable slice of the handicapping regimen: pace. Pace is primary in claiming races and important in the majority of nonclaiming races.

The author is an authentic expert, no small point. Brohamer has enlightened handicappers, including me, on vital aspects of pace analysis—the critical role of early pace (and how to analyze it), the importance of the second call, energy distribution, the relationships between running styles and track profiles, how pace standouts must be capable of controlling two race segments, not just one—and is widely recognized as a leading authority on pace among his colleagues and peers.

The documentation is excellent. Not only are the input, processing, and output tasks clear, but also the procedures have been related specifically to the handicapping purposes they support. In other words users understand not only what to do, but why.

The program development has been excellent. Programmer Ken Massa qualifies as a handicapper as well as a computer scientist, and the dual roles have come shining through. A split screen allows handicappers to enter data (or download) and view the output simultaneously. A set of standard times for each distance allows users to toggle with arrow keys to the actual times of races instead of entering raw times repeatedly, a greatly convenient feature.

Track variants can be estimated from Beyer Speed Figures. Horses can be scratched from rankings that form a major component of the output, forming new rankings that might be consistent with various outcome scenarios. Turn-times are calculated. Beaten lengths at today's first and second calls are projected. Velocity ratings and the corre-

MPH Software Output

			6 FURLONGS						
	09-03-94		**ON DIRT**		**DMR**		**CLAIMING**		
RACE#01	**FR1**	**FR2**	**FR3**	**A/P**	**E/P**	**S/P**	**F/X**	**H/E**	**E/E**
SKY KID	60.43	57.31	49.53	55.73	58.83	54.18	54.98	53.42	54.29%
ME AND M	60.08	57.10	50.37	55.82	58.55	54.46	55.23	53.74	53.76%
WHITE ST	59.29	57.69	50.40	55.79	58.48	54.44	54.85	54.05	53.71%
HE'S A G	59.03	57.98	51.48	56.16	58.50	54.99	55.26	54.73	53.19%
MUNROE F	58.72	55.95	52.28	55.62	57.30	54.79	55.50	54.12	52.29%
GEIGER T	58.42	57.72	52.99	56.38	58.07	55.53	55.71	55.36	52.29%
GOLDEN C	56.36	56.10	52.83	55.09	56.23	54.53	54.60	54.47	51.56%

	ESP	**1st-C**	**2nd-C**	**FIN-C**	**TURN**	**FINF**	**E/E**		**FIG/VAR**
		21.84	44.88	110.4	23.0	25.5	53.21%		
SKY KID	E	21.84	44.88	111.5	23.0	26.7	54.29%	79	
ME AND M	E	21.97	45.09	111.3	23.1	26.2	53.76%	80	
WHITE ST	P	22.26	45.14	111.3	22.9	26.2	53.71%	82	
HE'S A G	E	22.36	45.13	110.8	22.8	25.6	53.19%	85	
MUNROE F	P	22.48	46.07	111.3	23.6	25.2	52.29%	82	
GEIGER T	P	22.60	45.46	110.4	22.9	24.9	52.29%	87	
GOLDEN C	S	23.42	46.95	111.9	23.5	25.0	51.56%	77	

	ESP	**A/P**	**E/P**	**S/P**	**F/X**	**H/E**	**SCORE**	**LINE**	**BL-1**	**BL-2**
GEIGER	P	1	5	1	1	1	33	2.1	4.4	3.4
HE'S A	E	2	3	2	3	2	22	3.5	3.1	1.5
ME AND	E	3	2	5	4	6	13	7.0	0.8	1.3
SKY KID	E	5	1	7	5	7	11	8.0	0.0	0.0
MUNROE	P	6	6	3	2	4	9	9.9	3.8	6.9
WHITE S	P	4	3	5	6	5	8	11.0	2.5	1.6
GOLDEN	S	7	7	4	7	3	4	23.6	9.0	11.7

sponding fractional times and final times are displayed. It's a veritable sculpture of the probable pace.

An illustration of the MPH Software output can be found above.

Happily, the price is right. MPH Software costs $267 or thereabouts.

A download utility is available, and that piece of the software can select the representative pace lines from the horses' recent records. It's a skill too many pace analysts lack. Brohamer has become convinced the utility will select the proper pace lines with high reliability, a major step in the continuing development of MPH Software.

Having said all that, I retreat to my original position. MPH Software deals exclusively with pace analysis. To the extent that the outcomes of the races will not depend upon pace, the program does not apply. Much of the time, considerable additional handicapping will be warranted.

As do many contemporary applications programs, MPH Software presents its disciples with a fair-value betting line. The betting line has been derived from considerations of pace. The line must be juggled to reflect any other factors that matter.

Handicappers are best reminded that computer programs should complement comprehensive handicapping, but not substitute for it.

With full-card simulcasting bearing down on the handicapping experience, the kind of high-tech support that turns my head is the speed and pace report issued by Colts Neck Data ONLINE. The friendly, ready-to-use report I imagined would be delivered to handicappers years ago by the *Daily Racing Form,* Equibase, BRIS, or some alternative national database service has come instead from the office-in-home of a computer sleuth and excellent handicapper.

On page 288 examine a portion of a printout for horses entered at a mile at Bay Meadows, September 3, 1994.

```
-   Colts Neck Data ONLINE   -     +Performances+     pg 03      ID: CYLKE
```

```
-----------------------------ci  INCREMENTAL>       TOTAL EFFORT        ODDS
Sat 03Sep94-03BMx  8.0  23  1/3-mid-end>  5th  4th  3rd  2nd  1st    inc  tot
--------------------------------------------------------------------+----+---
1  NOT TOO PROPER      22*  20  16+ 14*> -22  -20   20   20   19  *++ 3.6  2.7 1
5  MISS SILVER BATTLE  23  18*  25   23 >            / 34"  23"       4.5  5.9 4
3  BABY SHEA           22+  20  15*  22 > -22   25"  18"  21"  24" ** 4.8  3.0 2
6  WILD FOREVER        27   21  23   22 >  28"  25"  25" -29   22      5.5  4.8 3
4  MAYDAY QUEEN        23   20  22  19+>  24"  26   27   20   27" +   9.5 12.8
2  TO CARO WITH LOVE   29   19  21   25 >  32   26  -23  -23   24      9.8 16.2
7  FOREVER UMBER       27  19+  24   26 >            / 35"  38"/     10.8 26.0
```

```
+-------------------------------------+
|  Sat 03Sep94-03BMx           8.0f   |          23
+-------------------------------------+           |
                                                  |
```

```
24               3_NOT TOO PROPER        +--------+---------bonde j
14 10Aug94-06BMx  9+fast  8.0  20 19 18     19  |
25 27Jul94-11SRx  3-fast  8.0  26 20 16     20  |              4x1  20:20:21
20 02Jul94-11Pln  3+fast  8.3  35 14 10     20  |              5x1  21:21:22
52 12Jun94-03GGx  8+firm  8.5T 23 16 21    -20  |              3x4  17:20:22
   +                                            +              6x1  22:24:25
27 21Apr94-09GGx  7+firm  8.5T 28 19 19    -22                 5x3  22:23:24
29 25Mar94-07GGx  0-good  8.0  36 19 10     22                 6x1  22:23:25
15 24Feb94-08GGx  2-fast  8.5  23 22 14     20 |              4x0  21:22:24
                                            +--------+---------+
```

```
38          3_TO CARO WITH LOVE           +--------+---------perez r
   +                                            +
32 27Jul94-11SRx  3-fast  8.0  19 21 31     |24                0x6  21:21:22
   +                                        +
13 25Jun94-07GGx  7+firm  8.5T 23 23 24    -23                 3x3  22:24:25
24 12Jun94-03GGx  8+firm  8.5T 24 26 20    -23                 4x3  22:24:25
43 19May94-02GGx 10+fast  8.5  24 25 28     |   26             6x0  26:26:26
   +                                        +
26 06Apr94-06GGx  5+fast  8.5  30 28 37         |         32   0x4  26:25:26
14 11Mar94-03GGx  8+fast  8.0  26 31 27             28         9x0  29:30:30
 7 25Feb94-02GGx  5+fast  8.0  30 33 30     |           31 |   6x1  32:31:30
                                            +------------+------+
```

```
71          3_BABY SHEA                   +--------+------hollendorfer j
   +                                            +
   +                                            +
15 24Jun94-04GGx  5+fast  6.0  23 25 25         |24"           5x0  25:22:24
11 09Jun94-08GGx  6+fast  6.0  23 14 26        21"             2x5  20:24:25
21 29May94-07GGx  2+fast  6.0  20 15 19    18"                 7x0  19:23:23
32 08May94-08GGx  5+fast  6.0  21 26 26         |   25"        3x6  23:20:22
   +                                            +
12 06Apr94-08GGx  4-firm  8.5T 16 26 26    -22                 4x1  22:22:23
30 25Mar94-07GGx  0-good  8.0  19 22 19     20 |              7x0  22:23:25
   +                                            +
12 23Feb94-04GGx  3+good  5.5  17 17 08    14" |              5x0  24:30:29
                                            +--------+---------+
```

At a studious glance, Colts Neck subscribers know that either Not Too Proper or Baby Shea should beat To Caro With Love and that Not Too Proper dispenses highly consistent speed figures.

That's because Colts Neck ONLINE offers a compelling visual portrayal of the recent records. The rectangular display of Not Too Proper's speed figures features a center line that represents par. As seen in the example just above Not Too Proper's rectangle, Colts Neck's par for the Bay Meadows mile is 23. Lower is better on Colts Neck's figure scale, and above-par figures are plotted to the left of the center line, while below-par figures are plotted to the right.

Handicappers quickly note that Not Too Proper has invariably outrun today's par, and To Caro With Love has never exceeded par.

Baby Shea is fascinating. Can she beat Not Too Proper? In her last seven races Baby Shea has exceeded today's par five times and she shows two figures Not Too Proper has not equaled. Baby Shea's best efforts may be too good for the consistent favorite.

As indicated by the numeral 71 (days away) to the left of Baby Shea's name, the filly has been idle for seventy-one days, a telltale feature of the report. If Baby Shea runs especially well fresh, she might be an attractive alternative to Not Too Proper. Leading northern California trainer Jerry Hollendorfer does not hurt the cause.

The various numbers are pace and speed figures, easily comprehended and interpreted. At the top, where the field has been ranked on early pace (I like that, too), a pair of odds lines appears at the far right. The first ("inc") reflects each horse's rank on pace ability, the second ("tot") on speed or final time. The ranks (1, 2, 3, 4) to the right of the final-time odds are based on speed figures.

Under "Total Effort" the Colts Neck report presents each horse's most recent five speed figures. The same figures are plotted in the rectangle left-to-right as above-and-below-par.

As with MPH Software, the Colts Neck betting lines reflect speed and pace comparisons only. The lines must be juggled by handicappers to reflect other factors that might be relevant today.

As with MPH Software, too, the price is right. In September 1995 the Colts Neck ONLINE reports could be downloaded for as many tracks as handicappers preferred for a flat fee—$100 a month. One of the service's loyal clients has suggested the Colts Neck handicappers may not be astute businessmen.

Maybe not. But they are first-rate handicappers. Monitoring the service intermittently at Del Mar for northern and southern California, I have been amazed at how well figure handicappers operating out of an office in New Jersey can play the races three thousand miles away.

But that's the promise of high-tech handicapping well done, and of on-line services that can download the goods to handicappers everywhere, saving them precious time and energy while equipping them with information they might rely upon to analyze the races and to make betting decisions.

Things are getting better.

INTERACTIVE TV

The notion that home betting represents the ultimate distribution system that will resurrect the fortunes of Thoroughbred racing, terminating the current decline and malaise, collapses on scrutiny as wishful thinking, but a much broader and strongly related concept may brighten the future after all.

Following the advent of pari-mutuel wagering, the Triple Crown, grass racing, exotic betting, and the Breeders' Cup, one of the great leaps forward for this reactionary industry may be interactive TV. The technology extends the promise of sending directly into the customer's home and office any and all varieties of handicapping and wagering information, *exactly as the customer wants it!*

Even more—quickly, conveniently, accurately, and at low cost.

One crucial point should be stressed up front. Every man and woman who imagines himself and herself a manager, director, or executive in this troubled industry should understand this. If interactive TV is developed solely as means of distributing pari-mutuel wagering opportunities to the home, forget it. The game will have been lost again.

Interactive TV represents the potential of providing nothing less than a management information system for the consumer. Not merely for the local tracks but for all racetracks. It's a tremendous opportunity, and the hope runs deep the executives will not blow it.

Let's imagine what interactive TV can do for the beleaguered horse players being buffeted and tossed about by the winds of full-card simulcasting. The technology can provide the following:

A HANDICAPPER'S DATABASE

The database must be relational, and it must be developed in consultation with excellent and leading handicappers. Third-rate handicappers need not apply.

In scope the database should permit handicappers to obtain any and all varieties of relevant information about horses, races, racetracks, trainers, and jockeys, not only for local tracks but also for all tracks. It's national, not local.

That means handicappers can access on TV the past performances, information reports, statistical summaries, speed figures, and any other combination of data items in the database. Customized, personalized reports would be accessible on demand, and handicappers would be capable of running applications programs across whatever portions of the database they judged pertinent.

An inquiry function would be a vital aspect of the system. Handicappers might ask numerous and specific questions of the database about horses, tracks, trainers, and jockeys. A couple hundred commands in English syntax could be embedded in the system. Handicappers would rely upon the inquiry function liberally and usefully, and at nominal cost.

The impediment to a system of interactive TV that makes sense and will make a difference is precisely the absence of a national relational database that covers the ground handicappers must cross when they play the races. The construction of that wonderful database becomes a critical priority. The industry should proceed with the task in haste, throwing money at it, so that racing's customers can access the relevant information as television pictures, study the pictures, and if they so choose, print them.

A VIDEO LIBRARY

The video system should contain every race run at any racetrack in the country. Handicappers can view the races they want to see. If a player at Thistledown in Cleveland wants to watch the fifth race at Louisiana Downs in Bossier City on August 7, he or she can call up menus of tracks and race dates within seconds and watch the race. Any cost will be nominal. Thousands of trip handicappers across the nation will have been well served. Without the video library the trip handicappers will have been poorly served. The difference matters.

CURRENT ODDS AND EXOTIC PROJECTIONS

The reference is obvious, but necessary. Planners might consider that the plague they have visited upon their best customers in recent times has not been too many races—although that detracts despairingly from the quality of racing—but too many underlays. Underlays are ruinous for regular racetrack bettors. Even when underlays win, the bettors lose, because they receive an unfair payoff.

So bettors need current odds and projections on combination bets. If betting has not begun, morning lines can be provided, but in too many situations these will be amateurish and awful.

LIVE RACES

Needless to say, interactive TV will present the races live. Full-card simulcasting. In the home or office. Handicappers and bettors should be able to view the replays of interest.

EXPERT ANALYSIS

A prerace analysis by authentic experts is always welcome. Especially if such analysis has been rooted in objective data, state-of-the-art know-how, reliable information, and not just the subjective swapping of opinions.

TUTORIALS

Interactive TV offers an excellent opportunity for the industry to repair decades of benign neglect of customer education.

Player development is a vital issue the industry has only recently bothered to address. Newcomers and beginners can be intimidated by the game, and they face severe educational needs.

Newcomers can learn to view the track layout and how to read the past-performance tables. They can be introduced to the kinds of races and types of wagers. They can discover the facts of pari-mutuel wagering as well as the distinctions between positive and negative strategies for betting the exacta, quinella, trifecta, Pick 6, Pick 3, and other pari-mutuel games that will be introduced. All of this requires ninety minutes.

Beginners and novices can pursue a deeper exploration of speed handicapping, class evaluation, pace analysis, form analysis, trip handicapping, pedigree, trainers, biases, and the rest. The educational potential of interactive TV will be far-reaching and dynamic.

Enough. The potential of interactive TV for racing's participative purposes should be obvious and great. Will it be realized?

Very probably not.

EQUIBASE

As much as any single person or factor, the near future of this sport and industry, the next decade or two decades, may depend upon the philosophy, direction, and management of the company called Equibase. It's a terrible burden to put on a youngster (Equibase is not ten years old), but I am more than happy to do it.

Thoroughbred racing is in trouble. The sport does not know how to grow new markets (young adults, women, baby boomers, the corporate-professional-technical elites), and it has not learned how to compete for market share with other forms of gaming. Worst of all, to an astonishing degree its managers and executives do not understand their own product and they do not understand their primary markets.

Under those circumstances it will be difficult to succeed. Equibase has the resources and the opportunity to come to the rescue. The company also faces severe and familiar obstacles, which will be elaborated momentarily.

Equibase is the brainchild of the Jockey Club, its parent and the ruling body of Thoroughbred racing. That is the company's impenetrable strength. The company's charter is to be the electronic information resource for the sport and industry in the information age. That charter brings the company into competition with other information providers, notably but not exclusively the *Daily Racing Form,* and ultimately face-to-face with racing's customers.

In a peculiar sense the main strength of Equibase may be its main weakness. The Jockey Club has been as distinctly removed from racing's customer base as a severed head from its body. Forgive the morbid comparison, but the historical dissociation means the contemporary connection may prove tenuous, uncomfortable, awkward, and ultimately unproductive. Will Equibase be able to serve the information needs of handicappers and bettors?

Maybe.

Only two companies possess a national data source for playing the races—the *Daily Racing Form* and Equibase. The element of competition serves racing's customers absolutely, but the critical question regards what Equibase will do with its data.

Handicappers already know, and greatly appreciate, what the *Daily Racing Form* has done with its data: the past-performance tables, the results charts, and lately data downloads. The past performances and result charts have formed the lifeblood of this sport and industry from the beginning. Yet times they are a-changing. Electronic communications have been replacing hard copy. Information takes precedence over data. Can Equibase offer racing's customers a timely electronic alternative?

Maybe.

The first several years have not looked promising. The practice of selling data (past performances) to racetracks that then publish the data in bloated crowded versions of the official track program not only qualifies as a poor man's replication of the *Racing Form*'s tables (half as many races or fewer, small and badly spaced and sometimes barely legible print) but has also suggested that handicappers might set their expectations of Equibase rather low.

I find the tacky data rows crammed into track programs clearly beneath the dignity of the Jockey Club. Comments from leading handicappers regarding the speed figures contained in Equibase's past performances have been uniformly critical, including those of Steven Crist, now an Equibase board member. Does anybody actually use the Equibase figures to make serious wagers? In 1994 Equibase experienced a change of management, and in the person of President Richard Le Ber handicappers can be encouraged to gaze upon the company with renewed hope. Le Ber cares about the information needs of handicappers and bettors, the regular handicappers as well as casual customers, a position that constitutes something of a first principle and merits respect from all of us.

A partner from McKinsey & Co., the leading international management consulting firm, and an information scientist, Le Ber first of all understands the vital distinction between data and information. As Le Ber has emphasized, data are a commodity. Data are cheap. Furthermore to obtain meaning, even for trackside bettors, data must be processed and converted to information, a time-consuming circumstance not compatible with full-card simulcasting. During his first year

Le Ber reduced the cost of downloading the Equibase past-performance data for a track's daily program to a dollar, a market-price reduction as great as 1400 percent. He deserved a reward.

Not only did the price reduction send a ringing message to other information providers, but it also reflected Le Ber's conviction that the future of Equibase cannot be hinged to downloading data, either to official track programs or to the applications programs of handicappers. That acknowledgment comes to handicappers like a blast of fresh air.

Listed below are the Equibase past performances as they appeared in *Post Parade,* the official track program of NYRA, at Aqueduct, for a stakes race simulcast to New York from Gulfstream Park, January 1994:

Encouraged that the future of Equibase cannot be hinged to downloading and selling data, handicappers and bettors can wonder instead what the company's agenda will be?

Presumably a major direction for Equibase will be product development. Information products. Products that handicappers and bettors can use to handicap more efficiently and to play the races more effectively. It's a bumpy road having a faraway destination. Unfortunately it's also a direction that Le Ber may be ill equipped to travel.

The new president of Equibase has virtually no experience playing the races, neither casually nor regularly. It's a severe limitation, and maybe a disabling one.

Moreover, and this is no small impediment, much of Le Ber's time, conversation, and professional associations will occur with racetrack executives and establishment figures, the majority of whom share the same debilitating limitation. Too many of these people have been a part of the problem and will not be a part of the solution. It's a sorrowful case of the blind leading the blind.

It won't happen, but I would urge Le Ber to take $5000 of his salary and play the races a couple of days a week until he either doubles his bankroll or blows it. The time would be well invested, far more valuable than staff meetings, symposiums, and other official business. Untutored but smart, Le Ber, by playing the races, will achieve a visceral appreciation of the knowledge, skills, and information resources horse players need to play well, indeed to cope with the game, to survive as a racetrack customer. Without playing experience, Le Ber will have difficulty identifying in any meaningful way with handicappers and bettors.

Back to reality.

The alternative remedy is a close association with leading handicappers. Crist on the board is a positive. Equibase's products will achieve resonance and a loyal following in the mature handicapping market only to the extent that the products prove to be genuinely helpful.

Here the competition is not the *Daily Racing Form*, but an assortment of products and services produced by experienced handicappers in local and regional markets—a veritable underground marketplace—speed and pace figures, trip and bias reports, trainer statistics, workout summaries, horses to watch, sire statistics, computer software, newsletters. The markets may be small, but the surviving products and services tend to be high-quality items, and the subscribers loyal. Equibase cannot blow these competitors out of the water very easily, and at this moment cannot even compete effectively.

The broader recreational markets—hobbyists, weekend warriors, casual handicappers, newcomers, the seniors, occasional visitors—constitute a different audience and altogether different problems. Uninformed, indeed misinformed, and poorly educated on the fundamentals of handicapping and pari-mutuel wagering, not to mention the fine points of handicapping and the interrelationships among the several factors, this large, diverse group cannot interpret and use information products effectively. Unable to use the products successfully, the recreational customers soon abandon them. In the broader recreational market, sadly, Equibase will discover few loyal customers.

Le Ber need only survey other large-scale information providers (the *Daily Racing Form,* BRIS, Track Master) for the ugly precedents. Subscribers last ninety days, six months, a year, maybe two years, but then many of them desert. Le Ber can blame the racetracks that have refused to educate their patrons for decades. When people have lost more money than they can tolerate, most of them stop playing.

The remedies are (a) new markets and (b) customer education. Until those twin directions have been pursued seriously and successfully, even the best information products will deliver minimal to modest returns. Le Ber can consider this dynamic to be axiomatic. Customer education drives information services. Without the know-how, the information means nothing. Equibase will serve its long-term interests best by bestowing relatively equal concerns and resources on education and information.

Lacking combat experience, Le Ber and Equibase will be susceptible to another misstep racetrack officials have been prone to indulge forever: the unending pursuit of secondary and tertiary markets. The primary markets of racing, in descending order of importance, are as follows:

1. Regular handicappers and bettors
2. Recreational handicappers and bettors (hobbyists)
3. Casual handicappers and bettors (irregular players)
4. Beginners and novices
5. Newcomers

The secondary and tertiary markets consist of:

6.   Occasional racegoers
7.   Transient racegoers

The top two use information products (electronic and manual) liberally, and casual handicappers would, provided the products were conveniently accessible at racetracks, at a nominal cost, and helped the users win more frequently. Tall order.

Beginners, novices, and newcomers represent a tremendous source of potentially loyal customers, but a deadening lack of knowledge and skill (education) thwarts too many of them before the information products can salvage their predicaments.

Each of the primary markets deserves recognition and attention. For some reason, curiously unexamined, never persuasively articulated, racing's marketing managers become preoccupied with the occasional and transient racegoers, people who are uninterested in playing the races as a game of knowledge and skill and do not care about racing as a sport and industry. Elevated to a position of prominence and concern they do not deserve, the occasional and transient racegoers are alluded to euphemistically and optimistically as the $2 bettors. The idea is to secure their greater allegiance. Information products cannot perform that trick. Le Ber has already fallen headlong into this vicious trap.

In the summer of 1995 at Del Mar, Equibase introduced a $2 information product targeted at the occasional racegoer. It was called *The Bettor Times (Official Player's Guide),* and it was a fine product, both an amplification of the traditional track program and a condensation of the past performances. Users could review the conditions and finishes of each horse's last three races, accompanied by a handicapper's commentary on the recent record.

For each race as well customers were provided jockey statistics and a computer-generated bar graph (Pick-To-Graph) of the probable finish. Sprinkled liberally throughout *The Bettor Times,* too, were instructional nuggets—definitions of basic terms, explanations of wagers, and a vocabulary feature called "Track Talk."

The Bettor Times came to life following a considerable corporate enterprise, involving research-and-development money, focus groups (of racetrack customers), and Equibase's impressive computer technology. It's an attractive product, with excellent production values, colorful covers, and even interesting articles.

Sales were disappointing, in part because the $2 cover exceeded by 33 percent the price of the traditional track program. That mistake was quickly corrected. But the long-term prospects of *The Bettor Times* are problematic, not due to price but due precisely to the nature of the occasional and transient markets that form its target groups.

The occasional customers are here today, gone tomorrow. They do not care enough about Thoroughbred racing. A loyal following does not accumulate. *The Bettor Times* is destined to exist as an alternative to the track program among people who know next to nothing about playing the races. Fair enough, and there's no point in criticizing the effort, except as it has been intended to substitute for the real reasons people flock to racetracks more than occasionally. They go there to handicap and to bet, the participative motives of their days at the races.

A PAGE OUT OF *The Bettor Times*/Del Mar 1995

Race Number		
3		

Wagering Options for this Race
($2 Minimum Wager Except as Noted)

Win	Your selection must finish first in this race. **Example:** Tell the clerk "$2 to win on 2". You cash your ticket if #2 finishes first.
Place	Your selection must finish first OR second in this race. **Example:** Tell the clerk "$2 to place on 2". You cash your ticket if #2 finishes first OR second.
Show	Your selection must finish first OR second OR third in this race. **Example:** Tell the clerk "$2 to show on 2". You cash your ticket if #2 finishes first OR second.
Exacta	Your 2 selections must finish first and second in order in this race. **Example:** Tell the clerk "$2 Exacta 2-5". You cash your ticket if #2 finishes first and #5 second.
Quinella	Your 2 selections must finish first and second in either order in this race. **Example:** Tell the clerk "A $2 Quinella 2-5". You cash your ticket if #2 finishes first with #5 second OR #5 finishes first with #2 second.
$3 Pick Three	Select the winner of this race, the 4th & 5th races. **Example:** Tell the clerk "A $3 Rolling Pick Three 2-1-5". You cash your ticket if #2 wins this race, #1 wins the 4th race and #5 the 5th race.
Parlay	Total proceeds of a successful wager are wagered on subsequent race(s).

(continued)

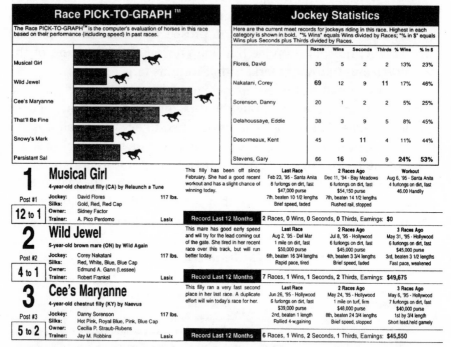

Race Description - Hall of Champions / John Longden

The 3rd race is for fillies (female horses under age five) and mares (female horses age five and up) three years old and upward. The field will compete at a distance of 6 furlongs (1 furlong equals 1/8 mile, therefore this race is 3/4 of a mile) for **a purse of $47,000.**

Dirt Course

6 furlongs (3/4 mile)

Race PICK-TO-GRAPH ™

The Race PICK-TO-GRAPH™ is the computer's evaluation of horses in this race based on their performance (including speed) in past races.

- Musical Girl
- Wild Jewel
- Cee's Maryanne
- That'll Be Fine
- Snowy's Mark
- Persistant Sal

Jockey Statistics

Here are the current meet records for jockeys riding in this race. Highest in each category is shown in bold. "% Wins" equals Wins divided by Races; "% in $" equals Wins plus Seconds plus Thirds divided by Races.

	Races	Wins	Seconds	Thirds	% Wins	% In $
Flores, David	39	5	2	2	13%	23%
Nakatani, Corey	69	12	9	11	17%	46%
Sorenson, Danny	20	1	2	2	5%	25%
Delahoussaye, Eddie	38	3	9	5	8%	45%
Desormeaux, Kent	45	5	11	4	11%	44%
Stevens, Gary	66	16	10	9	24%	53%

1 **Musical Girl**
4-year-old chestnut filly (CA) by Relaunch a Tune
Post #1
Jockey:	David Flores	117 lbs.
Silks:	Gold, Red, Red Cap	
Owner:	Sidney Factor	
12 to 1
| Trainer: | A. Pico Perdomo | Lasix |

This filly has been off since February. She had a good recent workout and has a slight chance of winning today.

Last Race	2 Races Ago	Workout
Feb 23, '95 - Santa Anita	Dec 11, '94 - Bay Meadows	Aug 6, '95 - Santa Anita
6 furlongs on dirt, fast	6 furlongs on dirt, fast	4 furlongs on dirt, fast
$47,000 purse	$54,150 purse	46.00 Handily
7th, beaten 10 1/2 lengths	7th, beaten 14 1/2 lengths	
Brief speed, faded	Rushed rail, stopped	

Record Last 12 Months | 2 Races, 0 Wins, 0 Seconds, 0 Thirds, Earnings: $0

2 **Wild Jewel**
5-year-old brown mare (ON) by Wild Again
Post #2
Jockey:	Corey Nakatani	117 lbs.
Silks:	Red, White, Blue, Blue Cap	
Owner:	Edmund A. Gann (Lessee)	
4 to 1
| Trainer: | Robert Frankel | Lasix |

This mare has good early speed and will try for the lead coming out of the gate. She tired in her recent race over this track, but will run better today.

Last Race	2 Races Ago	3 Races Ago
Aug 2, '95 - Del Mar	Jul 8, '95 - Hollywood	May 31, '95 - Hollywood
1 mile on dirt, fast	6 furlongs on dirt, fast	6 furlongs on dirt, fast
$50,000 purse	$45,000 purse	$45,000 purse
6th, beaten 16 3/4 lengths	4th, beaten 3 3/4 lengths	3rd, beaten 3 1/2 lengths
Rapid pace, tired	Brief speed, faded	Fast pace, weakened

Record Last 12 Months | 7 Races, 1 Wins, 1 Seconds, 2 Thirds, Earnings: $49,675

3 **Cee's Maryanne**
4-year-old chestnut filly (KY) by Naevus
Post #3
Jockey:	Danny Sorenson	117 lbs.
Silks:	Hot Pink, Royal Blue, Pink, Blue Cap	
Owner:	Cecilia P. Straub-Rubens	
5 to 2
| Trainer: | Jay M. Robbins | Lasix |

This filly ran a very fast second place in her last race. A duplicate effort will win today's race for her.

Last Race	2 Races Ago	3 Races Ago
Jun 26, '95 - Hollywood	May 24, '95 - Hollywood	May 6, '95 - Hollywood
6 furlongs on dirt, fast	1 mile on turf, firm	7 furlongs on dirt, fast
$39,000 purse	$48,000 purse	$40,000 purse
2nd, beaten 1 length	8th, beaten 24 3/4 lengths	1st by 3/4 length
Rallied 4-w,gaining	Brief speed, stopped	Short lead,held gamely

Record Last 12 Months | 6 Races, 1 Wins, 2 Seconds, 1 Thirds, Earnings: $45,550

Of the occasional transient customers who do become interested in playing the races, virtually all of them will abandon *The Bettor Times* in a heartbeat. The product can no longer serve their needs. They will now want greater handicapping nourishment than the Equibase program provides. And that's the essential flaw with information products and services ostensibly aimed at the occasional $2 bettors in oversimplified form. The moment those customers become interested in playing the races as a game of knowledge and skill at which talented players can win, they seek to improve their game, and they therefore seek the products and services that will help them win.

At that decisive juncture, equipping a beginner with *The Bettor Times* is tantamount to handing the beginning golfer a putter. How long will the duffer be satisfied with putting once he examines the golf course and sees so many other clubs in the bag? It does not take even an afternoon for the rookie golfer to realize he cannot play well with a putter.

And so it is with the great game of handicapping. All that will be left for *The Bettor Times* is tomorrow's share of the occasional transient market.

If I sound unduly hard on Equibase, it's deliberate. I expect a lot, perhaps too much. I expect Equibase and its bright new president from McKinsey & Co. to move this sluggish industry forward in important directions.

The Bettor Times is fine, within its limited reach, but I expect a wide array of information products and services that will stimulate racing's primary markets of regular players, recreational players, casual players, and that wildly heterogeneous pool of newcomers, beginners, and novices.

I also expect Equibase to take a front-and-center position in the education arena. If Le Ber has not yet recognized that racing's customers are badly misinformed and poorly educated, he should take a longer, closer look. Once he has made the vital connections—information and education—I expect the president will persuade the Equibase board and the leaders of the Jockey Club that it's their noble purpose and duty to do something about it.

I also expect Equibase to bring the Thoroughbred racing industry into the information age and onto the information superhighway in consummate professional style, and I'm satisfied that on this important matter Le Ber is equipped to bring the effort home a winner.

ADDENDUM: A VISION

W hat follows constitutes a dream perhaps, but no one is dreaming. I'm wide awake.

The reality behind the dream is the desire to create stars. Not equine stars. Playing stars. Handicapping and wagering stars.

Handicappers as stars. Is that a novel idea? And I believe I know how to do it, rather quickly.

Remember the 1994 proposal to add one-quarter percent to the national take, and use the money in a national marketing campaign that would promote Thoroughbred racing? Revenues were estimated at $25 million annually.

Handicappers and bettors by a wide majority were outraged. Beyond the unfairness, the promotional ideas, when they were mentioned at all, proved conventional, and therefore uninspiring. Traditional ideas can hardly be expected to create waves of new racegoers. The more things change, the more they remain the same, or grow worse. Even racetracks were opposed.

Suppose, however, the quarter percent was added to the national take and the $25 million was redistributed to the bettors in the form of prize money for an exciting schedule of TRA-sponsored handicapping tournaments at racetracks large, medium, and small, throughout the country.

Instead of outraged, handicappers and bettors would be supportive, because the new revenues would be awarded to talented players. Just as owners, horsemen, and racetracks extract meaningful money from the handle, so now would winning handicappers.

Not only that, in my reverie the handicapping tournaments represent nothing less than the most dynamically successful marketing strategy Thoroughbred racing has ever dispensed. New markets (of the types of individuals the sport has never been able to attract) are growing and people are beginning to flock to racetracks again. Within three to seven years, the current decline and malaise have been reversed.

The sport, the game, and the industry will never be seriously troubled again. Corporate sponsors have become sufficiently impressed to climb aboard as an additional source of financing. Instead of sponsoring just a stakes race, major corporations now sponsor several of the handicapping tournaments, and a few of them even sponsor individual handicappers. How about that!

This is what happens in my recurring dream.

It's the first major tournament of the new season, the $250,000-added Gulfstream Park Handicappers' Challenge, and everybody is there—the Gulfstream Park regulars, of course, plus all the leading players in the United States.

First prize is guaranteed at $100,000, as usual in the six majors, and second prize is $50,000. Third prize is $20,000, fourth is $15,000, and fifth is $10,000. Once the corporate coffers open wide, the prize money will be much greater. Special prizes of $5000 are awarded to the top female finisher and top twentysomething finisher, because these people represent two target groups horse racing desperately needs to attract.

Players proceed with a bank of $2000. It's real money, and they can wager 5 percent ($100) to 10 percent ($200) on a minimum of six races a day, until the final round, when no betting limits apply. Tournament bets are commingled with the regular Gulfstream pool, and players keep whatever profits they accumulate.

If two hundred players wager $1000 a day during the tournament, a lowball scenario, Gulfstream Park derives its customary on-track commission on a tournament handle upward of $800,000. The track benefits as well from the not-inconsiderable promotion, publicity, and media coverage. The handicapping tournaments, especially the majors, have become media events. The final rounds become fantastic shoot-outs as the leading players compete for the top prizes.

The field consists of roughly two hundred players. As usual, certain players have been exempt from qualifying: the top thirty finishers in last year's Gulfstream Park Handicappers' Challenge. In addition, winners of any TRA-sponsored tournament earn an exemption from qualifying for all handicapping tournaments for one year. Winners of any of the six major tournaments each year receive a special five-year exemption from qualifying for all other tournaments.

In the qualifying rounds at Gulfstream Park and at the other tracks on the tournament circuit, handicappers are required to make a minimum of sixty flat bets to win, of $50 each, during thirty racing days. Both Gulfstream races and simulcast races can be bet. All players producing a flat-bet profit qualify for the Gulfstream Park Handicappers' Challenge. Other eligible players include the top one hundred money winners in the national merry-go-round of TRA tournaments during the preceding calendar year.

The other major tournaments are held at Santa Anita Park, Hollywood Park, Churchill Downs, and Belmont Park (twice), but a generous handicapping tournament is held every week somewhere. Handicappers compete for good money, status, and prestige. As in golf tournaments and tennis tournaments, the same names find their way up the leader boards again and again. It's fair to say these individuals qualify as the best handicappers in the nation.

The wildly successful handicapping tournaments are predicated upon a single assumption that Thoroughbred racing has never before been willing to accept:

You can beat the races.

As the tournaments have demonstrated beyond dispute, many players do, and in every racing market throughout the country. The marketing strategy is elementary but elegant. Identify the winners, racing's best handicappers, and promote them.

Racing's customers do not identify with the horses. They do not identify with the trainers. They do not identify with the jockeys. But they would identify with excellent handicappers, with the winners.

And by identifying with winning handicappers, racing's customers have come to know at last that you can beat the races; that skillful players do win, many of them consistently; and that skillful play will be generously rewarded. As a result, the image of the racetrack has benefited from a positive change that has bordered on the revolutionary, and racing's economic future has been looking brighter than ever.

A crucial component of my dream may be unexciting, but it's indispensable.

In combination with the handicapping tournaments, all TRA tracks offer their patrons well-designed, professionally delivered programs of customer education. An unprecedented emphasis on player development drives the marketing effort.

Newcomers, beginners, and novices, for so long ignored, now can visit Newcomers' Centers at the tracks. The centers feature interactive learning and training activities. Newcomers can watch videos, engage computer programs, listen to audiotapes, and ask questions about playing the races and pari-mutuel wagering. Excellent local handicappers staff the premises. Interested customers can also sign up for a one-day class provided free every weekend and featuring simple techniques newcomers might use to play the races more effectively. The misinformation and bad habits that newcomers and novices have traditionally developed on their initial encounters with the racetrack have been replaced by simple, sensible programs that supply accurate information and fundamentally sound playing techniques. Newcomers and novices are extremely grateful.

The newcomers and beginners, along with journeymen and veteran racetrackers, so many of them badly informed and poorly educated on their favorite game, can now participate as well in a certificated program of instruction and training designed to transport racing's customers from novice to journeyman to expert within eighteen months.

First, participants engage in a six-week course on the fundamentals of handicapping and pari-mutuel wagering. The fundamentals course is provided at no cost to the participants. The course is subsidized by the TRA and by the local racetracks.

Participants next choose three of several methods courses, such as speed handicapping, class evaluation, pace analysis, trip handicapping, statistical approaches, high-tech handicapping, trainers and jockeys, and betting strategy and money management. The methods courses are scheduled for six weeks and involve extensive playing time at the races. Participants pay $99 apiece for the methods courses. The cost of completing the program amounts to $297.

The curriculum for each course is developed by leading handicapping practitioners and the classes are conducted by handicappers as teachers, who are paid a fee by the TRA or local tracks similar to instructors' fees in university extension programs.

Upon successful completion of the four-course program, participants are given a certificate that entitles them to free clubhouse admission at any TRA track for a calendar year. In addition, the graduates obtain an exemption to three handicapping tournaments. By this design, the tournaments stimulate the education process and the classes nourish the handicapping tournaments.

All of this has come to pass because the Thoroughbred industry awakened from its deep slumber and began to promote the participative motives of track attendance. The glorious shift has saluted the gaming aspects of a day at the races, and without abandoning the spectacle of the sport. Both facets of the racetrack experience can be promoted effectively, and finally both are.

A tremendous unanticipated payoff delivered by the tournaments and courses regards the changing image of the racetrack. The negative image of the track as a haven for dreamers, drifters, and gamblers is being effectively countermanded and significantly altered. Several of the handicapping tournaments are being contested and won by men and women who are also doctors, lawyers, engineers, accountants, teachers, writers, bankers, computer scientists, corporate executives, and successful businesspeople.

In interviews and conversations, off track as well as on track, virtually all of them identify the racetrack as comprising a meaningful slice of their lives. It's no longer uncommon for impressive tournament winners to tell broadcasters on television that they relinquished professional and corporate careers to play the races.

How about that!

One more delightful detail. I cannot awaken from my dream without first imagining that a number of the big-ticket handicapping tournaments have been won by me. I've yet to sweep the six majors, but invariably I'm high enough in the rankings to take down important money.

So I dearly hope this vision comes to life.

The sooner the better.